A Popular History of the Catholic Church

A Popular History of the Catholic Church

Carl Koch

Saint Mary's Press®

The publishing team for this book included Robert Smith, FSC, development editor; Jacqueline M. Captain, copy editor; Gary J. Boisvert, production editor, typesetter, page designer, and mapmaker; Maurine R. Twait, cover designer and art director; Ken Call, illustrator; Elaine Kohner, line art illustrator; Alan M. Greenberg, Integrity Indexing, indexer; pre-press, printing, and binding by the graphics division of Saint Mary's Press.

The acknowledgements continue on page 286.

Printed in the United States of America

5208

ISBN 978-0-88489-395-0

Library of Congress Catalog Card Number: 96-68895

God is so good that He not only brings us into existence by His act of creation but also desires that all of us come to the knowledge of truth. This truth is God Himself and all that He has willed to reveal to us through Jesus Christ, through His apostles, and through His church. God desires all of us to be taught this knowledge, that our minds may be enlightened by the light of faith.

(Meditations for the Time of Retreat) ■

John Baptist de La Salle:

Patron Saint of Teachers

Contents

1

Exploring Church History

Seeing the Church with New Eyes

Suppose that you had no idea of your own personal history, that you suddenly found yourself without any memory of your past. The following story gives some notion of what that would be like.

A woman in her twenties had been found nearly dead at the edge of a highway. With a severe concussion and other injuries, Jane Doe, as the woman was called, had gone into a deep state of amnesia. In the weeks following her rescue, doctors determined that Jane would have to re-learn even elementary actions like how to dress herself and tie her shoes. Because she could not read or write, her teachers started from the ABCs. Without identifica-tion, she would not be able to register for a driver's li-cense, open a bank account, request school transcripts, or fill out an application for a job. People perceived her as an adult, but in effect, she often functioned as a child. What was even more disheartening was that Jane had no known family or friends—no one to depend on in a world that was unfamiliar to her.

On one trip outside the hospital with her occupa-tional therapist, Jane lingered at a flower stand. On a whim, the therapist bought Jane a bouquet of daisies with a few roses mixed in. Tears of delight and gratitude brimmed in Jane's eyes. The next day, when the therapist arrived at Jane's room, she was startled by what she saw. The ordinary bouquet of flowers had been arranged cre-atively—professionally. Amazed, she asked Jane who had done the arrangement.

"I did. What do you think of it?"

"I think we just found out what kind of work you did before your memory loss."

Police investigators began calling florists. Eventually, they found, in another state, the floral shop where Jane had last worked. From there, they discovered her true identity as Clare Forrest, a woman with a real past, in-cluding devoted family and friends who had been search-ing for her for months. These people were eager to welcome her back into their world.

A week later, Clare's father, sister, and two brothers, along with several aunts, uncles, cousins, and assorted friends, crammed into her hospital room for a grand re-union. For hours, they reeled off family memories, helping her piece together the story of her life. They told about the time when, as a three year old, Clare had jumped into the neighbor's pool and nearly drowned (was that why she was afraid to get into the hospital whirlpool?). Clare heard about her own starring role in the high school mu-sical and her aspiration, back then, to sing on Broadway (no wonder she loved the sing-alongs at the hospital and had to fight off the strange impulse to jump up and lead the singing!). Sadly, her visitors relayed that her mother had died when Clare was only ten and that Clare had taken it hard (did that explain the tears that overcame her the other day as she observed a little girl in the lounge waiting to visit her mother in the intensive care unit?). Clare's relatives and friends told her about themselves too: who was married to whom, where they worked, what they and Clare used to do together when they were kids.

Over the hours, Clare's life began to come into focus for her. Memories flashed through her whole being. It would be a long time before her entire past would become clear to her, but she was beginning to remember. So much about herself and her reactions to things around her had seemed mysterious. Now she could understand why she was the way she was. She sensed that she was not living in a vacuum, that she was a person with a history and could therefore figure out where to go with the rest of her life. And this wonderful discovery had started with a simple bouquet of daisies and roses.

Why Study History at All?

Clare's experience of losing her memory and then regaining it can offer insight into the value of knowing our history, at both the personal and the societal levels.

Memory: A Key to Personal Identity

Finding Out Who We Are

Clearly, for all of us, our memory of our personal history plays a key role in telling us who we are and enabling us to function. And with a family and all the information they give us about ourselves over the years, we have recognition of our talents and our virtues. In short, we have a sense of our own identity.

We learn our identity from relating with other people. For instance, if you feel that you possess athletic ability, it is probably because over the years your family, and maybe some neighbors and coaches, said things like, "You can really shoot and dribble well." The more this aspect of your identity was reinforced by others' making similar comments, the more your identity as "athlete" became a part of who you are.

Of course, as a person suffering from amnesia, like Clare, you would lose this understanding of yourself as an athlete, and you would have to discover it all anew. Just as Clare did not know she was a natural performer, you would not recognize your athletic skill. Your memory would not automatically give you the confidence that comes with knowing where you have come from and what you can do.

Knowing the Why of Things

Besides giving us an understanding of who we are, a sense of personal history enables us to discover why we are the way we are, how it is that we have certain traits, reactions, or stumbling blocks. When Jane Doe discovered her history as Clare Forrest, a world of understanding opened up to her. She could then see the reasons for her fear of water, her love of singing before a group, her sadness at a little girl's emotional distress. What had been mysterious and cloudy came into focus, and Clare could see the why of the present.

Choosing Wisely

Knowing our personal history can also help us make better choices for the future. If you have a history of success in math courses, you can select a college major accordingly. Clare, knowing that at ten years of age she had lost her mother, might take special measures to make sure she is nurtured as an adult and not haunted by feelings of deprivation. When we know the why of things, we have the tools to figure out what to do in the future.

Group Amnesia and Group Recall Every family needs to cherish its own history as a family. Even though we may sometimes be embarrassed or bored by the old, well-worn tales that relatives tell at family reunions, each telling reminds us of who we are as a family. Some of the stories evoke tears: "I'll never forget Uncle Joe's last words, right before he died. He looked at me and whispered, 'Promise me you'll tell Helen I've always loved her and I always will, even when I'm gone.'" Other family stories urge us into laughter: "Remember when we were at Mass in the front pew of Saint Louis Cathedral and Jay got his mitten tangled in the collection basket? Yeah, Mom and Dad didn't know anything was wrong until they heard people laughing. Then they saw that there was Jay, stuck trying to get his little legs over the pew so he could chase the usher down for his mitt." Even such funny memories remind us of who we are as a family.

Forgetting Who We Are

Not only do families need to remember who they are, but cultures, societies, and nations must carry the memory of where they have come from and what they have experienced. Without this memory, they are doomed to forget who they are and repeat terrible mistakes. For instance, Christians must always keep before them the memory that Jesus was a Jew and that the roots of Christian faith are in Judaism. For centuries, some people who called themselves Christian persecuted Jewish people—most horribly in the *Shoah* (the

Hebrew, preferred term for the Holocaust) of six million Jews, which was perpetrated by the Nazis under Adolf Hitler. But how can it be possible to hate Jews without hating Jesus, who was a Jew? Today, anti-Semitism (prejudice against Jewish people) is still a problem in many parts of the world, including our own society.

Societal-Level Choices

By understanding the reasons for the way things are, societies and nations are in a better position to make wise choices. If we take the lessons of history to heart, we see how certain choices in the past led to certain outcomes, and we avoid the worst of both. Put another way, "those who forget the mistakes of history are condemned to repeat them."

So why study history? Knowing about history gives us a sense of our personal and cultural identity. It gives us insight into why things are as they are today. How fascinating it is to discover where a situation came from, to see that our conditions are not carved in stone and unchangeable just because they are "there." The present developed out of past events and can likewise be shaped and transformed by our own actions. Such an understanding of the why of things can be liberating; it can help us avoid making the same mistakes that were made in the past, because we see more clearly and understand our options more completely.

Why Study *Church* History?

Christianity is a historical religion, based on the life of a historical person: Jesus of Nazareth. The Gospels offer us faith-filled accounts of Jesus' life. Likewise, the story of the church, its history, provides us with a perspective on how Christians have lived out the Gospel message over the centuries. In fact, learning about the church is learning about the presence of Jesus Christ throughout history. Christ acts through and in the church's people; he lives in people's hearts and is seen in the actions of those who work in his name. Clearly, not all the actions of the church's members are Christlike—after all, the church is composed of regular, limited human beings. However, these same people have at times been the signs of the Lord's presence. Thus, knowing the church means knowing Jesus through his people.

Understanding Catholic Christian Identity

If you are reading this book as a Catholic, this study of Catholic church history can deepen your sense of identity as a Catholic Christian. You can see yourself as a member of a great religious movement that began with twelve disciples almost two thousand years ago and has grown to about one billion Catholics in the world today.

If you are reading this book as a non-Catholic Christian, much of the history described here, at least from the earlier periods until Christianity divided, will actually be your history as well. So the course will inform you about the parts of your own church's history that are shared with the Catholic church.

If you are reading this book as a non-Christian, you can gain some appreciation for the Catholic Christian identity of some of your neighbors, colleagues, and friends.

Learning the "Whys" of Catholic Faith

During the 1960s, many Catholic Christians were surprised to find significant changes in their church's liturgical practice. Many changes came as a result of a worldwide council of bishops, the Second Vatican Council, which met from 1962 to 1965.

New Developments in the 1960s

The altar, which formerly had been positioned against and facing the back wall of the church, was brought forward and turned around so that the priest could celebrate Mass facing the people. The language used in the Mass was no longer Latin but the local language. Instead of listening to a choir singing chants in Latin, the congregation was supposed to join in the music—sung in the language of the

When Christians refer to the Bible or the Christian Scriptures, they mean a whole collection of sacred writings that comprises what Christians have commonly called "the Old Testament" and "the New Testament." The Scriptures of the Old Testament are central to the Jewish faith and were originally written in Hebrew. Out of sensitivity to our Jewish brothers and sisters, we will call the two parts of the Christian Scriptures the Hebrew Scriptures and the Christian Testament, rather than terming them "old" and "new." ∎

Why These Terms for the Christian Bible?

people and accompanied by guitars, piano, drums, flutes, and other popular instruments. In some cases the names of the sacraments changed: penance became "the sacrament of reconciliation," and extreme unction was renamed "the anointing of the sick." Priests and members of religious orders adopted secular, or common, dress. The position of deacon, which had previously been restricted to men preparing for the priesthood, became open to all men.

These developments were quite disturbing to many Catholics because they thought that the essentials of their religion were being tampered with. They had thought that their church was unchanging—a steady sacred rock in the midst of a swirling sea of secular change.

Insight into the Historical Roots

Catholics with a good sense of the history of the church were not distressed by the changes in church practice, and their identity as Catholic Christians was not threatened. Wherever changes were introduced with an explanation of the historical roots of the changes, most Catholics not only accepted but welcomed the developments. They found out that the changes were an attempt to put the church back in touch with its roots in the faith and vision of the early Christian communities.

For instance, when Catholics during the 1960s discovered that the language of the liturgy was originally intended to be understandable, not mysterious, changing the Mass from Latin to the local language made sense to them. It was useful for Catholics to learn that Latin had come into use for the liturgy around the year 400 in the western part of the Roman Empire, because Latin was the language of Rome. It eventually became the official language of the Roman Catholic liturgy, and it remained so until the 1960s, even though most Catholics did not understand it. Yet, in the early decades of Christianity, the Apostles probably celebrated the Eucharist in Aramaic, not in Latin. And Saint Paul probably broke bread and wrote his Epistles using the Greek that was the everyday language of the communities he served.

Similarly, Catholics of the modern era were able to appreciate and accept new developments in the ordained ministry after knowing these facts: In the early centuries of the church, married deacons ministered to the people. The role of deacon was not just a step to the priesthood but was a permanent role. And up until the year 1200, many priests were married.

A Sense of the Essential

By learning the reasons for various church practices and how certain traditions originated, we can better sort out what is essential and unchangeable in Catholicism from what is not essential and therefore changeable. Besides, it can be just plain fascinating to discover how things got to be the way they are.

Choosing for the Church of the Future Understanding church history can liberate us to see more clearly what is required for the church. That is, if we understand how present realities came to be and we can distinguish the essential from the inessential, then we can choose more wisely for the future.

The church, over its long history, has been moved and shaped by the Spirit of God, acting in and through human beings like ourselves. We can shape the future by who we are to and for others, and by the care with which we choose the course of action for our lives.

The Story of a Relationship The history of the church is the story of a relationship between Jesus and the believers who have followed him over the centuries. As you read the history of Catholic Christianity, you will learn about people—those who have shaped the way that the world and the church are today. Some parts of the history may disturb you. Other parts may inspire you. Just remember that as in a friendship, we need to know about and learn from both the good and the bad. We need to be able to appreciate the church with all its limits, as we would learn to accept a friend who has faults as well as attractive qualities. Fundamentally, Catholics believe that God's Spirit has been with the church through good times and bad, guiding it in the most difficult and disastrous periods as well as in the apparently glorious eras.

Six Ways of Seeing the Church

Just as friendships are exciting because we always learn more about our friends, so exploring the church's life can be fascinating because we learn more about God and people. We can study the church, all the while realizing that it is so full of God's presence that we will never thoroughly know it. Ultimately, like a friend, the church is a mystery that cannot be completely analyzed or explained.

Although we can never totally know the church, we do have ways of studying it that can help us appreciate it more. While learning about its history, we can try to examine the church along a number of different dimensions, or models. In other words, we can see the church according to its various aspects.

Think of the models of the church as a device somewhat like the engineering plans for a new building. An engineering firm could make a number of drawings of the different aspects of the building. Perhaps one drawing would diagram all the electrical wiring, another drawing would show all the plumbing, and still another would indicate the steel frame and the placement of windows and walls. No single drawing would give us a complete picture of the building, but each one would add to our understanding of it. Taken together, all of these different drawings would give us a fairly good picture of the structure and inner workings of the building.

Let's consider six models of the church, with each one highlighting or emphasizing a different dimension of the complex, ultimately mysterious reality that we call the church of Jesus Christ.

1. The Church as Body of Christ or People of God

"We are related to one another as a family." In the Christian Testament, the church is often described as the Body of Christ. The community of believers—professing Christian faith, caring for one another, celebrating the Eucharist together, serving the poor—becomes the body of Jesus on earth. And the different parts of this body of Jesus are related to one another in the same way that members of an actual physical body are intimately dependent on one another.

In his First Letter to the Corinthians, Saint Paul says that all members, each with a different function, are important to the Body of Christ, the church. Therefore, just as people would care for their own body, they must take care of one another. No person alone can do everything necessary to be the embodiment of Christ in the world, but together, the church as a whole body can be the fullest expression of Christ.

In addition to being called the Body of Christ, the church community goes by another name that expresses a similar reality—People of God. This name recalls the identity of the Israelites as the Chosen People of God in the Hebrew Scriptures. In the Christian Testament, Jesus calls all people to God's love. Thus, those who believe become the People of God, members of God's own family.

2. The Church as Institution

"We are organized through formal structures." The word *institution* is used in a variety of ways. We speak of colleges and hospitals as institutions (meaning that they are highly complex and formally structured organizations). We hear praise for the institutions of democracy (meaning, in the United States, the secret-ballot elections, the three branches of government, and so on). In neither of these cases does *institution* mean simply a building. Rather, the term refers to the organized patterns, rules, and social structures that have developed to help carry out a group's or a movement's purposes.

Humans tend to "institutionalize" groups and movements that they hold as important and valuable. A group wants to maintain itself in an orderly way and accomplish its goals without constantly wrestling over how to proceed or who is in charge. Thus the church over time developed an institutional aspect, with rules, roles, and an authority structure. In fact, the church as Institution is probably the most familiar model of the church to us, because we associate the church with a hierarchy, or authority structure, of pope, bishops, and priests. When we speak of the church, we often mean the "official church," the church of the Vatican in Rome or of the diocesan office locally. We forget that this formal, institutional aspect is only one dimension of the church.

Even at its very beginning, the church was developing institutional patterns, although the first followers of Jesus would not have thought of themselves as an institution. Jesus gave Peter authority as leader and commissioned the Apostles to preach the Good News, which was a way of passing on authority to them. They in turn commissioned others. Formal roles—of bishop, deacon, and then priest— were established to do the work of the early church. Processes for entry into the church, as well as for being banned from the church for grievous offenses, had to be worked out. Forums such as church councils were developed for settling conflicts, even as early as the time of Saints Peter and Paul.

The institutional dimension of the church is the human way of ensuring that the church will be maintained and its mission will continue: the needy will be cared for, God will be worshiped, and the Gospel will be preached.

3. The Church as Sacrament **"We are a visible, tangible sign of God's love."** Human beings need tangible, flesh-and-blood reminders that God is with them. For this reason, Catholicism stresses the sacramental quality of life—that we find God in the concrete, the ordinary, the physical reality of existence. The seven official Catholic sacraments (Baptism, the Eucharist, Confirmation, Marriage, Holy Orders, Reconciliation, and Anointing) convey God's love through physical, tangible actions like pouring water, sharing bread, massaging with oil, and laying hands on a person.

Similarly, Jesus is sometimes referred to as the Sacrament of God, because in his human, physical existence here on earth, he embodied and was a sign of God's loving action in the world. Now the church, as the extension of Jesus in historical time, continues being a sign of God's presence in the world. Therefore, the church is a Sacrament, a physical sign of God's saving love. When the people of the church worship, serve, and preach, God's saving power is revealed as present. The people remember what Jesus was all about when he was on earth and thus what God is all about.

As a Vatican Council II document expressed it, the church "is a kind of sacrament or sign of intimate union with God, and of the unity of all mankind" (*Dogmatic Constitution on the Church*, number 1). We see this unifying action of the church in the celebration of the seven sacraments themselves. For instance, at the Eucharist, in sharing the body and blood of Christ, Catholics become united with God and with one another in Jesus. This sacrament expresses the reality of an actual living community—real people at a specific place and time, affirming their identity through activities they do in unison. Just as a volleyball team is identified as a team because it plays games regularly together, the Christian community maintains its identity through its liturgical celebrations.

4. The Church as Herald of God's Word

"We proclaim the Good News." You may have seen movies about medieval European castles and towns and the people who lived in them. When rulers wanted to send an official message to the people, they sent out a herald. The herald would blow a horn, ring a bell, or yell loudly to call people together. Usually the message was for everyone to hear, and it was considered very important.

The church is the Herald of Jesus Christ. It acts as a messenger to proclaim the word of God to all people everywhere. The first Christians spread the word by going out from Jerusalem to tell the Good News of Jesus to anyone who would listen. Eventually the Apostles proclaimed the Gospel as far as Rome. Later generations of Christians, right up to the present, have brought the Gospel "to the ends of the earth"—to every continent and every nation.

Belief in Jesus Christ and his Gospel comes about through hearing the word of God preached by credible witnesses to the Gospel. People will not believe in something they have never heard about, nor will they have faith in a vision that does not seem to affect the lives of the ones proclaiming the message.

The church acts as Herald in several ways. Jesus said, "'Where two or three are gathered in my name, I am there among them'"

(Matthew 18:20). So, on a simple level, any gathering at which Christians read the word of God or pray together is the church acting as Herald. During the liturgy of the word at Mass, for example, the church is Herald. Many church publications, TV programs, and radio programs herald the word. Missionaries still preach the Gospel to people who have not heard it. Finally, the loving, committed actions of Christians herald the Good News.

5. The Church as Servant   **"We are at the service of God and therefore of all humankind."** The night before Jesus died on the cross, he gave the Apostles an example of how to live and relate to others. Jesus, who was the disciples' "lord and master," washed their feet, taking the customary role that a servant would have in a Jewish household. In doing so, Jesus modeled for his followers the kind of persons that they must be—servants who give themselves and make sacrifices for others.

At another time, Jesus made it clear that when his followers serve others with compassion, they are really serving God:

"'I was hungry and you gave me food, I was thirsty and you gave me something to drink, I was a stranger and you welcomed me, I was naked and you gave me clothing, I was sick and you took care of me, I was in prison and you visited me.'" (Matthew 25:35–36)

The church, like the Apostles, is called to be a Servant to the world, to offer itself to humankind directly and compassionately out of love for God. The church serves human beings through its institutional structures but also through the efforts of individual Christians who put their life at the service of others.

The ways in which people become servants may vary a lot. Everyone has different talents, positions, and circumstances—from the laboratory researcher studying the effects of pollution on the environment, to the parent welcoming the neighborhood kids in for some snacks and fun, to the teenager offering to help a classmate with a difficult course. Christians need to look at their own abilities realistically and use whatever talents they possess in the best ways for the greatest good. People make their marks on history mostly through the service they give to humankind. In this way they also live out the reality of the church as Servant.

As an institution, the church has established many service organizations. Worldwide, the Catholic church educates millions of students in grade schools, high schools, colleges, and universities. Thousands of Catholic hospitals and clinics treat sick people. The church runs orphanages and homes for aged and chronically ill persons. It also operates literacy programs, agricultural development projects, publishing houses, and so on. At one time, when slavery was common, some religious orders dedicated themselves to freeing those in bondage. As needs arise in the world, the church seeks to meet those needs.

6. The Church as Community of Disciples

"We are followers of Jesus." A disciple is a devoted follower of a teacher or master; a disciple strives to live according to the beliefs and lifestyle of the person followed. Jesus' disciples took on his way of life; they learned his values, traveled with him, and dedicated themselves to his vision. As a consequence of following Jesus, they went against the grain of the wider society. Eventually all of them suffered for their beliefs, and most of them died for those convictions.

Any group of people who feed the hungry, love one another, share their goods, stand up for those treated unjustly, and live simply, peacefully, and with respect for their environment are bound to stand in contrast with the rest of society. Because they do not follow the standards of the rest of the world but instead look to an alternative vision, they may not be successful in terms that the rest of the world understands. They may be failures economically; they may even get in trouble for challenging injustice when they see it.

Such is the call of the church—to be a Community of Disciples of Jesus, a people whose lifestyle stands in contrast with the rest of society. Overall, Jesus' message and way of life are immensely challenging, and not necessarily popular.

Jesus never imagined that his disciples would have it easy. Life for them would be fulfilling, yes. Easy, no. The cost of following Jesus over the centuries has often been paid in blood by martyrs, who have died for the cause of the Gospel. In our own time, committed followers of Jesus suffer consequences, in some instances even torture and death, for the lifestyle to which they commit themselves. But more typically in our society, the consequences of following Jesus are likely to be seen in situations such as less material success or loss of popularity because of the stands one takes.

To believe in Christ and work for his vision of peace and justice and love demands sharing in the sufferings of Jesus. The church as Community of Disciples bears witness by its own lifestyle that the "good life" is about more than television sets, expensive cars, the latest fashions, smooth skin, a nice body, a great sound system, and a high-status job.

The church as Community of Disciples may be the most challenging dimension of being church. But faithful, hopeful, and loving people have chosen to be different, have chosen to be disciples of Jesus throughout the almost two thousand years of the church's history.

Church History and the Models As you read about the history of the Catholic Christian church in this book, these models will be referred in order to highlight different dimensions of the church's role in history—as Body of Christ or People of God, Institution, Sacrament, Herald, Servant, and Community of Disciples.

You will see that over the centuries the church has developed in different directions and according to a variety of emphases. For instance, as the church has grown, the Institution model has become much more obvious. At particular times, the missionary activities of the church have highlighted the Herald model. Most of the adaptations in the church through history have come about so that it could be a more effective Body of Christ, Institution, Sacrament, Herald, Servant, and Community of Disciples. Yet the church is more than the sum of its parts—more than all the models put together. Ultimately, the church remains a fascinating mystery.

Conclusion This book aims to help you see the church with new eyes. Like someone on a fascinating search to find his or her family's roots, perhaps you will discover with surprise some insight into who you are and why "the family" of the church is the way it is today. You may be troubled to find stories of family tragedy or conflict, delighted to discover brave and inspiring ancestors, and appreciative of the struggles that have shaped the family over the years. You may find dimensions of the family that you never noticed or that you took for granted. Finally, you may find that this journey into the past will enable you to see the future more clearly and commit yourself to it with a wiser mind and heart.

Questions for Reflection and Discussion

1. In what ways are your personal story and your family's story important to you?
2. What are some of the biggest changes in the Catholic church that you can remember happening after Vatican Council II? How did they affect you?
3. Which of the six models of the church do you feel most comfortable with? Which model represents your present experience of the church?
4. What is it that most attracts you to explore the story of the church?

2

A Church of Converts

Widening the Circle of Jesus' Followers

IN THE BEGINNING of its history, the church was not even thought of as a church. Rather, while Jesus was alive, the band of disciples who gathered around him thought of themselves simply as followers of Jesus of Nazareth. It was not unusual in those times for movements and followings to develop within Judaism, which was the religion of Jesus and his disciples. Most of these movements were tolerated within the religion; Judaism was known for the diversity of groups and beliefs within it. Jesus' truthfulness and integrity, however, would eventually get him into big trouble with the authorities, both religious and civil.

Rather than squelch the fledgling movement of Jesus' followers, the Roman authorities' execution of Jesus seemed only to bring more followers to the Way—the way of life that Jesus had shown them. The disciples of Jesus spread the Good News that he had been raised from the dead and had appeared to them. Surely, they declared, this man was the long-awaited Messiah, sent by God to save the Jewish people from oppression.

These claims, though welcomed by many new Jewish followers of the Way in Jerusalem, presented an intolerable threat to the Jewish authorities of the Sanhedrin, the supreme council of the Jews. Within a couple of years of Jesus' death, scenes like the following one were occurring, as the Sanhedrin tried to stamp out the growing movement of Jesus' followers:

A young man stood undaunted in front of his accusers, members of the Sanhedrin, who encircled him. Their faces showed a mixture of hate, fear, and grudging admiration. The young man, Stephen, did have courage. He was sure of himself. Indeed, his confidence itself made his listeners fearful and uneasy. They felt strongly that Stephen and his kind had to be crushed before their ideas about this Jesus spread far.

Stephen had been selected by the community of Jesus' followers to be a deacon. His duties included taking care of widows, orphans, sick people, and those members of the movement who were in prison. Although challenging the Jewish authorities was a dangerous move, Stephen felt compelled to speak out, convinced that Jesus was the way and the truth. The crowd of accusers claimed that Stephen spoke "blasphemous words against Moses and God," so Stephen attempted to show them that even Moses had been rejected by the people of Israel. He further unsettled the crowd by claiming that God did not

Timeline . . .

27
- Jesus begins his public ministry.
- Peter's leadership role is foretold.
- Jesus dies and is resurrected.
- Pentecost transforms the disciples.

- General persecution follows Stephen's stoning.
- Saul encounters Risen Jesus, is converted to the Way.

- Peter first baptizes

40 Gentiles.

- Antioch believers are termed Christians.

- Paul and Barnabas bring famine relief to Jerusalem.
- Paul begins his first missionary journey.

50
- Council of Jerusalem decides Jewish Law is not essential for Christians.
- Paul begins his second missionary journey.
- Paul writes his first Epistle.

- Paul begins his third missionary journey.

need a Temple in which to be worshiped. God existed everywhere and could be worshiped everywhere.

Over the shouts of the hostile council members, Stephen ended his speech with words that only further inflamed them: "You stiff-necked people . . . you are forever opposing the Holy Spirit, just as your ancestors used to do. Which of the prophets did your ancestors not persecute? They killed those who foretold the coming of the Righteous One, and now you have become his betrayers and murderers. You are the ones that received the law as ordained by angels, and yet you have not kept it."

Many of the dignified men of the Sanhedrin had covered their ears to prevent hearing such blasphemy. Enraged, they grabbed Stephen and dragged him out of the city. They snatched up large stones; first one and then the rest began hurling the stones at Stephen. Soon the stones rained down upon him. Blood poured from his wounds.

"Lord Jesus, receive my spirit," Stephen prayed, and then in a loud voice he cried out, "Lord, do not hold this sin against them." A large stone, thrown with all the force of anger and fear, crushed the back of Stephen's skull.

When the young man finally lay still, those who had stoned him gazed silently at his broken and bleeding body. Slowly, they began drifting away. Many had laid their coats at the feet of a young man named Saul, who came from Tarsus. Saul had heartily approved of the execution. In the days that followed, he joined the vigilantes who broke into homes and dragged Jesus' followers off to prison. He was determined to put an end to the Way, this fanatical movement whose followers dared to challenge the most sacred beliefs of Judaism. (Based on Acts of the Apostles, chapters 6–7)

In spite of persecution and martyrdom, and perhaps even because of it, the community of Jesus' followers persisted in their message. The movement grew. It developed in unexpected ways into a church whose identity would one day be worldwide, going far beyond the boundaries of Palestine and its original Jewish membership.

Let's step back, however, to see what was behind this movement, what gave the disciples of Jesus determination to follow him no matter what the cost.

The Original Circle: Those Who Walked with Jesus

The church began with the group who gathered around Jesus: the twelve Apostles and other disciples who knew him personally. The beliefs that united them came from Judaism, and they saw themselves as Jewish to the core. Like other Jews, the disciples longed for the coming of a Messiah, who would rescue them from oppression by their Roman occupiers. Gradually they would come to recognize Jesus as that Messiah, the redeemer sent by God. Thus, church history began in a powerful personal experience—the disciples' living, talking, and walking with Jesus. Even today, Jesus' followers personally experience him, though in different ways than the original band did.

Peter: First Among the Faithful Among the twelve Apostles—those followers associated most closely with Jesus—the most prominent one was Simon Peter, also known simply as Peter. When Jesus first called him away from his fishing nets in Galilee, Simon would certainly have laughed if anyone had told him how his life would change. As odd as it may seem, this illiterate, hot-tempered, married fisherman was to be the "rock" on which Jesus would build the church. (Peter, the name Jesus gave to Simon, literally means "rock.") Jesus called Peter and Peter's brother Andrew from their fishing occupation, promising, "'Follow me and I will make you fish for people'" (Mark 1:17). And Peter and Andrew left behind a whole way of life to follow him. Jesus must have been a striking, magnetic person.

The Christian Testament tells us that Peter was to be central to the new group of believers, after Jesus would be physically gone. In Matthew's Gospel account, Jesus says:

"I tell you, you are Peter, and on this rock I will build my church, and the gates of Hades will not prevail against it. I will give you the keys of the kingdom of heaven, and whatever you bind on earth will be bound in heaven, and whatever you loose on earth will be loosed in heaven." (Matthew 16:18–19)

Jesus knew Peter and loved him, even with Peter's many weaknesses, including his ignorance, angry moods, and betrayals. After all, Jesus had come to save sinners, and Peter was clearly one of them.

The Apostles: Witnesses to Jesus' Death and Resurrection

Together at the Last Supper

As Jesus rode triumphantly into Jerusalem toward the end of his life, the crowds who acclaimed him were huge. But crowds do not necessarily make up a church of genuine believers. So the night before he died, Jesus gathered the twelve Apostles together to celebrate the Passover. At the Last Supper, in a ritual meal that was to be repeated in remembrance of him, Jesus showed the Apostles how they should serve one another and share the word of God. This was the coming-to-birth church, celebrating its first Eucharist.

A Disappointing Group of Friends

In the Garden of Gethsemane, where Jesus went to pray after the Last Supper, Peter and the other Apostles disappointed Jesus. Instead of keeping vigil with him, they all went to sleep—abandoning their leader to lonely agony, for he knew that the time of his betrayal by one of his own followers, Judas, was at hand. After the Roman soldiers came and took Jesus away, Peter and perhaps some of the others followed. But when pressured to identify himself with Jesus, Peter denied that he even knew him. The Apostles were probably at the Crucifixion, but we are sure only of John's presence there.

Amazed by the Risen Lord

In the Gospels, we have an image of the Apostles, scared and worried, huddled together, when Mary Magdalene and two other women came rushing back from the empty tomb to announce that Jesus had risen. Peter "got up and ran to the tomb; stooping and looking in, he saw the linen cloths by themselves; then he went home, amazed at what had happened" (Luke 24:12). Later, the Risen Jesus appeared to his followers on the road to Emmaus, and then again in a room where they were staying—the place where "doubting Thomas" insisted he would have to touch Jesus' wounds to believe that Jesus was risen. In one amusing story of Jesus' appearing to the disciples after the Resurrection, Peter spots him on shore from a fishing boat and, in eagerness, jumps in the water to go meet him.

The Resurrection, Jesus' being raised from the dead, was the crucial event for the church. Without it, the Apostles would have certainly disbanded, and Jesus would be a forgotten religious fanatic who was executed for threatening the established order of things. However, for the church to really take off, one more event—Pentecost—had to happen after the Resurrection.

Transformation at Pentecost After the joy of experiencing Jesus with them again, the Apostles were disheartened and frightened when Jesus ascended to God and no longer walked with them. For days the Apostles drifted like boats that had lost their rudders. Nonetheless, these disciples and Jesus' mother, Mary, gathered to celebrate the traditional Jewish feast of Pentecost, in thanksgiving for the year's harvests. What happened in that anxious gathering was completely unexpected, but it transformed those present, who had known Jesus personally, as no other experience could:

When the day of Pentecost had come, they were all together in one place. And suddenly from heaven there came a sound like the rush of a violent wind, and it filled the entire house where they were sitting. Divided tongues, as of fire, appeared among them, and a tongue rested on each of them. All of them were filled with the Holy Spirit and began to speak in other languages, as the Spirit gave them ability. (Acts 2:1–4)

The coming of Jesus' Spirit, or the Holy Spirit, upon them suddenly turned the timid, discouraged, scared followers into bold, confident, zealous heralds of the Good News. This was the conversion that the Apostles needed if they were to have the strength and vision to carry on in Jesus' footsteps. Therefore, the Christian feast of Pentecost, which recalls the wonderful event that transformed the Apostles, is frequently called "the birthday of the church."

The Circle Expands: Jews Who Did Not Know Jesus

On the day of Pentecost, the Apostles were not the only ones who were converted in a new way to Jesus. Their hearts were set with such a fire that for the first time, they had the courage to go out into the world and proclaim Jesus to all who would listen. The Apostles could no longer keep the Good News to themselves.

The First Christian Baptisms Leaving the building where they had been moved by the Holy Spirit and going into the streets of Jerusalem, the Apostles encountered their fellow Jews, many of whom were originally from countries besides Palestine. Amazingly, the foreign Jews heard the Apostles speaking about God's great deeds, each in the hearer's own native language. Peter addressed the crowd powerfully, speaking to the people in the context of their own Jewish tradition—about how Jesus had been sent as the Messiah, and God had raised him from the dead and placed him at God's right hand. With these words, Peter invited the assembled Jews to follow Jesus, a man they had never met:

"Repent, and be baptized every one of you in the name of Jesus Christ so that your sins may be forgiven; and you will receive the gift of the Holy Spirit. For the promise is for you, for your children, and for all who are far away, everyone whom the Lord our God calls to him." (Acts 2:38–39)

The Acts of the Apostles, which gives an account of the early years of the Christian community, records that about three thousand persons were baptized that day. Through his actions on Pentecost, Peter became a central figure for Jesus' followers, and the circle of Jesus' followers expanded.

Jewish *and* Christian   It is important to recognize that the first-to-be-baptized followers of Jesus did not think of themselves as converting from Judaism to Christianity or as starting a new religion. They saw themselves as still within Judaism but following Jesus' way of life and teachings. In fact, as noted earlier in this chapter, their movement was known as the Way. (The term *Christian* did not come into use until about ten years later, when it was applied to the believers at Antioch. For our purposes, however, we will refer to Jesus' followers as Christians at this point.)

Before long, Christianity would spread far beyond Jerusalem's gates and beyond Palestine to many other places in the Roman Empire where Jewish communities existed. Those spreading the word would usually preach to their fellow Jews in local Jewish synagogues, because the Jews could understand the prophecies about the Messiah and see Jesus as a fulfillment of their religious hopes.

As a minority movement within Judaism, the earliest followers of Jesus met regularly in Jerusalem at the Temple, the center of Jewish worship, to pray, and they kept the Jewish religious laws. In other towns, they went to the local synagogue to pray. The followers also met in private homes to share meals and special prayers.

Trouble with the Authorities   In Jerusalem, the Jewish authorities began harassing the growing community of Jesus' followers. What upset the authorities was that the leaders of the group, especially the fisherman Peter and a fellow named John, kept telling people that Jesus of Nazareth was alive, that they had seen and talked with him, even eaten with him—all this after everyone knew that he had been executed and buried. Peter and the others also claimed that Jesus was the Messiah, sent by God to give freedom to the Chosen People. In addition, Jesus' followers were able to cure the sick. The cures could not be denied, because there were too many eyewitnesses.

Due to all of this trouble, some of the Jewish leaders had the Apostles jailed, but the Apostles managed to escape and continued to teach in the Temple. Finally, a powerful member of the Sanhedrin, the Pharisee Gamaliel, urged the Jewish leaders to leave the movement alone. If Jesus was the Messiah, he reasoned, the Sanhedrin could not do anything about it, as it would be fighting against God. On the other hand, if Jesus was not the Messiah, his followers would disband and eventually die out. In spite of Gamaliel's wise advice, incidents such as the stoning of Stephen, the first Christian martyr (from the story at the beginning of this chapter), took place and set off a round of persecution.

When the harassment, imprisonments, and executions began in Jerusalem, the Apostles stayed on there, but most of the other Christians fled into the countryside and waited for the persecution to die down. The Christians, remember, thought of themselves as faithful Jews, so they must have been grief-stricken and horrified that they were being persecuted by members of their own religion.

Paul: The Link Between Jewish Christians and the Wider World

The Acts of the Apostles notes that after the stoning of Stephen, Saul (whom we know as Paul) ravaged the Christian community by going house to house and dragging Christian men and women off to prison. He even obtained warrants from the Sanhedrin to go north into Syria and arrest any Christian refugees he could find in the city of Damascus.

Who Was Paul? Who was this zealous defender of Jewish orthodoxy? Saul was a well-educated Jew from Tarsus, a major trading city in Asia Minor (now Turkey). He was steeped in the Jewish tradition, having studied under Gamaliel at the Temple as a boy. In addition, he was knowledgeable of and comfortable with Greek and Roman ways, because of having grown up in a major trading city. His everyday language was Greek, and he enjoyed the privileges of Roman citizenship, including having the Roman name *Paul*. He had been around many Gentiles (non-Jews) in his life, but Saul's first allegiance was to his Jewish faith. As a teacher and leader in the synagogue at Tarsus, he loved the Jewish Law and greatly revered the covenant between God and the Chosen People.

On the Road to Damascus **Forever Changed**

Something happened to Saul as he approached Damascus to persecute the Christians, and the event would change him and the community of Jesus' disciples forever. In the Acts of the Apostles, Saul tells about his experience:

"While I was on my way and approaching Damascus, about noon a great light from heaven suddenly shone about me. I fell to the ground and heard a voice saying to me, 'Saul, Saul, why are you persecuting me?' I answered, 'Who are you, Lord?' Then he said to me, 'I am Jesus of Nazareth whom you are persecuting.' Now those who were with me saw the light but did not hear the voice of the one who was speaking to me. I asked, 'What am I to do, Lord?' The Lord said to me, 'Get up and go to Damascus; there you will be told everything that has been assigned to you to do.' Since I could not see because of the brightness of that light, those who were with me took my hand and led me to Damascus." (Acts 22:6–11)

In a state of shock, blind, and too stunned to eat or drink, Saul realized that his old world was coming to an end. He had been doing what he thought was right—protecting his religious heritage. With the startling experience on the road to Damascus, his thoughts must have gone around in circles always ending with Jesus. Jesus really was alive. Now what?

After Saul had suffered three days of shock and blindness, a man named Ananias came to visit him. Ananias claimed to have been sent by Jesus. Saul felt the man's hands on his face, and suddenly he could see again. Not only could he see the physical world, but a spiritual insight was given to him. Acknowledging Jesus as the Messiah, he received baptism from Ananias.

When Saul was well again, cared for by the people whom he had come to harm, he needed time to rebuild his life. In a letter to the Galatians, written years after his conversion, he says that he left Damascus and went to Arabia, the desert area east and south of the city. He does not say what he did there, but he likely went back to making tents, which was the trade of his family in Tarsus. He probably read, again and again, what the prophets said about the Messiah in the Hebrew Scriptures. Above all, he must have prayed and reflected deeply on his experience at Damascus.

Saul, who eventually went by his Roman name, *Paul,* was vigorous, determined, and dynamic. When he came out of the desert after studying and praying, all the energy he had put into persecuting the followers of Jesus was directed toward spreading Jesus' message. Paul's whole life and destiny were changed. He would travel thousands of dangerous miles, mostly on foot, to spread the Good News that had knocked him off his feet on the road to Damascus.

Gentile Converts: Beyond Judaism's Limits

While Paul was living in the quiet desert country, unexpected things were going on elsewhere among the people of the Way.

First the Samaritans, Then the Gentiles As Jesus' followers fled from persecution in Jerusalem, all along the way they spoke of Jesus to whomever would listen. For example, a deacon named Philip stopped in Samaria. For centuries the Samaritans (who were despised "distant cousins" of the Jews) and the Jews had been enemies. But the Samaritans listened to Philip's Good News about Jesus. Many asked to be baptized. Peter and John were sent by the Jerusalem community to find out what was going on at Samaria, and they saw the great belief the Samaritans had in Jesus. Spurred by the acceptance of the Good News, Philip went west to the towns on the Mediterranean coast, speaking to both Jews and Gentiles.

Following in Philip's footsteps through the coastal towns, Peter taught and healed the sick, and even brought a dead woman back to life. At Caesarea, the Roman capital of Judea, Peter baptized some Gentiles, including the Roman commander Cornelius and his whole family. Much to the amazement of the Jewish members of the Way, these newly baptized Gentiles then received the Holy Spirit and began speaking in foreign tongues.

Today we think of Paul as the person who brought the Gospel to the Gentiles. His role in that process was certainly most significant, but he was not the first to preach to them.

Controversy Brews over the Gentiles

Peter in Jerusalem

When Peter returned to Jerusalem, turmoil in the community greeted him. How could Peter baptize Gentiles—people who were not Jewish? Even if the Gentiles accepted belief in the One God, they were not the Chosen People. Jesus had come to the Jews. Besides, didn't Peter break the Jewish Law by visiting Gentiles and eating with them? (The Gentiles were considered unclean because they did not follow the strict dietary laws of the Jews. In addition, the Gentiles did not follow the Jewish practice of circumcision, which was a sign of the covenant with God and was essential for Jewish males.)

Peter defended his actions, telling the community that in a vision God had instructed him not to call anyone profane or unclean. Peter was growing in the conviction that although Jesus had come among the Jews first, his gift of salvation was meant for all people, not just the Jews. Peter reminded the Jerusalem community that Jesus had eaten with sinners, tax collectors, and Samaritans and had commissioned the Apostles to go out to the whole world. Those reminders probably stung the Jerusalem community. Although the members were followers of Jesus, they still thought of themselves as religious Jews, not as members of a new religion. Peter's explanation calmed the group for a while, but the problem did not end there.

Paul's Mission: Initially to a Jewish Audience

When Paul emerged from his time of reflection in the desert (after about three years), he was on fire with faith in Jesus. He started preaching to the Jews in Damascus, the city of his conversion. So powerful were his words that some people complained to the governor. Paul's friends warned him that a special guard at the city gates had orders to arrest him on sight. So in the deep of night, Paul's allies managed to lower him over the high city walls in a large basket ordinarily used to carry vegetables.

Having escaped Damascus, Paul headed south to Jerusalem, where he met Peter and James and spent two weeks with them. Undoubtedly they told Paul many things about Jesus as they remembered him, but Paul also had his own unique experience of the Risen Jesus on the road to Damascus to carry with him the rest of his life.

Soon Paul was on the run again, to escape a plot by some Jews to kill him. Paul, who previously had persecuted other people for preaching about Jesus, became a marked man himself. After these initial experiences with preaching the Gospel, Paul spent several years back in his hometown of Tarsus.

Antioch: The First Jewish-Gentile Christian Community

Some of the Jewish Christian refugees from Jerusalem had gone to Antioch, the third largest city in the Roman Empire, to escape persecution. Situated on a river not far from the Mediterranean Sea, Antioch was beautiful and impressive. The city had a mixed population of Gentiles and Jews. Some of the Gentiles even attended the synagogue with the Jews, but they usually did not convert to Judaism, because they felt that the Jewish Law was too difficult to observe and that too many of the laws did not make sense.

The Controversy Reopens

When the Christians from Jerusalem arrived at Antioch, they spoke of Jesus to the mixed Jewish-Gentile audience in the synagogue. Consequently, those asking for baptism included people from both groups. The Christian community in Jerusalem was upset when it heard about this, reopening the controversy that the community had earlier with Peter over whether to welcome Gentiles into the Way. An influential and committed Christian, Barnabas, was sent by the Jerusalem community to make inquiries into the questionable goings-on at Antioch.

A Remarkable Community

Barnabas saw clearly that the Jews and Gentiles at Antioch were united in their faith in Jesus. He was glad. In fact, he decided to stay in Antioch to teach and encourage the people in their new way of life. As the Antioch community grew, Romans and other outsiders remarked about how different this group was compared with the rest of the Jewish community. Therefore, to distinguish this community from the other Jews, the general population began to call the members *Christians,* that is, "followers of Christ." It was the first time the term was used.

Charity and Solidarity Grow

Barnabas enlisted the help of Paul, living then in Tarsus, to minister with him to the flourishing church of Antioch. Before long, the Antioch community was responding to news of a crop failure in Jerusalem that was putting the Christian community there in danger of starvation. The Antioch community collected money and sent Paul and Barnabas to deliver it to the hungry and persecuted Christians of Jerusalem. This charity must have been greatly appreciated by the community at Jerusalem, who not long before had questioned the legitimacy of the mixed Jewish-Gentile church of Antioch.

The Christians in Jerusalem were hurting. The Apostle James was beheaded by the Jewish king, and Peter was imprisoned. Although Peter escaped miraculously, he knew that he had to flee Jerusalem. So he appointed another man, also named James, as head of the Jerusalem community. In such a time of crisis, it must have been consoling for the Christians in Jerusalem to know that they could rely on other Christian churches, even those far away like the one in Antioch, for material and spiritual support. The Christian community learned about compassion and solidarity early on.

Paul's First Journey: A Growing Gentile Audience With the community at Antioch solidly established, the missionary team of Paul and Barnabas could turn their attention to spreading the Gospel to other cities in more unfamiliar territory. The trip they undertook is known as Paul's first missionary journey. They had the advantage of traveling within the bounds of the Roman Empire, which had good roads, seas that were relatively free of pirates, and a common language—Greek. From this point on, Paul and Barnabas would be preaching to mixed populations: Greeks, Romans, and people from distant lands. Nevertheless, in many places, they would find Jewish congregations with whom they could stay.

Beginning with a successful effort on the island of Cyprus, Paul and Barnabas then worked their way through the seaside towns of Asia Minor (modern Turkey), staying in each place for several months, and then went on to the plateau prairie lands.

Rejection by Jews

Paul and Barnabas's plan was first to preach in the synagogues on the Sabbath. Some Jews accepted Jesus as the Messiah; many did not. Those who rejected Paul and Barnabas's teaching ignored them or forbade them to speak in the synagogue again. Others who rejected the message, usually a small minority, became violent. Paul wrote later of being driven out of towns, beaten, and even stoned and left for dead. Somehow he and Barnabas survived all of the violence.

Acceptance by Gentiles

The Gentiles who accepted Jesus were relieved that they did not also have to accept the many laws that their Jewish neighbors followed. Paul and Barnabas did not encounter the violent rejection of their teaching from Gentiles. Mixed communities of Jewish and Gentile Christians began to form their own worship groups, distinct from the synagogues. Paul and Barnabas stayed in each town for a while, teaching, praying, and counseling the new Christians. Paul often paid his way by working as a tent maker.

At the end of the first preaching tour, Paul and Barnabas ended up back in Antioch. While they had been gone, more controversy had been brewing over what was expected of Gentiles entering the church.

Crisis over the Jewish Law

By the time Paul and Barnabas finished the first missionary journey, the Christian community at Jerusalem had supposedly accepted the fact that the Way would be open to Gentiles as well as Jews. But the issue never seemed to really go away; it flared up particularly around the issue of exactly what would be expected of the Gentiles entering the church, such as those in Antioch. Although the Gentile Christians were not Jews, would they be obligated to keep the Jewish Law, in effect becoming Jews?

Dietary Laws and the Requirement of Circumcision On a visit to Antioch, Peter discovered that the Gentile converts there ate food forbidden by the Jewish Law—for example, pork and shellfish. In the first century, meals were considered very important in human relations. People who ate together shared their lives just as they shared food at the table. Thus, meals were signs of unity.

The members of the small Christian community in Antioch enjoyed having meals together. Peter joined them. As had happened earlier, a group of Jewish Christians from Jerusalem reprimanded

Peter for eating with Gentiles. He was breaking the law that forbade Jews to eat with non-Jews. This was a serious charge against the man designated as leader of the Apostles.

Dietary laws were not the only controversial issue. The Jerusalem delegation of Christians insisted that the male Gentile Christians be circumcised. All Christians, according to the Jerusalem group, had to observe the entire Jewish Law. Shock ran through the Antioch community. In fifteen years of its existence as a Christian community, no one had made this demand. In effect, the Jerusalem group was saying that biblical laws were even more important than faith in Jesus.

Peter must have immediately grasped the gravity of the situation: The Gentiles would never accept obedience to the Jewish Law as a prerequisite to being believers in Jesus and active members of the Way. The work of Peter, Paul, Barnabas, Philip, and all the other missionaries would be destroyed. Most importantly, didn't Jesus come to save all who would believe, even if they did not follow the Jewish Law? The issue had to be settled finally.

A man of action, Paul lost no time in bringing the issue before the whole Christian community in Antioch. As might have been expected, the Jerusalem group turned against Paul as well. Arguments followed. After more wrangling, the Antioch Christians sent Paul and Barnabas to talk to the leaders in Jerusalem about the problem.

The Council of Jerusalem

A Turning Point for Christianity

The Christians in Jerusalem called a meeting about the question of the Gentiles' not observing the Jewish Law. The Council of Jerusalem, held in 50 C.E., would later be considered the first official church council, that is, a gathering of the leaders of the church to decide on major issues of doctrine or religious practice.

Debate and Decision

At the Council of Jerusalem, Paul and Barnabas described their work among the Gentiles, stressing the enthusiasm and faith of the people who had turned away from their idols and converted to belief in Jesus and the one true God. One group at the meeting insisted that everybody, including Gentile converts, had to keep the Law that was given to Moses. After lengthy debate, Peter stood up and addressed the council:

"You know that in the early days God made a choice among you, that I should be the one through whom the Gentiles would hear the message of the good news and become believers. And God, who knows the human heart, testified to them by giving them the Holy Spirit, just as he did to us; and in cleansing their hearts by faith he has made no distinction between them and us. Now therefore why are you putting God to the test by placing on the neck of the disciples a yoke that neither our ancestors nor we have been able to bear? On the contrary, we believe that we will be saved through the grace of the Lord Jesus, just as the [Gentiles] will." (Acts 15:7–11)

James, the head of the Jerusalem community, supported Peter and proposed a solution that was accepted by the assembly and then stated in a letter to the Gentile Christians.

The letter assured the Christians of Antioch, Syria, and Asia Minor that they had to do only what was essential for the followers of Jesus. They did not have to observe the complete Jewish Law, and circumcision was not required of them. The communities were asked to live together in peace. Thus:

"It has seemed good to the Holy Spirit and to us to impose on you no further burden than these essentials: that you abstain from what has been sacrificed to idols and from blood and from what is strangled and from fornication. If you keep yourselves from these, you will do well." (Acts 15:28–29)

The Gentiles gladly accepted these conditions and rejoiced at the encouragement the decision gave them.

Conflict Resolved, Essentials Defined

A major rift in the community had been healed, and as a result Paul was completely free to speak about Jesus to Gentiles everywhere. Perhaps most important, the essential criterion for being a Christian had been defined: the criterion was belief in Jesus Christ, which did not include adherence to the Jewish Law.

The decision made at the Council of Jerusalem represented a major turning point in the history of the church's development. It was a turning point that eventually would enable the church to spread throughout the world. Soon Gentiles outnumbered Jews in the Christian communities. The Christian congregations began to develop their own non-Jewish identity. As Paul would say in one of his letters, "There is no longer Jew or Greek, there is no longer slave or free, there is no longer male and female; for all of you are one in Christ Jesus" (Galatians 3:28).

Conclusion   Under the inspiration of the Holy Spirit received on Pentecost, the disciples in Jerusalem began actively telling people about Jesus. They formed a community that was nourished by their mutual care and the sharing of the Body of Christ. The

Way proved to be so dynamic that the religious authorities of the time wanted to wipe it out.

The young church was also expanding its understanding of itself. Beginning with the small band of Jewish followers who had walked with Jesus in his lifetime, the community welcomed other Jews who professed belief in Jesus. But the identity of the Way as a strictly Jewish movement soon gave way to a broader, more inclusive identity. The missionary Apostles Peter and, especially, Paul found that Gentiles were even more receptive to the Gospel than Jews were.

The major issue surrounding the acceptance of Gentiles into the church focused on whether they would have to follow the complete Jewish Law. In a pivotal moment for the church, the Council of Jerusalem settled the matter, truly opening the church to all believers. Thus the church became "catholic" in the root sense of that word—"universal" or "all-inclusive." From then on, belief in Jesus Christ became the defining characteristic of a Christian.

Questions for Reflection and Discussion

1. What kinds of issues cause tension in the church today? What does the way in which the Council of Jerusalem handled controversy suggest to us about dealing with these modern issues?
2. Stephen is regarded as the first Christian martyr. Who are some modern Christians who have been persecuted for their faith?
3. How would you compare the authority structure of the early church with the structure today? What has happened?
4. The early days of the church saw many conversions, some dramatic and some gradual. What experiences in your life have and are calling you to conversion? Is God calling you to new life?

3

The Lasting Legacy of the Apostles
Christian Communities and Scriptures

As WE SAW in chapter 2, Christianity began as a movement within Judaism, but before long, the new church opened itself to a wider world, the world of the Gentiles. In a momentous decision, the Council of Jerusalem, in 50 C.E., declared that Gentiles did not have to follow the Jewish Law in order to be baptized as Christians. This shaped the direction that Christianity would take.

With that decision, an explosion of growth began in the Christian church. Missionaries such as Paul and his companions made their way across the Roman Empire from city to city, port to port, spreading the Good News and gathering together those who would believe in Jesus Christ. Small Christian communities sprang up, most of them either Jewish and Gentile or entirely Gentile in membership. Before the Gospels of the Christian Testament were written, these vital communities passed on to the next generation of Christians, by word of mouth, the stories they had heard about Jesus.

Why did the Gentiles find Christianity attractive, so much so that they were willing to leave behind their old, familiar ways and take up a completely new way of life and belief? For some Gentiles of the Greco-Roman world (the Roman Empire, which was heavily influenced by Greek culture), religion had degenerated into stories of the high jinks of wicked gods, and then into worship of corrupt, powerful human beings—the emperors. Paul recognized that in such a world, people had little of substance to believe in. They were drowning in cynicism. They desperately needed what he had to offer them—the Good News of the One God, who loved them and wanted them to love one another. In fact, many Gentiles already had a strong attraction to the God of Judaism, but not many were willing to adopt the Jewish Law in its entirety.

Jesus gave the One God a human face. And unlike the Greek and Roman gods, Jesus had lived in the real world, not simply in people's imaginations. He had walked the earth, healed sick people, embraced and forgiven sinners, died, and been raised from the dead. What was most appealing was that Jesus offered *all* people eternal salvation. Jews and Gentiles, rich and poor, slaves and free persons, women and men could be freed from the bonds of sin and death and be raised to new life as Jesus had.

When Paul stepped off the boat at Philippi, he was a man with a mission. He spoke with conviction because his God and Jesus, the Messiah sent from

Timeline . . .

50
- Council of Jerusalem decides Jewish Law is not essential for Christians.
- Paul begins his second missionary journey.
- Paul writes his first Epistle.
- Paul begins his third missionary journey.
- Paul is arrested in Jerusalem, imprisoned in Rome.
- Rome burns, Nero persecutes Christians.
- Peter and Paul are martyred.
- Mark's Gospel is written.

75
- Romans destroy Jerusalem, Jewish Temple.

- Matthew's and Luke's Gospels are written.

- Christians break with Judaism.

- John's Gospel is written.

100
- Roman law makes Christianity illegal.

39

God, stood in stark contrast to the Gentiles' gods. Each time that Paul spoke, he defined more clearly who Jesus was and how great was the gift of Christ to all persons.

Small Christian Communities: Prayer and Mutual Love

Driven by Paul's missionary zeal, Christianity spread like wildfire across the empire, particularly among the Gentiles. Other Apostles also contributed to the evangelizing. But Paul is remembered as the key missionary, perhaps because his letters, written to members of small, local Christian communities, have survived as part of the Christian Testament and have inspired Christians for almost two thousand years.

Even before Paul's letters were written or the Gospels were recorded, however, Christian communities were alive and well. Thus, the church was flourishing before there was a Christian Testament. The Christian communities, in fact, were the places where the Christian writings would be born. The Christian communities were the first gift of the heritage given by the Apostles.

The Major Cities of Paul's Travels

We do not know the details of how the early communities developed or what they were like. From the Acts of the Apostles and Paul's letters, though, we have some idea of how Paul worked with the communities and nourished them during his second and third missionary journeys, and even during his final years in Rome.

The Communities on Paul's Second Journey On Paul's first missionary journey, covered in chapter 2, Paul was accompanied by Barnabas. On the second missionary journey, which lasted about four years, Paul was joined by Silas, a leading member of the church of Jerusalem, and Timothy, a young man of Jewish and Greek parents. (Over time, Timothy would become a valuable assistant and lifelong dear friend to Paul.) Luke, who would later write the Acts of the Apostles, also seems to have joined Paul at some point.

Philippi would be a major stop on this second journey. It was also the first place that the Good News would be preached on what later became known as the continent of Europe.

Love Brings Conversion in Philippi

In Philippi, Paul was well received by the small Jewish community that met him on the riverbank, where the community worshiped because it was too small to have a synagogue. One of those who came to hear Paul preach was Lydia, a devout woman who had converted to Judaism. After she and the members of her household were baptized as Christians, she offered Paul and his companions hospitality in her home and would not take no for an answer. Perhaps some of Paul's warm feelings about the community, reflected in his letter to them some years later, came from the hospitality of people such as Lydia.

In one incident in Philippi, Paul and Silas were beaten and jailed in chains for expelling a demon from a slave girl. The girl was a source of moneymaking for her masters because, under the influence of the evil spirit, she could tell fortunes for a price. So Paul and Silas were locked up not for helping the girl but for hindering the greed of her masters.

That night in the jail, the missionaries had the opportunity to escape when a violent earthquake burst open the doors. Their jailer was so afraid that he would be blamed for the escape that he was on the point of suicide. Feeling compassion for their jailer, Paul and Silas did not leave the jail. Their love for the distraught guard won him over, and they had another convert to the Way. That night the jailer and his family were baptized. The next day the authorities, learning that Paul was a Roman citizen, released Paul and Silas.

Run Out of Thessalonica

Another stop on Paul's second journey was the coastal city of Thessalonica. Paul was well received by Gentiles there, but the Jews were hostile to him. Far from accepting his teaching that Jesus was the Messiah, the Jewish leaders charged Paul with treason. They said he was trying to substitute worship of Jesus for loyalty to the emperor. Under threat of severe punishment, Paul and Silas were smuggled out of town in the night's darkness. Soon Paul boarded a ship bound for Athens, the most famous city of Greece.

Rejection in Athens

Athens was a special city filled with ancient temples and majestic buildings. In many ways, Athens was the birthplace of Western philosophy and what we now know as democracy.

The Athenians proved to be too skeptical to believe Paul's message. They loved to debate and listen to lectures on the latest ideas, but when Paul began to tell them about the Resurrection of Jesus, some of them burst out laughing. Being skeptical of anything they could not perceive with their senses, they thought Paul's story bizarre, even funny. Although a few Athenians accepted the Way, Paul was not very successful and failed to start a community. He moved on to Corinth.

Challenge in Corinth

As was often the case in seaports, the vices of prostitution, gambling, drinking, and brawling flourished in Corinth, but it was a prosperous town for some people. Paul's attempt at preaching to the Jewish congregation failed, so he turned to the Gentiles, especially the poorer people. After Paul had labored in Corinth for eighteen months, the Christian community grew quite large. Paul took up his old trade as tent maker in the shop of Priscilla and her husband, Aquila. The community met for worship at Priscilla and Aquila's house, and the couple became missionaries with Paul.

Years later, while on his next journey, Paul would be distressed that the community he had founded in Corinth was splitting into factions. His response, an eloquent message (in the First Letter to the Corinthians), is one of the most well known descriptions of love. Evidently, though, his reminder that charity should characterize Christian communities did little to improve the situation. Even when Paul made a personal visit, the troublemakers rejected his help. Things did settle down after a while, and Paul's next letter to the Corinth church expressed happiness over the renewed spirit of community.

The Communities on Paul's Third Journey   In his fifties, Paul was on foot again for the third time in eight years, heading west from Antioch to the cities of Asia Minor in which he had previously spent time. On this third missionary journey, he probably wondered if he would ever see Antioch or Tarsus again. Fifty was an old age for persons then, and Paul's life was far from easy.

Taking on the Magicians in Ephesus

Paul had made an earlier brief stop at Ephesus, but on this journey he was to stay about two years. Ephesus was an important port city in Asia Minor, a meeting place for eastern and western travelers and traders. Among its impressive buildings were a huge temple to Diana, who was the Roman goddess of fertility, and an outdoor theater that seated twenty-four thousand spectators.

Again, Paul began by preaching in the Jewish synagogue, and when he was rejected there, he taught Gentiles at a lecture hall. Paul's preaching at Ephesus made a strong impression on the whole Roman province of Asia because his words were spread by the many travelers coming to and from the city, and his deeds of healing the sick made his words convincing. But Paul's gift of healing created envy among some of the Ephesians.

God did extraordinary miracles through Paul, so that when the handkerchiefs or aprons that had touched his skin were brought to the sick, their diseases left them, and the evil spirits came out of them. Then some itinerant Jewish exorcists tried to use the name of the Lord Jesus over those who had evil spirits. . . . But the evil spirit said to them in reply, "Jesus I know, and Paul I know; but who are you?" Then the man with the evil spirit leaped on them, mastered them all, and so overpowered them that they fled out of the house naked and wounded. When this became known to all residents of Ephesus, both Jews and Greeks, everyone was awestruck; and the name of the Lord Jesus was praised. Also many of those who became believers confessed and disclosed their practices. A number of those who practiced magic collected their books and burned them publicly; when the value of these books was calculated, it was found to come to fifty thousand silver coins. So the word of the Lord grew mightily and prevailed. (Acts 19:11–20)

The magicians, who proclaimed themselves as healers, envied Paul's real ability to heal people and felt threatened. The local silversmiths felt threatened too. They made a good living by producing silver statues of Diana (who was also called Artemis). When people converted to Christianity, of course, the demand for statues of Diana declined dangerously, and the silversmiths lost business. The silver-smiths held an angry protest meeting against Paul. As a result, Paul sadly had to leave the Christian community of Ephesus and head off farther west.

House Churches

In the cities Paul visited where a Christian community had developed, eucharistic worship often took place in a member's home, such as Priscilla and Aquila's house in Corinth. The following description from the Acts of the Apostles gives a picture of a house church, and it incidentally shows that even Paul's sermons could go on far too long!

On the first day of the week, when we met to break bread, Paul was holding a discussion with [the believers]; since he intended to leave the next day, he continued speaking until midnight. There were many lamps in the room upstairs where we were meeting. A young man, . . . who was sitting in the window, began to sink off into a deep sleep while Paul talked still longer. Overcome by sleep, he fell to the ground three floors below and was picked up dead. But Paul went down, and bending over him took him in his arms, and said, "Do not be alarmed, for his life is in him." Then Paul went upstairs, and after he had broken bread and eaten, he continued to converse with them until dawn; then he left. Meanwhile they had taken the boy away alive and were not a little comforted. (Acts 20:7–12)

This gathering of Christians to break bread and share the word was typical of the early communities' worship. Christians formed close-knit groups whose shared life testified to God's love for all.

Troubles for Paul in Jerusalem

A Mission of Mercy

Since the early time that the community of Antioch had taken up a collection for the Jerusalem community when it was threatened with starvation, Paul had pledged that the Christian communities would help one another; indeed, this was an essential part of the Way. The people of Jerusalem were once again suffering from famine, and Christians in Greece and Asia Minor contributed generously to a fund for the community in Jerusalem. Paul set out to deliver the donations to that city at the end of his third missionary journey. He also wanted to go to Jerusalem to discuss a recurring problem—that Jewish Christians were still demanding that Gentile Christians submit to the Mosaic Law (or the Jewish Law). Even the earlier decision of the Council of Jerusalem was not persuasive enough.

A Touching Farewell

Paul knew that trouble lay ahead for him in Jerusalem. As he told the elders of Ephesus in a farewell address:

"I am on my way to Jerusalem, not knowing what will happen to me there, except that the Holy Spirit testifies to me in every city that imprisonment and persecutions are waiting for me. . . .

"And now I know that none of you, among whom I have gone about proclaiming the kingdom, will ever see my face again." (Acts 20:22–25)

Obviously, the people Paul had ministered to in Ephesus held great affection for him:

When [Paul] had finished speaking, he knelt down with them all and prayed. There was much weeping among them all; they embraced Paul and kissed him, grieving especially because of what he had said, that they would not see him again. (Acts 20:36–38)

The person who had brought them hope, love, meaning, and faith in Jesus was leaving them. They would have to continue the struggle to witness to Christ without Paul.

A Mob Attack and Roman Protection

Paul was warmly welcomed by the Christian community in Jerusalem, and undoubtedly the donations he brought from the other churches were accepted gratefully. Although Paul wanted to help settle the dispute over the Jewish Law in Jerusalem, he never had the opportunity to do so. Shortly after arriving there, he ran into a protest against him by some Asian Jews at the Temple, and he was dragged outside the Temple gates by a mob. The Asian Jews viewed Paul as an enemy and a collaborator with the Romans because of his position that converts to Christianity did not need to adhere to the Jewish Law. He was saved from death by Roman soldiers because of his Roman citizenship, whereby he was protected under Roman law.

Paul was escorted under heavy guard to Caesarea, the Roman capital of Palestine, where he lived for two years at the governor's palace under house arrest. When he finally had the opportunity to go back to Jerusalem to defend himself before the Sanhedrin, Paul decided instead that as a Roman citizen with the right to a Roman trial, he wanted his case heard in Rome, the capital of the empire.

Paul's Final Years   ### House Arrest in Rome

Paul did arrive in Rome, but not before going through violent winter storms at sea and being shipwrecked on the island of Malta. In Rome he was confined under an easy house arrest. He lived in a rented house, and it soon became a busy place. Paul's most regular visitors came from the Roman Christian community, which had most likely been formed by Peter. Although we do not know much about what happened to Paul during his last years, we do know that after a couple of years under house arrest, he was freed and was able to visit some Christian communities in Greece and Asia Minor.

Death in Nero's Persecutions

One night in 64 C.E., probably soon after Paul had left Rome on his visits, a raging fire spread through about two-thirds of the city. Someone had to be blamed. People grumbled that Emperor Nero himself had arranged for the fire to be started, perhaps so that he could rebuild the city the way he wanted it. To squelch the rumor, Nero accused the Christians, who clearly lived differently than other Romans and were an easy target as a small group whose activities were suspect. Many Christians were arrested and quickly executed. This inaugurated the era of persecution of Christians by Romans.

Despite all the dangers, many Romans converted to Christianity. They avoided the pagan religious ceremonies honoring the many Roman gods, even though attending those ceremonies was considered the patriotic duty of every Roman citizen. Consequently, Roman Christians were viewed as treasonous.

Peter and Paul both died in Nero's persecutions. According to legend, because Peter was a Roman subject, not a citizen, he was crucified. Paul, a Roman citizen, was beheaded. No one recorded Paul's last words and actions, but several years earlier he had described his attitude toward death to his friends at Philippi: "To me, living is Christ and dying is gain" (Philippians 1:21). Paul's faith gave him confidence that at last he would see Jesus face-to-face forever.

The Christian Testament: Letters, Stories, and Inspiration

While Paul and other missionaries were building up Christian communities across the Roman Empire, a most significant development was going on: the Good News as it was given to the Apostles was being handed on, both orally and in writing. The written word gradually evolved into the form that we know today as the Christian Testament. Letters written by Paul and other Christian leaders; stories of Jesus' life, death, and Resurrection; accounts of the church's beginnings; and other writings intended to inspire were developing within and for the Christian communities of the first century.

Eventually, by the end of the second century (about the year 200), church leaders would agree on the writings that were considered particularly special and authoritative. Not until the end of the fourth century, however, would the church finally and formally approve the collection of twenty-seven books called the Christian Testament. This collection is often referred to as the Christian canon. (The word *canon* comes from the Greek word for "rule" or "standard.") Ultimately these writings would be the heritage of Christians for all time.

Paul's Epistles: Letters of Love to the Christian Communities During Paul's second journey, an important event took place: in about 51 C.E., when he wrote his first letter, or epistle, to the Christian community at Thessalonica, he was composing the first document that would eventually be included in the Christian Testament. Paul certainly would have been shocked if someone had told him that he was writing part of the Bible. The only Bible he knew was the Hebrew Scriptures that he had grown up with.

Written to the Local Assembly

Paul addressed his letter to the Christians of the city of Thessalonica in particular, and he addressed his later letters to each of the other churches that he eventually wrote to: "To the church of God that is in Corinth" (2 Corinthians 1:1) or "To the churches of Galatia" (Galatians 1:2). Paul's word *church,* in Greek, means "assembly." When Christians of the first century called themselves "a church," they saw themselves not as a building for worship but primarily as an assembly of people gathered to celebrate their belief in the Good News of Jesus Christ.

Paul wrote his epistles to the Romans, the Corinthians, the Ephesians, and the other churches to address issues relevant to each particular church. For instance, Paul wanted to moderate the Thessalonians' enthusiasm about what they thought would be the immediate second coming of Jesus. They believed that Jesus would come to earth again very soon and would bring his followers with him to heaven. Consequently, some of them had quit working and had lost interest in the world around them. Paul wanted to affirm the Christian belief that Jesus is coming; however, he realized that we do not know exactly when. Therefore, he urged the Thessalonians to go about their business, living as Christians but not ignoring daily concerns.

When the Christian communities received Paul's letters, his words were read during community prayers and at times of the Eucharist. Copies were circulated to neighboring communities. As a result, one

In the church of the first and second centuries, Sundays began early. Christian worship started before sunrise. The community would meet in someone's house; the location would vary because persecutions occurred periodically. When all the believers were gathered for the Eucharist, the leader of the assembly would read the sacred writings, sometimes called the memoirs of the Apostles—letters from Paul; parts of the Good News from Mark, Matthew, Luke; or the most recent Gospel, by John. Then the leader would explain the meaning of the texts. Prayers for all the people followed. This first part of the worship might include singing too. The pace was unhurried, and people sometimes joined in the discussion of the readings. After the discussion, those who had not been baptized left the celebration and were given instruction in the Christian life; these uninitiated persons were called catechumens.

The second part of the worship service of early Christians was described as follows by Justin, a martyr who died in the second-century.

> At the end of the prayers, we greet one another with a kiss. Then the president of the brethren is brought bread and a cup of wine mixed with water; and he takes them, and offers up praise and glory to the Father of the universe, through the name of the Son and of the Holy Ghost, and gives thanks at considerable length for our being counted worthy to receive these things at his hands. When he has concluded the prayers and thanksgivings, all the people present express their joyful assent by saying Amen. . . . Then those whom we call deacons give to each of those present the bread and wine mixed with water over which the thanksgiving was pronounced, and carry away a portion to those who are absent.
>
> We call this food "Eucharist," which no one is allowed to share unless he or she believes that the things which we teach are true, and has been washed with the washing that is for remission of sins and unto a second birth, and is living as Christ has commanded. For we do not receive them as common bread and common drink; but as Jesus Christ our Saviour. (*The First Apology*, chapters 65–66)

Sometimes the worship service was followed by another meal, called the agape. At this gathering, the community ate together, talked, and generally had a good time being with people of the same faith. The agape was a chance to support one another too, for the times were quite threatening to the new, small communities. ■

Sunday in the Early Church

hundred and fifty years after he wrote the letters, a sizable collection of them was in circulation throughout the Mediterranean cities.

Paul's Message Summarized

Because Paul wrote each epistle in response to the unique issues facing each community, no one letter contains Paul's entire message about Jesus. And we cannot even guess how many of his letters got lost along the way. By considering all of his known writings together, though, the modern reader can see the main themes of Paul's preaching and writing:

Only one God exists. This God has faithfully loved us from the creation of the world. Even so, humans have rejected God's love and have turned to violence and destructive ways. In an act of complete love, God sent Jesus to give a human form to God's love on earth. Jesus preached, lived, died, and rose to show us what life in God is all about. Belief in Jesus, not adherence to the Law, is what saves us. Jesus gives us the Holy Spirit to inspire us and the church to be his body now and in the future.

Treasures Passed On

The letters of Paul—as well as those of Peter, James, John, and Jude—were treasured by the Christian communities. Copies were made by hand and circulated year after year. Letters in general were rarely received in those times, so ones from important people like the Apostles would have been especially cherished. While Paul was still alive, there were no Gospels; beginning in about 65 to 70 C.E. these would be written down.

In Paul's time, only a minority of the population of the Roman Empire could read and write. To write letters, most first-century people went to professional scribes, scholars who specialized in beautiful handwriting. Because experts today find several different styles in Paul's letters, they believe that he, out of necessity, used varying methods for his writing. In some cases he seems to have dictated slowly, word for word. In other instances, he probably had ideas coming so fast that the secretary recorded only Paul's general thoughts and then later put them into words of his own. Finally, some of the epistles that we credit to Paul were probably written by his followers, perhaps after his death. These writers knew Paul's thinking, and they felt that they should put his name on the teachings they had learned from him years earlier, in order to give the letters more authority.

The Gospels: Who Was Jesus? During the last third of the first century, after the deaths of Peter and Paul, Christians in various churches began to put into writing the story of Jesus Christ. Eventually these writings became known as the Gospels, meaning "good news."

The Good News Told, Then Written Down

Composing the Gospels was a long process (they were not completed until about 100 C.E.). People wrote down the Good News for two compelling reasons: First, only a few of the people who had known Jesus personally were still living. If the firsthand experiences of Jesus were to be preserved, they had to be written down. Second, like Paul's letters, the Good News could reach many more people throughout the Roman Empire if it was in written form.

Many stories about Jesus had been kept alive in the Christian communities by public recitations. Indeed, talking and storytelling were the most important sources of entertainment and information before the advent of printing presses. As a result, people of the early times developed astonishing memories. Of course, storytellers frequently added their own twists or interpretations to the original tales. The interpretation presented by a storyteller frequently depended on his or her audience.

Eventually people began to write down certain incidents in the life of Jesus that they considered most important. They likely first wrote about the sufferings of Jesus, his death on the cross, and his Resurrection. Christians also described some of his healings and recorded many of the things he had said. All of these writings were just bits and pieces—nothing like a full scroll or book. However, they were useful to the communities, especially in the liturgy, when these notes were read, discussed, and prayed about. Finally, the pieces were compiled and edited into the four Gospels as we know them.

Different Gospels, Different Audiences

The Gospel of Mark was probably composed in Rome after Peter's death, between the years 65 and 70. It was directed particularly to the Gentiles who had become Christian. Being the earliest written Gospel, it became a source document for the Gospels of Matthew and Luke.

The Gospel of Matthew was written between 80 and 100, apparently in Antioch for a Jewish and Gentile community. The writer tried to show how Jesus, as the Messiah, fulfilled the hopes and prophecies of the Jewish tradition.

The Gospel of Luke is ascribed to Luke, a companion of Paul in the later years. Luke was a Gentile and probably a doctor who wrote in about the year 85, very likely in southern Greece. Using writings from Mark and Matthew and his own interviews, he tried to help his Gentile Christian readers understand that Jesus had come to save everyone, regardless of race or social status.

The Gospel of John was the last Gospel to be written, at the end of the first century. Many scholars believe that it was based on the teachings of the Apostle John, put into final form by John's followers after his death. The purpose of the Gospel was to help people believe in Jesus as divine, as God-made-flesh.

After each Gospel was written, copies were made by hand and distributed to various churches in the Roman Empire. Other accounts of the life and teachings of Jesus were written later, but only the four Gospels were accepted as authoritative by all the churches. In time the Gospels came to be appreciated as inspired by the Holy Spirit.

Other Writings of the Christian Testament   In addition to the thirteen epistles of Paul and the four Gospels of Matthew, Mark, Luke, and John, other elements of the Christian Testament, eventually to consist of twenty-seven books, were in the making in the first century.

The Acts of the Apostles is Luke's account of the early days of the Christian community, both the church's initial development in Jerusalem and the spread of the Good News throughout the Roman Empire. Paul's missionary work is highlighted in Acts, which is commonly seen as a companion piece to Luke's Gospel.

Epistles written or inspired by authors other than Paul make up eight of the books of the Christian Testament. James, Peter, John, and Jude are attributed as authors of seven of these letters, mostly written to a general audience of believing Christians. The Letter to the Hebrews is a kind of extended sermon of unknown authorship.

The Book of Revelation was the last work of the Christian Testament to be written, probably around the end of the first century. This book, filled with highly symbolic and mysterious images, inspired Christians who were under persecution by the Romans to remain firm in their belief. It addresses the expectation that Jesus will return in glory at the end of time to fulfill God's work on earth.

By the end of the first century, through the work begun by Jesus and carried on by the Apostles, the movement known as Christianity had two essential features: small, local communities of believers in

Jesus, and the Scriptures of the Christian Testament. Combined with the Hebrew Scriptures that were the heritage of the earliest Christians, the Christian Testament would become central to the worship life of the small communities, as well as become the basis for what would later be known as the Christian Bible.

The Final Break with Judaism: Christianity as a New Religion

The later part of the first century saw a dramatic alteration in the relationship between Christianity and Judaism: Christianity was no longer defined by Christians or others as a movement within Judaism. Rather, by the end of the century, the break between Christianity and Judaism became final and complete. Christianity was on its own, rooted in the Jewish tradition but a new religion nevertheless. Let's trace the reasons for the split that occurred in the first century.

Jesus the Jew   Jesus was a Jew. While he was growing up, his parents taught him to speak the language (Aramaic) used by the Jewish people, to read the Hebrew (Jewish) Scriptures, and to pray Jewish prayers. Though as an adult he criticized a rigid strictness regarding religious rules, he himself kept the Jewish Law, also called the Torah. Jesus' friends were all Jews. So were his earliest followers. It made sense for the Jewish Christians in Jerusalem to continue to live as Jews.

The Breach Widens   Though tension did exist between the first Christians and the Jewish leadership, the separation between Jewish Christians and the majority of Jews did not become pronounced until 62 C.E. That was when James, the leader of the Christians in Jerusalem, was arrested by the Jewish high priest for blasphemy, thrown from the roof of the Temple, and then stoned to death. During the next four years, many Christians fled Jerusalem and settled in a Gentile town about sixty miles away. Meanwhile, strong rebellious feelings against the Roman Empire were swelling among the Jews in Jerusalem.

A Matter of Survival   In 66 C.E., a group of Jews at the Temple committed an official act of rebellion against the Roman Empire by discontinuing the daily sacrifice to Emperor Nero. Shortly after, a massive Roman army attacked Jerusalem. For four years Jerusalem

This passage, written by the Roman historian Tacitus, who called Christianity "a deadly superstition," illustrates how Christians were persecuted by the mad Emperor Nero:

> To kill the rumours [that Nero had started the fires that destroyed much of Rome], Nero charged and tortured some people hated for their evil practices—the group popularly known as "Christians." . . .
>
> . . . In their deaths they were made a mockery. They were covered in the skins of wild animals, torn to death by dogs, crucified or set on fire—so that when darkness fell they burned like torches in the night. Nero opened up his own gardens for this spectacle and gave a show in the arena, where he mixed with the crowd, or stood dressed as a charioteer on a chariot. As a result, although they were guilty of being Christians and deserved death, people began to feel sorry for them. For they realized that they were being massacred not for the public good but to satisfy one man's mania. (*Annals*, 15.44)

The following excerpts from an anonymous letter of the second century indicate the admiration that some nonbelievers had for Christians.

> They love every one, but are persecuted by all. They are unknown and condemned; they are put to death and gain life. They are poor and yet make many rich. . . . They are dishonoured and yet gain glory through dishonour.
>
> . . . They are attacked by Jews as aliens, and are persecuted by Greeks; yet those who hate them cannot give any reason for their hostility.
>
> To put it simply—the soul is to the body as Christians are to the world. The soul is spread through all parts of the body and Christians through all the cities of the world. The soul is in the body but is not of the body; Christians are in the world but not of the world. ∎

Two Views of the Early Christians

held out, but finally, in the year 70, the Roman army took the city and leveled the Temple. With the center of Judaism gone and thousands of Jews killed or imprisoned, it seemed that Israel as a nation would disappear forever.

If Judaism as a religion was to survive, it had to be unified. Conformity of belief was required. Thus, within a few years after the fall of Jerusalem, the synagogues no longer welcomed the nonconforming Christians. The Jewish Christians who had followed the Law all their life were hurt and angered by this rejection. In the year 90, as part of the effort to unify Judaism, the Jewish leadership settled on the canon of official Jewish sacred Scriptures. The break between Jews and Christians was final. And—as often happens when people who were once close begin to exclude one another—distrust, bitterness, and even hatred often took the place of love.

Conclusion The followers of Jesus began to be identified as Christian, and their numbers grew rapidly. The God of Israel and the Messiah, Jesus, held tremendous appeal not only for many Jews but, increasingly, for Gentiles in the Roman world. Paul and the other Apostles continually preached, often at great hazard to themselves. Indeed, spreading the word of God cost them their life. They would leave behind a great legacy: first, the gift of those small communities of worship and service that were to nourish the life of the growing church, and second, the gift of the Christian Testament, inspired by God and produced within the Christian communities as the written expression of their faith. The Way, at first a movement within Judaism, was becoming a religion in itself, with its own organization, rituals, Scriptures, and tradition. As the fledgling church entered the second century and new fires of persecution, it had all the means necessary to sustain its members: an informal but functioning organization, meaningful rituals, the Scriptures, zeal for spreading God's word, and the grace of Jesus Christ.

Questions for Reflection and Discussion

1. If Paul landed on the shores of this country today, would he find an audience in many ways similar to the one he found in Philippi, Corinth, and the other cities he visited? How would these audiences respond to his message and his passion?
2. How is missionary work today similar or dissimilar to Paul's missionary endeavors? Can you think of any contemporary missionaries? If so, how do they approach their ministry?

3. Ponder this question: To what degree am I willing to suffer for what I believe in?
4. Why is it important for a Christian today to remember that Jesus was a Jew?
5. What advantages do small communities like the early "house churches" have over large congregations? Are there any disadvantages?

4

Gold Tested in Fire

Courageous Faith and Clear Doctrine

BY THE END of the first century, which was also the end of the era of the Apostles, the young Christian church had developed its own community way of life and worship. Its own Scriptures were evolving into the form we know as the Christian Testament. And the church, opening itself more and more to the Gentile world, was finally separated from active participation in the Jewish community, though not from its Jewish roots and Scriptures.

To the first-century Christians, hostility and persecution from outside the community, as well as conflict over ideas and directions within the community, were no strangers. Such difficulties foreshadowed what was to come in the next two centuries—a period of greater suffering as Christian martyrs would die for their faith in an empire that was hostile to them. In those centuries, even ordinary Christians would wrestle with questions of who Jesus was, their different beliefs creating divisions among Christians. But from the intense heat of Roman persecution and internal conflict over doctrine would emerge "the gold tested in fire," the courageous faith of the early Christian church and a clarity of understanding about who this Jesus was that Christians were dying for.

The story of Blandina, a slave, and the other martyrs of Lyons (in the part of the Roman Empire known as Gaul, now France) dramatizes the horrors of the persecutions, but also the impressive strength of belief those early Christians held. This account of Blandina's martyrdom, in the year 177, is excerpted from a long letter written at the time by one who survived a terrible persecution.

There can be no adequate description, either in word or writing of the magnitude of the suffering here, of the animosity of the pagans towards the saints, or of the steadfastness of the blessed martyrs. . . .

[Forty-eight Christians were dragged before the Roman governor. Every one of them confessed faith in Christ, knowing that they would thus be condemned to torture and public execution. The Christians were tortured in hopes that it would force them to reject Christianity.]

We were all in a state of terror . . . lest, Blandina, by reason of her physical frailty, would not be able to make a bold confession of faith. But she was filled with such power, that even those taking turns to torture her in every possible way from morning till night had to admit defeat. . . . Her whole body was a mass of open wounds. . . . Yet this blessed woman was renewed in her vigor through her confession of faith. Indeed the very saying of the words "I am a Christian—we have done nothing to be ashamed of" was itself a restoration. . . .

[After being tortured, the Christians were tied up in the arena to be devoured by wild beasts.]

. . . Blandina, hanging from a stake, was exposed as bait for the wild beasts which had been loosed for the attack. She seemed to hang there in the form of a cross and continued to inspire . . . those still struggling. . . .

But since none of the beasts had touched her, Blandina was taken down from the stake and led back to prison. . . . This woman, little, weak, easily despised, had put on . . . the mighty and invincible warrior, Christ. . . .

. . . Blandina was brought back again together with Ponticus, a boy of fifteen. Every day they had been brought in to watch the rest being tortured, and these had been attempts to force them to take the oath by the pagan idols. . . .

After the scourging, after the wild animals, after the red-hot grid, finally [Blandina] was cast into a net and exposed to a bull. She was severely tossed by the animal yet was hardly aware of what was happening because of her hope and her grasp of all that she believed in and her communion with Christ. At last she was sacrificed, but the pagans themselves confessed that never had any woman suffered so much and so intensely. . . .

After the bodies of the martyrs had been subjected to every possible insult and had lain exposed to the elements for six days, these wicked people burned the remains and swept the ashes into the Rhone [River] which flows close by. They were determined that not a trace be left on the face of the earth.

Blandina died in Lyons, but Christianity could not be put to death. The blood of the martyrs became the seed of Christianity.

Courageous Faith
amid the Fires of Persecution

Why were the Christians such a threat to the Roman Empire that the Romans felt it necessary to torture and execute them? The empire at that time, though seemingly all-powerful, was in fact coming apart at the seams, strained by its own corrupt emperors and by "barbarian" attacks from the north.

The Roman Demand for Conformity The thinking of the Roman authorities proceeded like this: Common religious observance fostered unity in the empire. Refusing to observe the Roman religious sacrifices and pay homage to the "divine" emperors was thus unpatriotic, even treasonous. Unpatriotic people caused disunity in the empire.

In addition, the Roman citizens believed that the gods sent blessings on them only if they offered sacrifices. They feared that the gods would curse them for tolerating the Christians' refusal to offer sacrifices.

As a result of the Romans' thinking, the faith of Christians was regularly tested in the fires of torture and persecution.

Periodic Persecutions

A law against being Christian was in effect for two centuries, although it was enforced only periodically. The outright persecution of Christians was limited to those periods. But throughout the two centuries, much of the Roman world looked upon the Christians with deep suspicion. Christians never knew if someone might turn them in for being Christian, or when the next persecution would come.

Despite the constant possibility of harassment, suffering, torture, and even death, Christian communities took root in Syria, Asia Minor, Greece, Italy, Gaul, Spain, and the coast of Africa.

Well-known Early Martyrs

Among the early martyrs were many bishops, including Ignatius of Antioch, who was taken to Rome to be eaten by lions in the amphitheater, for the amusement of the crowds at the circus. Not concerned about himself, on the way to Rome, Ignatius wrote letters to the Christians of each of the seven towns at which he and his captors stopped; he encouraged those groups of Christians to be united with their own bishop.

At one point on his journey, Ignatius summed up the type of belief that sustained not only him but many of the early martyrs:

Now I begin to be a disciple. . . . Come fire and cross, gashes and rendings [tearing of the flesh], breaking of bones and mangling of limbs, the shattering in pieces of my whole body; come the wicked torments of the devil upon me if I may but attain unto Jesus Christ.

Another renowned martyr of the period was Justin. Born of non-Christian parents, he studied all kinds of philosophies in his search for the meaning of life. He found his answers in Christianity. In

Rome he started a school of philosophy that would be a bridge between Christianity and pagan philosophy. Arrested for being Christian, Justin and six of his students refused to sacrifice to an idol, and all of them were executed. Justin was one of the earliest, most important apologists, or "defenders of the faith," well-educated people who knew Greek philosophy and could debate with non-Christians on an equal basis.

Church Structures and Roles Develop

Besides their strong faith in Christ and strong sense of community in the midst of a world that was hostile to them, the Christian churches were held together by the organizational structures and roles that had evolved by the second century.

Bishops

Each community selected one of its members to be a bishop. (*Bishop* comes from the Greek word for "supervisor.") The bishop led the community's worship and, as the Greek meaning implies, supervised the life of the Christian congregation. The communities generally were small enough that all the members of a given community could meet at one location for the Eucharist, so each city needed only one bishop. The position of priest did not develop until later.

Deacons and Deaconesses

Assisting the bishop were deacons and deaconesses. Like Stephen, the first martyr, deacons and deaconesses attended to the welfare of the community's poor, widowed, orphaned, and sick persons. The bishops, deacons, and deaconesses were not full-time ministers; in most cases, they continued to support themselves through their own labor.

The Bishop of Rome as Peter's Successor

Another development was the increasing importance of the bishop of Rome. Before Jerusalem was crushed by the Romans in 70 C.E., the bishop of Jerusalem was considered most important of all the bishops. After Jerusalem's fall, the bishop of Rome became more and more central in the church. This was because Peter died in Rome, and Rome was the imperial capital. Most significantly, the bishop of Rome was considered to be Peter's successor. Because, according to tradition, Peter had been appointed by Jesus as head of the church, his successors would have that role also.

Barbarians Threaten the Empire's Order   For most citizens besides the Christians, life in the Roman world from approximately 100 to 200 C.E. was peaceful enough. Prosperous cities ringed the Mediterranean. The various ethnic groups were held together by Roman law. A single currency was used in the empire, and roads led everywhere. Commerce flowed throughout the empire. The "peace of Rome" did not bring justice and peace to Roman subjects in any deep sense; after all, they were living under the boot of a powerful dictatorship that could execute people at will for dissenting. But there was peace in the sense of relative order.

Nevertheless, nomadic tribes from the north posed a constant threat as they gathered strength to attack Roman territory. They were known as barbarians, from the Greek word meaning "hairy ones." The term referred to any non-Roman who spoke an unfamiliar language and who was unshaven. (Now it is synonymous with "brute" or "savage," an association that is probably unfair to the tribes.)

The barbarians lived on the northern frontier formed by the Rhine and Danube rivers. The Romans built forts and walled cities to protect the empire's northern border. Sometimes the Romans even hired barbarian tribes to help guard the frontier border. Later on, barbarians were recruited for the imperial army. However, most barbarians lived free of control and liked to make quick raids across the borders into Roman lands. The Romans' fear of the barbarians and of any dissent fueled the suppression of minority groups like the Christians.

The Decline into Chaos   The years from 100 to 200 had seen persecutions of Christians. The next one hundred years brought the emergence of worse emperors and crueler persecutions, but a sharp decline in the real influence of the Roman Empire. A tyrannical emperor was assassinated; then one inept emperor followed another. The empire was rotting from the inside, and on the outside the nomadic tribes were sharpening their swords.

No Tolerance for Nonconformity

Corrupt as the Roman emperors were, each of them demanded complete loyalty from all citizens. In 250 C.E., the emperor required each citizen to carry a certificate showing that he or she had sacrificed to the gods. Faithful Christians, of course, refused to take part in the pagan rites. Another strike against the Christians was their

Christians in the early church did not escape the prejudices of their culture any more than Christians do today. Consequently, not many women make appearances in the few documents that we have from those early centuries. Paul mentioned the good work done by specific women who spread the word of God. Agnes and Cecilia were two among many women martyrs honored by the early church. We know that deaconesses had responsibilities similar to those of the deacons. And women were almost certainly part of the deliberations in the Jerusalem community.

However, throughout much of Western history, most women were kept in the background and allowed to be skilled solely at homemaking. Their purpose in life was to please their husband by being subservient, obedient, and the mother of sons. So women appear infrequently in historical accounts, although there are notable exceptions. For the most part, in recorded histories of Western civilization, it has been a man's world. This has been no less true in recorded church history. Again, with rare exceptions, such as the women featured in this book (contemplatives, educators, founders of religious orders, and so on), we know little about what women thought, felt, or did during much of church history.

When women are featured in documents or histories of the early church, they are often being preached at about their place in the scheme of things. The belief that Eve was responsible for original sin and that women were the sources of temptation—especially sexual temptation—for men, led some early Christian writers to urge women to wear chaste dress, to assume quiet ways, and to keep orderly houses for their men. An example of this comes from an essay written by Tertullian, a theologian who died in about 230. Here are a few things he had to say about female dress:

> Very many women . . . have the boldness so to walk in public as though chastity consisted only in the bare integrity of the flesh and in the avoidance of fornication. . . . In their gait they display the same outward appearance as Gentile women, in whom the sense of true chastity is lacking. . . .

The desire to please by outward charms, which we know naturally invite lust, does not spring from a sound conscience. Why should you rouse an evil passion? Why invite that to which you profess yourself a stranger? . . .

You must not overstep the line to which simple and sufficient elegance limits its desires, the line which is pleasing to God. Against Him those women sin who torment their skin with potions, stain their cheeks with rouge, and extend the line of their eyes with black coloring. Doubtless they are dissatisfied with God's plastic skill. . . .

. . . Bow your heads before your husbands, and you will be sufficiently adorned. Busy your hands with wool; keep your feet at home; and you will please more than if you were arrayed in gold.

Tertullian's words indicate that women were typically treated as sex objects by men, and his advice is intended to show a different option for Christian women—that their bodies, created by God, should be treated as God's creations. However, typical of the men of his time, Tertullian blamed women for men's lust and relegated women to the home and the commands of their husband. (It should be noted that Tertullian was probably at the extreme of strictness within Christianity. In fact, eventually he joined a heretical group, the Montanists, who discouraged marriage and all things related to worldly pursuits.)

Tertullian was a product of his times; we are products of ours. In written accounts of the church, the most prominent figures are men, with a few remarkable exceptions. This does not mean that women were not active in and essential to church life; it simply illustrates that the history of the church was recorded by men, primarily for men, in a world where public deeds (governmental proclamations, service in wars, and so on) were performed mostly by men. ■

Women in the Early Church

resistance to joining the army or, if they did join, their participating in only a noncombat capacity. Pacifism—the belief that it is wrong to kill another human being in war or for any purpose—was, for the most part, the tradition of the early church. This commitment won the Christians the contempt of society, because helping to fight the barbarians was deemed a patriotic duty.

A general persecution of Christians was ordered, in which the bishops of Rome, Antioch, and Jerusalem were martyred. Other periods of persecution followed.

Diocletian's Persecutions

As the 200s came to an end, the Roman Empire finally had a competent ruler, Diocletian—who was competent in the sense of being able to get things done. He managed to hold off the barbarians' invasions, which was something his immediate predecessors had failed to do. He reorganized the government, moving from military to civilian administration.

But Diocletian demanded complete conformity to his will, which he mistakenly thought would bring unity to the empire. Naturally Diocletian turned his attention to the dissenting Christians. In his last two years of rule, he ordered churches destroyed, sacred books burned, and leaders executed. The persecutions were especially horrible in North Africa and in the East. Ironically, some of Diocletian's own relatives were Christians.

Christians Who Sacrificed to Idols: What to Do?

Besides mourning for martyred or enslaved family and friends, Christians had to face a new problem resulting from the persecutions: What should they do with Christians who had sacrificed to the idols to save their life? Should those people be allowed to re-enter the Christian communities? Most of these apostates, or people who had renounced their faith, wanted to repent and return to the church. Some bishops said that their sin of denial could never be forgiven. Other bishops disagreed.

Sharp debate about this issue ensued for many years, but the decision of the bishop of Rome became generally accepted: apostates could be reunited with the Christian communities after repentance. The public penance and ritual of re-entry were the first forms of what we now know as the sacrament of reconciliation.

Christians on the Brink of a Revolution

By now the church had endured, even thrived, during three centuries of persecution. The suffering had tested the convictions of anyone who wanted to be a Christian. Little did the Christians of the early 300s realize that a revolution in their identity and power was about to begin. They would soon change from a church of nonviolent martyrs with no political power into a church entwined with the culture, politics, and wars of Europe for many centuries.

Constantine's Conversion: A New Era for the Church

One person can be singled out as initiating a whole new era for the church. Although not a Christian himself at the time, Constantine's conversion would alter the church's power and status dramatically. How and why did this radical reversal of fortune for the church come about?

A Claim of Victory Through the Son of God After Diocletian's rule, several contenders grasped for the imperial throne. Constantine was chosen to be emperor by the Roman troops in Britain, but he faced the superior forces of a rival emperor when he reached Rome in 312 C.E. to make his claim to the throne.

The story is told that before the decisive battle, Constantine had a vision promising him that he would conquer through a special sign—the sign of Christ. (Constantine's mother, Helena, was a Christian, but Constantine, himself a pagan, worshiped the sun god.) Trusting the vision, Constantine instructed his soldiers to put the first two Greek letters of Christ's name—XP (or chi-rho)—on their banners and shields. Out of the battle, Constantine's smaller army emerged victorious. The Roman senate erected a triumphal arch to Constantine, which attributed the victory to the sun god. Constantine shocked them by honoring the Son of God instead. (Although he then supported Christianity, Constantine would not be officially baptized until shortly before his death in 337.)

Christianity Becomes Legal **The Edict of Milan**

Constantine at first agreed to share power with a general, who would be emperor of the Eastern part of the empire while Constantine would be emperor of the Western part. Shortly after assuming power, in 313, Constantine and the Eastern emperor issued the Edict of Milan, granting freedom of worship to Christians in the Roman Empire. Christians could no longer be punished by law for practicing or preaching their religion. They had moved from a secret, or "underground," status to an open and legitimate, or "aboveground," status. Further privileges

The Spread of Christianity

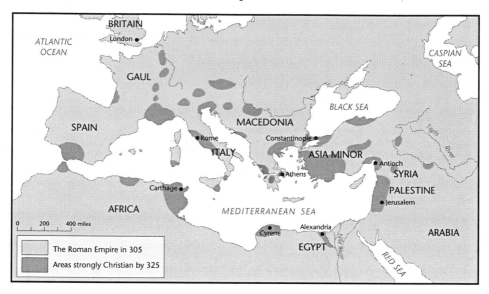

followed, with Christian clergy being exempted from paying taxes and many churches being built by Constantine, especially in Rome and Palestine.

A New Capital for a Fresh Start

In 324, Constantine defeated the Eastern emperor, united the empire, and became sole ruler. But problems still plagued the empire. Rome itself was run-down; many people lived in crumbling slums. Feeling that a fresh start was needed, Constantine decided to move to a new capital in the Eastern part of the empire, closer to the centers of population. For the site he chose a little town called Byzantium. He named his city New Rome, even modeling the public buildings after Roman structures. Constantinople, as it came to be called, became the new center of the empire.

Church and State Entwined

Like emperors before him, Constantine saw religion as a way of unifying the people from various cultures who were under his domination. Therefore, Constantine began to interfere in church matters. Previous emperors had dominated the Roman pagan religions, so Constantine was following suit by trying to run the church. The Christians, finally legitimate and enjoying Constantine's good favor, were of course grateful to him and therefore not inclined to resist his influence. This development, though, was an enormous one. Christianity, which had been powerless, poor, and nonviolent for three centuries, became allied with the Roman Empire. The tension between being true to the faith versus being loyal and subservient to the government was to saturate church history for centuries.

The Official Religion of the Empire

By the end of the fourth century, the reversal of fortune for the church was complete. The emperor Theodosius declared paganism illegal and made Christianity the official religion of the empire in 380. Christianity was not only tolerated but enforced! By the year 500, in another ironic twist for the once generally pacifist church, only Christians were allowed to serve in the army.

Thus, while Constantine's conversion saved the church from the horrors of persecution, a new era began when the church became intimately connected with worldly power and, too often, with the corruption of power. By the mid-300s, Christian bishops ranked high in public life, some of them holding civil positions as judges. Staying free from political pressures and influence proved difficult. The church was also given lands, and the revenues from these properties were to be used for the upkeep of the church. However, the accumulation of property sometimes led to greed. The church in 350 was a far cry from the band of Apostles who had wandered with Jesus, having no place to lay their heads.

Clarity of Doctrine amid the Fires of Heresy

In its early centuries, even as the church was suffering persecution from outside itself, it was not immune to conflict within. The early Christians were not uniform in their belief, and various splinter groups challenged the beliefs of the majority. So the church had to sift through the varieties of beliefs, keeping those that seemed consistent with the message passed on from the Apostles but vigorously opposing those that did not square with basic aspects of the faith. Beliefs contrary to some essential belief of the faith are called heresies.

Gnosticism: A Denial of Jesus' Humanity   As early as the second century C.E., one splinter group was the Gnostics, who believed that all material things, including the human body, were evil. They claimed that if Jesus came from God, he could not have taken on a body, which was evil by nature. Therefore, the apparently human figure of Jesus was just an apparition. To the Gnostics, Jesus was divine but not human.

The Gnostics believed that human beings remained totally ignorant of God because God was so removed from material things. The exception to this, they claimed, was that the Gnostics themselves had a special secret knowledge of God and of their own spiritual destiny. Salvation was not the gift of Jesus to all persons but the special privilege of the Gnostics.

The Gnostic denial of Jesus' humanity was considered a heresy because it was contrary to the understanding of Jesus as human that we get from the Gospels and the Epistles. Irenaeus, a Christian who became the bishop of Lyons, particularly opposed Gnosticism.

Challenges to Christian belief, such as Gnosticism, caused turmoil but also led to clarity and unity in the church because the basic beliefs of the church then had to be agreed upon and expressed. As a result, by the year 200, Christians had formulated a statement of faith—the Apostles' Creed. This creed became part of Christian worship, and candidates seeking baptism had to understand it and accept it publicly before they could join the church.

Arianism: A Denial of Jesus' Divinity   Gnosticism thrived during the period of the persecutions. But another heresy, Arianism, arose after the persecutions, around the time of Constantine, and ended up dividing the church for centuries. A year after he became sole emperor, Constantine called the bishops together in a council to discuss a divisive problem that was especially troublesome in the East. The problem had to do with the teachings of an Alexandrian priest named Arius, whose followers were thus called Arians.

Neither Divine nor Human

Whereas the Gnostics had denied Jesus' humanity, the Arians denied Jesus' divinity. The Arians did not believe that the unknowable, unreachable, and unchangeable God could ever take the form of a human being. And to the Arians, Jesus was made or created by God and subordinate to God. Calling Jesus divine was merely a courtesy. He was neither God nor human, but somewhere in between.

The Council of Nicaea and the Nicene Creed

The ecumenical (worldwide) council called by Constantine met in 325. Bishops gathered at the small town of Nicaea, across the water from Constantinople. More than three hundred bishops came, mostly from the East. It is important to remember that the church was still mostly made up of North Africans, Syrians, Palestinians, and residents of Asia Minor and Greece. As might be expected, because of the great number of council participants and their varied cultural backgrounds, disagreements occurred.

After much discussion, Arius's beliefs were condemned as wrong. They were inconsistent with the understanding about Jesus that was traditional in the church at large. When Arius refused to alter his stand, he was declared a heretic. The bishops also wrote a more elaborate creed than the earlier Apostles' Creed, one that would incorporate the understanding of Jesus as both God and human being. The Nicene Creed is still recited at Mass. The part of the creed that Arius rejected states:

> We believe in one Lord, Jesus Christ,
> the only Son of God,
> eternally begotten of the Father,
> *God from God*, Light from Light,
> *true God from true God*,
> begotten, *not made, one in Being* with the Father.

> (Emphasis added)

This passage expresses the Christian belief that Jesus was not *made* by God but is *one with* God, being both divine and human.

The Council of Nicaea was a major defining moment for Christianity, and belief in the Nicene Creed has been an important definition of membership in the Christian community for over sixteen hundred years.

Athanasius: Jesus as the Brilliant Reflection of God

Emerging from the Arian controversy as a great church thinker and leader was Athanasius, bishop of Alexandria, Egypt. As a young deacon present at the Council of Nicaea, he had forcefully and clearly opposed the Arians. His position began with this belief: the Word of God "had become man so that you might learn from a man how a man may become God." He proclaimed that Jesus—God present as a human being—made truth of the passage in Genesis that says human beings are made in the image of God (Genesis 1:27).

To counter the Arians, Athanasius tried to help his listeners understand that *Jesus is related to God as brightness is to light:* The two realities cannot be separated. Jesus is the brilliant reflection of the light that is God. The Scriptures state that if we know Jesus, we know God.

When Athanasius was chosen to be a bishop, he was constantly harassed by Arian bishops from the East. To force him out of office, they brought all sorts of false accusations against him. As a result of such plotting by the Arians, Athanasius was removed from office five times—the last time at the age of seventy—by four emperors in turn. In all, he spent seventeen years of his life in exile, sometimes safely hidden by people in the city, other times escaping to the Egyptian desert. During the last seven years of his life, he brought peace to the conflict-ridden church in Alexandria.

By 392, Emperor Theodosius had outlawed Arianism along with paganism. Arianism continued to grow outside the empire among the barbarians who had been taught by missionaries from Constantinople years before. But within the empire, by the end of Theodosius's reign in 395, what we now call the Catholic faith was the only religion allowed in the Roman Empire.

Conclusion　The three centuries from 100 to 400 C.E. saw dramatic changes for the church. It was transformed from a persecuted minority religion, an "underground" church, to the official religion of the Roman Empire, with other religions barely tolerated. The pivotal incident for the church was Emperor Constantine's conversion to Christ and then his legalization of Christianity through the Edict of Milan. This ended the persecutions of the Christians. The courageous faith of the early Christians was found to be strong and pure, like gold tested in fire.

But Constantine's welcome move also set the stage for the increasing involvement of the state in the affairs of the church. The church and the empire were, in a sense, wedded from the time of Constantine on. That relationship gradually turned the church from a politically powerless but very alive countercultural way of life into a powerful, wealthy mainstream institution. Naturally the emperors tried to use the church to their advantage. Sometimes the Gospel was compromised as emperors hastened to attach church approval to whatever they did. Some church leaders were only too happy to cooperate with imperial power.

The period from 100 to 400 saw the faith of the church tested in another way: The church had to respond to challenges to its understanding of Jesus, causing reflection and the refining of its faith into statements that Christians still recite today—the Apostles' Creed and the Nicene Creed. The Nicene Creed in particular was worded with precise philosophical language as a means to answer the philosophical arguments about the nature of Jesus.

Lying ahead for the church after 400, as it emerged from the fires of persecution and doctrinal controversy, was a period of creative growth, both in numbers and in its spiritual and intellectual heritage. Chapter 5 will focus on the richness of that period.

Questions for Reflection and Discussion

1. Do you see any evidence today that people continue to be persecuted for their religious beliefs?
2. Constantine used religion to unify his empire. In what positive ways can religion serve as a unifying factor in a culture? What are the dangers in trying to have religion serve a unifying role?
3. The early Christians held diverse religious views and expressed their beliefs in different ways. What are some areas of Christian religious belief about which diverse views exist today? How did the early church respond to diversity? How should the church respond today?

Building the City of God

Holiness in the Wilderness, Leadership in the World

AS WE SAW in the preceding chapter, Christianity was made legal in 313 and was even declared the official religion of the Roman Empire by the end of the fourth century.

By the close of that century, another kind of resolution had occurred in the church. This one regarded the church's beliefs about Jesus. Although other challenges to the church's beliefs about Jesus would be raised in centuries to come, by 400 the church had affirmed, in the Nicene Creed, that Jesus is "one in Being with the Father"—that is, divine. Arianism, an offshoot of Christianity that denied Jesus' divinity, was still a force to be reckoned with, especially among converted barbarian tribes. But the Catholic belief—the position of the mainstream church, which was in continuity with Peter and the Apostles—was clear.

In addition to clarifying its beliefs, by 400 the church also had discerned which of the Christian writings were inspired by God and therefore belonged in the official canon of the Christian Testament. So as the church entered the fifth century, it was legal, it had a well-defined set of beliefs, and it had settled on the twenty-seven books of the Christian Testament as its own unique Scriptures. The Christian church was ready for a burst of creative growth.

Monasticism: The Quest for Holiness

Even before the fourth century, a new kind of Christian witness, or testimony to the faith, was beginning to emerge in the deserts of North Africa, and then later in the wastelands of Syria and Palestine. This new Christian witness was an attempt to follow Jesus by retreating from the everyday business of the world in order to find truth and meaning in the silence of the wilderness. The new kind of followers of Christ struggled with these questions: Who am I really? What do I truly believe? Where is my God? What are my "demons," the things that keep me away from God? How do I find out what my faith is really made of?

These men and women took as their examples Moses, the prophets, and of course Jesus, all of whom had gone into the wilderness to confront who they were in the face of God. Moses had encountered God in a burning bush on a desolate mountain. Ezekiel the

Timeline . . .

300
- Antony of Egypt organizes colony of hermits.
- Constantine legalizes Christianity through Edict of Milan.
- Council of Nicaea condemns Arian heresy, writes Nicene Creed.

350
- Basil develops his monastic rule.
- Ambrose is made bishop of Milan.
- Jerome translates the Bible into Latin.
- Ambrose forces Emperor Theodosius into public repentance.

400
- Church settles on books of Christian canon.
- Augustine writes his *Confessions*.
- Rome falls to the Goths.
- Augustine writes *The City of God*.
- Leo the Great becomes pope.

450
- Council of Chalcedon affirms Jesus' human *and* divine natures.
- Pope Leo negotiates peace with Attila the Hun.

- Western empire falls.

500

73

prophet had taken refuge on Mount Horeb. Jesus had gone into the desert to fast and pray before he began his ministry, and there he had been tested by Satan.

The movement of men and women away from the world to pursue holiness came to be known as monasticism. The term comes from the Greek word *monos*, meaning "alone" or "single." And in fact, at first most of the men and women (monks and nuns) did live alone, as hermits. Soon, though, a different form of monasticism emerged, in which monks or nuns banded together in small communities to live under a common rule, or guideline for living. Tens of thousands of people entered this way of life in the fourth century. As the monastic movement developed over the centuries, it would prove to be one of the greatest contributors to and shapers of the church and society.

Antony of Egypt   Pioneer Hermit

Antony of Egypt was one of the earliest of the religious pioneers. His lifetime spanned the last part of the third century and the first part of the fourth, so he experienced Christianity in both its persecuted and its legal conditions. He moved to the desert around the year 270, while he was still a young man.

"Sell All You Own"

How did Antony become a hermit? When he was about age eighteen, both of his parents died. Suddenly he had to manage a farm and take care of a younger sister. One day, while walking to the Eucharist, he thought about how Jesus' Apostles had sold their possessions and given the money to poor people. The Gospel reading Antony heard that day, about Jesus' words to a rich young man, struck home with him: "'There is still one thing lacking. Sell all that you own and distribute the money to the poor, and you will have treasure in heaven; then come, follow me'" (Luke 18:22).

Antony took these words as a sign from God that he should do exactly what Jesus said. So he sold his farm, gave the proceeds to help needy people, found a group of Christian women with whom his sister could live, and left home to seek out his destiny.

For a long period Antony lived near a wise old man who taught him about virtue and discipline. Antony prayed persistently and raised his own food. By learning from these experiences, he became known by nearby village folk as "God-loved," "son," and "brother."

As Antony grew older, young people sought him out to be their teacher. They built huts or found caves near him, and they watched him—how he prayed, what he said, and how he treated people. His fame grew and grew, and stories abounded about his confrontations with demons, his acts of healing, and his wise teachings.

Why Monasticism? As mentioned earlier, men and women at first went out into the desert as hermits, seeking to wrestle individually with their own "demons" and to follow Christ to holiness. Initially no special rules guided their search, and no single reason explains the enormous growth of their number (about fifty thousand monks gathered to celebrate Easter around the year 390). One contributing explanation for the growth is that after Christianity was made legitimate in the empire and the possibility of martyrdom was a thing of the past, some people longed for a way to be authentically Christlike. The ending of the period of martyrdom made many Christians complacent about Christian living. Moreover, the clergy, during and after the reign of Constantine, were given positions of prestige and power. The move by laymen and laywomen from the cities to a monastic lifestyle in the wilderness was a way of rejecting a complacent, "soft" Christianity.

Toward "Purity of Heart"

Thomas Merton, perhaps the best-known modern monk, explained the early monks' call this way:

These were [people] who believed that to let oneself drift along, passively accepting the tenets and values of what they knew as society, was purely and simply a disaster. . . .

. . . They did not reject society with proud contempt, as if they were superior. . . . On the contrary, one of the reasons why they fled from the world of men was that in the world men were divided into those who were successful, and imposed their will on others, and those who had to give in and be imposed on. The [monks and nuns] declined to be ruled by men, but had no desire to rule over others themselves. (Pages 3–5)

[The goal] of all this striving was "purity of heart"—a clear unobstructed vision of the true state of affairs, an intuitive grasp of one's own inner reality as anchored, or rather lost, in God through Christ. The fruit of this was quiet: "rest." (*The Wisdom of the Desert*, page 8)

Love as the Fruit of Prayer

In the solitude of the desert, the hermits' main focus was prayer, particularly contemplation—that is, being silently present or attentive to the loving God. The most important lesson the hermits hoped to learn through contemplation and their simple life was love. In finding God, they would find love because, as Jesus said, God is love. So all monks and nuns were invited to love, to identify themselves with their neighbors. Hospitality toward travelers and poor or sick people became central in the monasteries that later developed for communal monastic life.

Basil's Rule for Communal Monastic Life Despite its purpose of fostering love, in the beginning monastic life could be quite eccentric, with individual monks sometimes becoming obsessed with harsh practices intended to free them from their "demons." A fourth-century monk and bishop, Basil, recognized that the practices of monastic life should not be determined by individual monks' ideas of what would lead to holiness. Rather, a rule for monks to follow in community was necessary in order to avoid excesses and guide them in their path to God.

Before becoming a monk, Basil had studied at Constantinople and Athens to become a teacher. After teaching for a few years, he left his post and became a hermit in Cappadocia, in Asia Minor. Soon other young men joined him in this new kind of Christian lifestyle. Basil decided to form them into a religious community. He developed a rule of life stressing simple living: own almost nothing, eat only what is necessary, and obey the abbot of the monastery. The abbot's role was to apply the supreme rule of the Gospel to everyday life.

The monks' main work was to seek God in their heart by listening in the silence of prayer, but the monks were also to help the poor and care for the sick. Significantly, the scholarly Basil encouraged them to do intellectual work, which was a departure from the earlier monks' refusal to study.

Basil's Rule has been observed for centuries, especially in monasteries in the East—that is, in Greece, Palestine, and Egypt.

Jerome The Monk as Scholar
Another fourth-century monk, Jerome, who lived as a hermit, made a tremendous contribution to the life of the church through his scholarship, especially his study and translation of the Bible.

Student and Convert

As a pagan boy growing up in northern Italy, Jerome was sent to Rome to be educated in Latin and Greek by some of the best pagan teachers of the time. However, more and more people were converting to Christianity. After serious study, at age eighteen, Jerome decided to follow in the footsteps of his mother, who had been baptized a Christian.

After more travel and study, Jerome went into the desert, where as a hermit he prayed, fasted, and began studying Hebrew. Next he went to Constantinople for further study, and eventually he went to Rome, where he served as the pope's secretary.

A Bible for the Common Person

The pope encouraged Jerome to translate the Christian Testament and the Psalms into Latin from the original Greek and Hebrew. This would make the Scriptures more available to the common person, because Latin was the language of most people in the West at the time.

The translating project led Jerome to begin teaching the Bible to interested noblewomen of Rome. A monk at heart, he encouraged the women to form a contemplative convent—a move that caused considerable opposition from the noblemen! Before long, Jerome traveled on to Bethlehem, in the Holy Land, where he built a monastery for religious men and several convents for the women who followed him from Rome.

In Bethlehem, Jerome toiled away day and night in a cave, studying and writing. He and his students continued translating the whole Bible into Latin from the original Hebrew and Greek, receiving help with the Hebrew from Jewish rabbis living nearby. The Latin version of the Bible, which took fifteen years of work to finish, became known as the Latin Vulgate, the version in the common language of the people of the West.

As the monastic movement grew and changed, it gradually affected the whole church. Monasticism also influenced agricultural methods, arts, music, scholarship, and architecture. In fact, as will be seen in later chapters of this book, the entire Christian society felt the impact of the monasteries and was in some way shaped by them.

The Legacy of Ambrose and Augustine

Early monasticism certainly had its scholars, such as Jerome, but the primary emphasis of the ancient desert monks and nuns was not on "right thinking" or "right belief" but on "a right heart." This focus on conversion at the personal, spiritual level was a valuable contribution of the early monastics. However, it was not the whole picture of what Christian identity was about.

While men and women were going out into the desert by the thousands to seek "a right heart," two intellectual giants were focusing on "right belief," giving further shape to what it means to be a Christian. These men were developing a strong theological tradition that Christianity would stand on for centuries. One of them, Augustine, is one of the most significant figures in Christian history. The other, Ambrose, was his mentor. We will turn to Ambrose first.

Ambrose The Reluctant Leader

How Ambrose, the unbaptized governor of Milan, came to a position of leadership in the church is a fascinating story in itself.

The People's Choice

In the mid-300s, the Roman Empire was still divided into East and West, with one emperor for the East and another for the West. Arianism was alive and well, in spite of being rejected as heresy by the Council of Nicaea in 325. Whether the bishop of a given diocese was an Arian or a Catholic (the latter being the mainstream of Christianity) depended largely on the will of whoever was emperor at the time. Most Christians, especially in the West, considered themselves Catholic, not Arian. So when the Western emperor decided that an Arian should become bishop of Milan, the people protested. Fighting broke out in the streets.

To subdue the violence, the governor of Milan, whose name was Ambrose, led his military guard to the cathedral, where a large, angry mob was milling about. He succeeded in calming the crowd. When the people then began shouting, "Ambrose for bishop! Ambrose for bishop!" he was naturally shocked—for he was not even baptized. Nonetheless, the people chose him.

Ambrose tried all means of dissuading the people and finally fled the scene and hid, hoping they might rethink their decision. It was no use; the people found him and persuaded him to accept the office of bishop. In great haste, he was baptized, confirmed, given the Eucharist, and ordained bishop!

Administrator, Student, Teacher, and Pastor

As an experienced administrator, Ambrose could manage a diocese, but he realized that his career as a lawyer and governor was not an ideal preparation for his new role as a spiritual leader. Thus he began his lifelong study of Christianity. He learned quickly. In the midst of a busy life, he managed to write numerous books on theology, some of the most important works written for the church. As a scholar and writer, Ambrose helped people understand their relationship to Jesus and to the church.

Bishop Ambrose was not only a scholar; he was a pastor as well. Times were hard, famines were frequent, and barbarian tribes were becoming bolder. At one time, Ambrose sold the gold and jewels given to his church, so that he could ransom people held captive by the barbarian Goths.

Courage in the Face of Imperial Power

As might be expected, Ambrose continued to have problems with the Arians and Arian emperors. When Ambrose was commanded to turn over one of the churches in Milan to the Arians, he flatly refused. To support Ambrose, the people of Milan crowded into the church, occupying it day and night—praying, singing hymns, and listening to Ambrose speak about the Holy Trinity. Civil disobedience and Ambrose's keen arguments forced the emperor to back down. In the midst of this dispute with the emperor, Ambrose gave a sermon against state interference in religious matters. His words included a famous caution that, unfortunately, often went unheeded in the centuries to come: "The emperor is in the Church, not over the Church; and far from refusing the Church's help, a good emperor seeks it."

On several other occasions Ambrose showed his courage in the face of imperial power. For instance, one emperor, Theodosius (who had done Christianity the favor of declaring it the official religion of the empire), ordered several thousand people of a city killed, to avenge the murder of one of his generals there. Hearing this, Ambrose refused to offer Mass in the church that the emperor attended, until the emperor would repent in public. Theodosius, knowing Ambrose's high standing with the people, did several weeks of public penance—a humiliating experience for an emperor. Clearly the church had become a force to be reckoned with, for even emperors obeyed it. At Christmas, Ambrose gave the emperor Communion, to the great joy of the huge crowd gathered in Milan's cathedral. Citizens felt insecure when the church and Rome were at odds, and finally things were "right" again.

Ambrose deserves a major place in Christian history as a theologian and leader in his own right. Nonetheless, what he is perhaps best remembered for is that his preaching and teaching inspired a confused young man named Augustine to become a Christian.

Augustine Longing for "the City of God"

Augustine was born in a region of North Africa often called Roman Africa because it was home for people whose everyday language was Latin and who embraced Roman customs. Augustine's father was a local Roman official and a pagan until shortly before dying. Augustine's mother, Monica, was a Christian.

In Search of Meaning

From the time Augustine started going to school, he easily led his class. Yet at sixteen he had to leave school because his father could not pay his tuition. During this year of idleness, Augustine visited prostitutes, drank, and gambled. When he returned to school, he studied to be a lawyer and, finishing his studies at age eighteen, became a teacher. He also took a mistress, which was not uncommon among non-Christians of the time, although Monica had tried to raise Augustine as a Christian.

Augustine next became a Manichaean, believing that one god created good and another created evil, and that therefore no one was responsible for his or her sins. Monica could only pray for her son's conversion; he was too brilliant and stubborn to be influenced easily. Then, without telling anyone, Augustine moved to Rome with his mistress and their young son. A year later he went to teach in Milan. Two strong influences came into his life there: his study of Plato and his meeting Bishop Ambrose.

For Augustine, Manichaeism was increasingly dissatisfying; Plato's philosophy was not. Plato claimed that a world exists beyond what we see, that human beings have a spiritual part beyond their body, and that God is a spirit. After Augustine became convinced that there is a single God and that humans have a spiritual side, he was ripe for meeting Ambrose. Monica had followed Augustine to Milan, and the two of them would sometimes visit Ambrose at his house. In addition, Augustine began attending Sunday Mass just to hear Ambrose preach.

Gradually Augustine, through the truth of Ambrose's message and the influence of Monica's love, began trying to reform his life. For one thing, he decided to marry and then to be baptized. The legal waiting period before marriage, however, was too much of a test for Augustine; instead he took another mistress, so the marriage plans were broken. Augustine was at a low point in his life; he wanted to reform, but his "lust"—as he said—was too much for him.

From Convert to Bishop

Augustine continued his studies and teaching, but his heart was still restless. At last, though, he had a turnaround. In his autobiography, *The Confessions,* Augustine wrote that he was sitting on a bench in his backyard one day when he heard some neighborhood children chanting over and over a little song: "Take and read, take and read." Almost without thinking, he picked up the Bible next to him and opened it at random. Paul's advice to the Romans stood out on the page:

Let us live honorably as in the day, not in reveling and drunkenness, not in debauchery and licentiousness, not in quarreling and jealousy. Instead, put on the Lord Jesus Christ, and make no provision for the flesh, to gratify its desires.

Welcome those who are weak in faith, but not for the purpose of quarreling over opinions. (Romans 13:13–14; 14:1)

This passage struck Augustine as the solution to his confusion. He could turn his great passion to something wonderful by loving God and serving his neighbors.

At the age of thirty-three, Augustine was baptized by Ambrose. After Monica died, Augustine left Italy for his hometown in North Africa, where he organized a small monastery. Soon the people of the town urged him to become a priest. (Later he would claim that he was caught and made a priest.) Although most priests were married during that period, Augustine decided to remain single. Four years after joining the priesthood, he was elected bishop of Hippo by the congregation of that city.

An Answer to Life's Longing

Augustine's own weaknesses perhaps made him more sensitive to other people. His failures certainly made him aware of his own need for God. The Scriptures gave him a guide, and love of God gave him inspiration. His long search for truth and love led him to say:

It is not with doubtful but with assured awareness, O Lord, that I love you. You pierced my heart with your Word and I loved you. . . . But what do I love when I love you? . . . I do love a kind of light, melody, fragrance, food, embracement when I love my God; for He is the light, the melody, the fragrance, the food, the embracement of my inner self: Where that light shines into my soul which no place can contain, and where that voice sounds which time does not take away, and where that fragrance smells which no wind scatters, and where there is that flavor which eating does not diminish, and where there is that clinging that no satiety will separate. This is what I love when I love my God. (*The Confessions*, book 10)

One of Augustine's most well-known sayings speaks a familiar truth to anyone who has ever searched with longing for fulfillment but come up empty over and over: "Our hearts are restless, O Lord, until they rest in you."

Augustine led a directionless, morally confused life before his conversion. He wrote *The Confessions* in order to explain his change in life and to show people that God's grace is there for all.

Thomas Merton, a leading Catholic figure of the twentieth century, lived from 1915 to 1968. Much like Augustine's, his youth was spent without clear purpose. He did his share of wild living, and, like Augustine, he fathered a son out of wedlock. Merton was as brilliant as Augustine too, and as restless about what he really wanted in life.

After periods of depression about where his life was going, Merton undertook a serious study of Christianity and began the process of conversion. Eventually he entered the Trappist monastery at Gethsemani, Kentucky. In more than twenty years as a monk, he wrote some of the twentieth century's most influential books on Christian living. Toward the end of his life, Merton was trying to explore the relationship between Buddhist and Christian monasticism. He was visiting Buddhist monasteries in Bangkok, Thailand, when he was killed in an accident.

Like Augustine, Merton wrote about his conversion—in a work entitled *The Seven Storey Mountain*. Here are some passages from that autobiography that show parallels with Augustine's story:

> Three or four nights a week my fraternity brothers and I would go flying down in the black and roaring subway to 52nd Street, where we would crawl around the tiny, noisy and expensive nightclubs that had flowered on the sites of the old speakeasies in the cellars of those dirty brownstone houses. There we would sit, for hours, packed in those dark rooms, shoulder to shoulder with a lot of surly strangers and their girls, while the whole place rocked and surged with storms of jazz. . . .
>
> It was a strange, animal travesty of mysticism, sitting in those booming rooms, with the noise pouring through you, and the rhythm jumping and throbbing in the marrow of your bones. . . . If we got hangovers the next day, it was more because of the smoking and nervous exhaustion than anything else. . . .
>
> . . . There is nothing so dismal as the Flushing bus station. . . . There were always at least one or two of those same characters whose prototypes I had seen dead in the morgue. . . . Among all these I stood, weary and ready to fall, lighting the fortieth or fiftieth cigarette of the day—the one that took the last shreds of lining off my throat.

The thing that depressed me most of all was the shame and despair that invaded my whole nature when the sun came up, and all the laborers were going to work: men healthy and awake and quiet, with their eyes clear and some rational purpose before them. . . . I was spiritually dead. (Pages 157–158)

[Because of this despair, Merton began reading the works of Christian authors; time passed.]

Sometime in August, I finally answered an impulse that had been working on me for a long time. Every Sunday, I had been going out on Long Island to spend the day with the same girl. . . . But every week, as Sunday came around, I was filled with a growing desire to stay in the city and go to some kind of church. . . .

. . . With the work I was doing in the library, a stronger desire began to assert itself, and I was drawn much more imperatively to the Catholic Church. (Page 206)

[More time passed; his studies continued.]

I took up the book about Gerard Manley Hopkins [a poet]. . . . He was thinking of becoming a Catholic. . . .

All of a sudden, something began to stir within me, something began to push me, to prompt me. It was a movement that spoke like a voice.

"What are you waiting for?" it said. "Why are you sitting here? Why do you still hesitate? You know what you ought to do. Why don't you do it?" . . .

And then everything inside me began to sing—to sing with peace, to sing with strength, and to sing with conviction.

. . . Then I turned the corner of 121st Street, and the brick church and presbytery were before me. I stood in the doorway and rang the bell. . . .

. . . "Father, I want to become a Catholic." (Pages 215–216) ■

Thomas Merton's Conversion:
Catholic Social Teaching in Action

Challenges to Erring Groups

Over and above his work as a bishop, Augustine turned his great learning into writings that challenged two erring groups: the Donatists and the Pelagians. These belief factions were schismatic, or splinter, groups within Christianity.

The Donatists · The Validity of the Sacraments

The Donatists (named after Donatus, a bishop of Carthage, in North Africa) were Christians who had had their own churches in Africa for almost a hundred years. Their separation from the Catholics grew out of a dilemma that arose during the Roman persecutions of the Christians. As seen in the preceding chapter, some Christians in that period had denied their faith in the face of torture or execution. The Donatists maintained that such a denial could never be forgiven, and thus that bishops who had been disloyal or who had cooperated with the Roman authorities could never again give real baptism. The validity of any given sacrament, in other words, depended on the worthiness of the priest or bishop who administered it.

The Donatists held on to their ideas for years and violently opposed the Catholics, even though most bishops, including the bishop of Rome, had said that the sacraments are actions of Christ that come to us through human beings, who are liable to sin. The validity of a sacrament, in Augustine's teaching, did not come from how good or sinless the minister was. Rather, its validity came from God, who works through weak and imperfect human beings. Augustine, who was greatly aware of his own failings, recognized that to expect perfection of those who administer the sacraments is to be constantly disappointed. Furthermore, by basing a sacrament's reality on the holiness of the minister, the Donatists' position seemed to leave no room for God's power and grace. Gradually, through the influence of Augustine, the Donatists' position died out. By engaging himself in refuting this heresy, Augustine helped clarify the Catholic theology of the sacraments.

The Pelagians · The Power of Grace

Another group of Christians against whom Augustine argued were the Pelagians (named after the monk and preacher Pelagius). They said that a person could get to heaven without the special inner help of God—the help that Christians call grace. In other words, the Pelagian belief was that getting to heaven or being saved was a matter of working hard enough at it and achieving it through one's own efforts.

The Pelagians, it should be noted, were reacting against an attitude of moral laxity that pervaded the Roman culture. They were trying to get across that people are indeed responsible for their moral acts and cannot just "leave it all up to God." As with most heresies, this one held a grain of truth, but the Pelagians extended the argument too far by denying the need for God's grace to save people. This denial was contrary to the belief held by the large majority of Christians from the Apostles' time onward.

Augustine wrote detailed discussions of grace. In that context he affirmed the church's doctrine of original sin, that human beings, because of the fall of Adam and Eve, have inherited a tendency to sin. Furthermore, without God's grace, humans are powerless to overcome this tendency. Augustine's main point stayed clear: "The grace of God through Jesus Christ our Lord must be understood as that by which alone men are delivered from evil, and without which they do absolutely no good thing." He argued that without God's grace, even more sin and injustice would be in the world: war, crime, dishonesty, greed, lust, and all the rest.

The issue of "grace versus works" or "God's power versus human effort" would be taken up again, in a somewhat different way, centuries later during the time of the Protestant Reformation. The theme persists even into our own day. The claims of Pelagianism have a modern ring to them in our culture, which places such emphasis on self-reliance and self-development. The twentieth-century assumption that we can do everything on our own, that we do not need God, might be considered a modern-day form of Pelagianism—our own "demon" that keeps us from God and from authentic living.

"The City of God"

In the year 410, the city of Rome fell to the barbarian Goths, who looted and burned it. This event sent shock waves through the whole Roman world, because the Western part of the empire no longer had a stable government to provide some kind of order. Many pagans blamed Christianity for the fall of Rome, charging that the barbarians had overpowered Rome because Christianity's God did not protect the empire like the old pagan gods had. Even Christians themselves wondered how God could possibly have allowed this disaster to happen.

Augustine responded to this challenge with his greatest work, *The City of God,* written over a period of about twelve years. *The City of God* remains regularly in print today and is considered one of the most important books ever written in the West. In this book Augustine answered those people who blamed Christianity for the downfall of Rome.

History, according to Augustine, can be understood as an ongoing struggle between two realms: "the city of God" and "the city of Man." The first is made up of those who place their faith in God and live in service and love; the second is made up of those who pursue only selfish interests, their own gratification. It is not possible to separate these two realms in the real world, although their values are radically opposed. Both of these cities are woven together in time, but only the city of God is destined to last forever. At the end of time, at the Last Judgment, the two cities will be separated.

Augustine saw the Roman Empire as symbolic of the city of Man, and thus he was not surprised at its crumbling. The church was, for Augustine, a sign of the city of God and of God's love for the world, though the church was not identical with the city of God. (After all, elements of the city of Man could be found right within the church!) The whole purpose of Christianity was to build the city of God, and the state's role was not to get in the way of God's purposes.

Christians' desire for a city of God became more intense as various barbarian groups continued invading. Not only did the nomadic tribes steal, rape, and pillage, but they even set up separate kingdoms inside the boundaries of the Roman Empire itself. The barbarian Franks were in northwest Gaul, the Goths in southern Gaul. The Vandals (from whose name we get our modern word for destructive groups) plundered their way through Spain, then crossed over into North Africa and began their siege of Hippo at the time Augustine was nearing death.

The City of God helped Christians see that they were building something good, that their story had a purpose, even in the midst of a crumbling earthly empire.

The Rising Influence of the Papacy

With the fall of Rome in 410 and the progressive crumbling of the Roman Empire in the West, a vacuum of leadership was created. Gradually the church would begin to fill that vacuum because it was the one stable and generally respected institution that could provide governance. The office of pope, the bishop of Rome, would assume increasing importance.

Leo the Great   Redefining the Pope's Role

One person, Leo the Great, or Leo I as he was known during his years as pope, stands out as shaping the role of the papacy into a force for leadership of the Western world. He became pope in the year 440. Leo was intelligent, tough, and courageous; he had to be all of these and more to face the challenges of his times. The Roman Empire was being attacked from all sides and from within. The faith too was under attack.

Leo came to his job as pope with impressive credentials as a mediator and leader. Before becoming pope, he had been called to settle a dispute between a Roman general and the Roman governor of Gaul. He was famous for his short but eloquent sermons that packed churches. The church needed such a capable person because the role of pope was becoming more complicated. The bishop of Rome was expected to be a statesman, spiritual leader, administrator, scholar, and saint all in one.

The "Supreme Pontiff"

The papacy was seen as so significant that Leo began to use the title *Pontifex Maximus*—a title previously used by Roman emperors to indicate their role as high priests in the Roman religion. (Literally, the Latin words *pontifex maximus* mean "highest bridge maker"; in the Roman religion, a high priest was seen as a bridge between the gods and human beings.) Even today the English translation of *Pontifex Maximus,* "Supreme Pontiff," is used in reference to the pope. This title indicated the greatness of Leo's power, particularly in the Western part of the empire.

The earlier title *pope* came from the Greek word *pappas,* a respectful but affectionate term for "father." The title *pope* had come into use when the community in Rome was small and the bishop was a well-known, friendly figure leading the persecuted local church there. Clearly, when "papa," or Pope Leo, also became Pontifex Maximus, there was a changed understanding of the office of the bishop of Rome. Leo was a spiritual father but also a powerful state official.

The Pope as Peacemaker

An example of the heightened importance of the papacy and the power of the pope to wield influence in affairs of state came when the beleaguered Western emperor asked Leo to intervene and make peace with Attila the Hun. Attila the Hun was the fierce leader of a barbarian tribe that was invading Italy.

The Huns had come into the grasslands of Europe because of unfavorable climate changes in Asia. They were wanderers who looted and burned towns in their path, taking people as slaves or killing as they pleased. Attila had stormed westward and had been stopped briefly in Gaul by the Romans and Goths. But soon he had marched into Italy, which was weakly defended. The Western Roman emperor, not having enough troops to stop Attila, asked Leo to negotiate peace.

Leo traveled more than two hundred miles north of Rome to a military camp not far from the city of Milan. There he stood face-to-face with Attila, who had a huge army behind him. Leo approached Attila unarmed. No record exists of what Leo and Attila said to each other, but the fact remains that the Huns turned back. Rome was saved.

Within ten years, Leo was again required to be a peacemaker for a Roman Empire that could no longer defend itself. When an army of Vandals from North Africa tried to sack Rome, Leo faced the enemy virtually alone. Though Leo could not prevent them from looting and taking slaves, the Vandals did agree not to kill people unless attacked. They pillaged surrounding areas of Italy but not Rome itself, then sailed back to Africa.

The fact that emperors in the West had to rely on Pope Leo to turn back barbarian attackers made it obvious that the government was unable to face its enemies. The stature of the papacy had never been higher. From that point on, the pope became one of the key figures in almost all governmental matters within the Western empire.

Leo and Church Controversies   Despite the rising stature of the pope as a leader in secular affairs, conflicts within the church also occupied Leo's attention. The old problem of theological differences regarding the nature of Jesus persisted. We saw this controversy played out in the long-term conflict between Catholics and Arians. Recall that the Arians said that Jesus was not divine. Although Arianism was a factor throughout the empire, East and West, the movement tended to be concentrated in the East and among the barbarian tribes that had been converted by Christians from the East.

The Council of Chalcedon: Jesus Has Two Natures

In Pope Leo's time, another challenge to the doctrine of the Incarnation—the belief that Jesus is both God and man—was raised from the opposite end of the spectrum. A group in the East asserted that Jesus had a divine nature but not a real human nature—that the divine somehow had absorbed the human part of Jesus as he grew up. After much wrangling in councils and even a riot in which the patriarch of Constantinople (bishop of Constantinople) was fatally injured, Pope Leo in 451 called the Council of Chalcedon to rule on the matter.

The bishops at the council rejected the notion that Jesus did not have a human nature. They stated that Jesus has two natures, human and divine—that he is a real human and the real Son of God. Some bishops from Syria and Ethiopia did not agree with this position, however, and split from the main body of Christians. Today we still have the results of that division in the Jacobite church and the Coptic church.

Toward Conflict Between Eastern and Western Christians

One decision of the Council of Chalcedon that Leo disagreed with would have far-reaching effects over the next six centuries. The bishops declared that the bishop of Rome was pre-eminent among all Christian bishops, and that the patriarch of Constantinople was second in authority. This represented a change, because formerly the bishops of Antioch and Alexandria had been considered the two highest authorities after the bishop of Rome. Constantinople, after all, had not even been founded until the church was three hundred years old.

Leo strenuously objected to elevating the patriarch of Constantinople to second in authority, because the decision to move Constantinople up in prestige was motivated solely by politics. Giving Constantinople greater authority would mean that the Roman emperor of the East, who lived in Constantinople, could interfere more with religious matters. Leo could do little to prevent the politicking that would come, and this change from custom would lead to five centuries of fighting and disputes between Christians in the West, led by the bishop of Rome, and Christians in the East, led by the patriarch of Constantinople. Eventually there would be a complete break or schism between the churches of the East and the West.

Conclusion   The period following the legalization of Christianity saw a burst of growth in the church—spiritually, intellectually, and institutionally. This growth would influence the spread of Catholicism for centuries to come.

Monasticism began as a movement of individuals out of cities and into the wilderness to follow the way of Christ more closely as hermits. Within a century or so, thousands of men and women had taken up this lifestyle, at first organizing themselves informally and later living together in orders under a common rule of life.

While the primary emphasis of the monastic movement was on seeking "a right heart," a scholarly tradition that focused on "right thinking" was also emerging in the church. Ambrose and Augustine were two intellectual giants of the movement to develop and clarify the church's theology.

At the same time, the Roman Empire was increasingly under barbarian attack, and it was clear that the government in the West could no longer hold things together. The role of the pope grew in significance as Pope Leo the Great filled the vacuum of leadership and made the papacy a crucial position for maintaining peace and order in the empire.

Doctrinal challenges still plagued the church, however. Although the issue of Jesus' human and divine natures was clarified by the Council of Chalcedon, under Pope Leo, theological and political tensions between the church in the East and the church in the West were building. The church, in the dark days ahead, would be challenged to keep society together even as it struggled with its own internal divisions.

The movements and events of the period discussed in this chapter would have impact through the centuries. As the Roman Empire fell more into ruin, the church's leadership grew and became indispensable. The next chapter discusses further how the church held things together in the face of the empire's crumbling.

Questions for Reflection and Discussion

1. What did the hermits hope to discover in the desert? Have you ever craved solitude and quiet? What has drawn you to seek time alone? Do humans need such times of being alone?
2. In what ways can solitude and contemplation help us to find love?
3. What was Augustine trying to get at when he declared that "our hearts are restless, O Lord, until they rest in you"? Do you agree?
4. What are ways in which contemporary culture is guilty of Pelagianism? How can modern Pelagianism be countered?

Growth in a Crumbling Empire

Spreading the Faith,
Bringing Order to Chaos

CHRISTIANITY MOVED RAPIDLY into a position of strong world influence in the fifth century, as the church developed its moral, intellectual, and political leadership. As we saw in chapter 5, monasticism, church scholarship, and the role of the papacy flourished even in the midst of increasing pressures on the Roman Empire, especially in the West.

In fact, the years from about 450 to 700 saw the complete disintegration of the Western Roman Empire. (The Eastern empire held together, but it was gradually weakening as well.) Barbarian invasions tore apart and destroyed what remained of the old Roman political, economic, and social fabric. All of what is now Europe was divided into areas or city-states ruled by local kings, who often warred with their neighbors. In the midst of all this chaos, the church was often the one stable element in people's lives.

However, the church in both the East and the West became thoroughly entangled with politics. As princes who formerly were pagans accepted Christianity, they brought their subjects into the church with them, and the church grew in number. Bishops and monasteries were granted large tracts of land. Land meant wealth and power. Some bishops and abbots even tried to exert their power to raise up or bring down kings. All too frequently the church's mission to be a sign of Jesus' love in a dangerous, violent age became lost in these struggles for dominance.

Indeed, the church and society had entered what would later be termed the Dark Ages. That period, however, was not as thickly dark and chaotic as would be assumed from that moniker. Despite the church's own version of "darkness"—its ongoing involvement and entanglement with politics and feuds, and its growing power, influence, and wealth—certain great and enlightened Christian figures provided leadership and inspiration. The church served as a means for warring kings to negotiate with their enemies, it supported monasteries that preserved the learning of ancient times, and it offered spiritual guidance and hope to people whose lives were usually brief and hard.

Timeline . . .

450
- Patrick begins missionary work in Ireland.
- Pope Leo negotiates peace with Attila the Hun.
- Western empire falls.
- Clovis converts, Frankish subjects follow suit.
- Brigid founds double monastery at Kildare.
- Justinian authorizes Justinian Code, rebuilds Hagia Sophia.

550
- Benedict issues his Rule at Monte Cassino.

- Gregory the Great is elected pope.
- Pope Gregory sends mission to Britain.

- Muhammad lays foundations of Islam.

650

- Muslims conquer Mediterranean, lay siege to Constantinople.
- Boniface begins missionary work in Germany.
- Charles Martel stops Muslim advance in Gaul.

750
- Boniface crowns Pepin king of Franks.

A Picture   History generally gets told as a record of the move-
of Christian Life   ments and decisions of kings, generals, and religious
leaders. Very little, at least in ancient times, was ever
written about the common folk, so we do not know much about
them. But we do have some knowledge of what it meant to be a
typical Christian in the midst of the Dark Ages. The following four
sections give some picture of Christian life.

God as Ruler

In the early Dark Ages, at the beginning of the sixth century,
people had little control over disease, their environment, or their fate
in general. Most people did not live past age forty-five, and they had
to scrape for their food day by day. Moving to a higher position in
society was almost unheard of. Consequently, people had a strong
sense that God ruled creation; clearly *they* did not rule it. They identified with the suffering Jesus and hoped to go to heaven as a reward
for enduring a life of hardship.

Certainly, sixth-century people also laughed, fell in love, cherished their children, and shared in all the other normal activities of
life. They believed that God "looked down from above," protecting
and blessing good persons and punishing the wrongdoers. The people of the Dark Ages had a strong sense of God's grace but also of
the devil's presence and power.

The Mass and the Sacraments

Worship, especially eucharistic worship, was central to Christian
life in the sixth century. On Sundays, people went to Mass, as it had
been called since the fifth century. (The term *Mass* came from the
Latin word *missa* in the farewell given by the presider at the Eucharist: *"Ite, missa est,"* or "Go, you are dismissed.") The form of the
Mass was fairly standardized by the sixth century for both the West
and the East. In the West, the Mass followed roughly the same form
as today, except that the language used was Latin, not the people's
local language.

In the East, there were some differences in the Mass. Curtains
and decorated wall panels separated the sanctuary and the altar from
the congregation. The liturgy of the word was celebrated in front of
the panels, but the eucharistic celebration took place behind the panels. This added to the sense of mystery surrounding the eucharistic
rite. The language used in the Eastern churches was generally Greek,
although other languages were also used, depending on the place.

In the West, the rituals of the sacraments besides the Eucharist
were somewhat different from the sacramental rituals today. The
sacrament of reconciliation, for instance, was usually performed in

public and only in cases of the most serious sins. The penances were quite severe by our standards, such as eating and sleeping less, refraining from marital relations, and renouncing involvement in business or politics. Not until a few centuries later would private confession become popular.

Veneration of Saints

Another increasingly important part of worship was the veneration of saints, especially martyrs. By the year 600, many saints were called upon in prayer and remembered during the liturgy because they were seen as intercessors in heaven, who could bring a person's needs directly to God. The relics of saints, which might be small pieces of cloth from their clothing or even particles of their bones, were treasured. People and localities adopted favorite saints and celebrated their feast days (the anniversary days of the saints' death).

The Clergy

From the fifth century to the beginning of the seventh century, qualifications for the priesthood gradually became stricter and more standardized. Early in the fifth century, the minimum requirements for priests were that they not have done public penance in their lifetime, not have served in the army since the time of their baptism, not have paid for public pagan games, and not have been a pagan priest. If married, they had to have married a virgin, not a twice-married woman or a widow. Nearly a century later, the list of qualifications was expanded to specify that no woman, no illiterate person, no proven criminal, and no physically deformed man could be a priest.

In those centuries, priests were often chosen by the townspeople or by the ruler of the local castle. Enforcement of the qualifications by the bishops was frequently weak because communications were poor. During Gregory the Great's papacy, as we shall see, the training of priests improved somewhat, and celibacy (staying unmarried) was encouraged, although not required.

Before considering how the church led and inspired people throughout the period from about 450 to 700, let's review the political developments that were the backdrop for the church's work.

The Political Scene, West and East

Barbarian Pressures in the West The two Roman empires, West and East, took different political directions, with the state being much weaker than the church in the West but stronger than the church in the East. In the West, as seen in the preceding chapter, waves of barbarian invasions put great pressures—social, economic, and political—on the empire. Small barbarian kingdoms were popping up in various parts of the Western empire, in what we now know as France, Spain, and England. The emperors were too weak to stop the invasions. As the state lost the ability to hold things together, the pope and the church ascended in power and influence, with the church becoming the stabilizing force for order and peace.

Control of the Church in the East The emperors who ruled the Eastern empire from Constantinople were generally more capable than the emperors in the West. The Eastern emperors were so strong, in fact, that they dominated the church, taking a "super-bishop" role. The emperors were involved in church doctrinal disputes, called church councils to deliberate over the disputes, appointed bishops, and so on. These Eastern emperors were often Arians (heretical Christians who denied the divinity of Christ), and their appointments of bishops reflected that theological bias. So the Arian heresy, though condemned by the Council of Nicaea in the year 325, was still alive and influencing church developments in the East.

Furthermore, the missionaries of the Eastern empire who went out to convert the barbarian tribes to Christianity were often Arian, so when the barbarians converted, it was typically to an Arian variety of Christianity, not to Catholic Christianity. Thus the barbarian tribes were not only invading Roman territory in the West but also spreading Arianism.

Chieftains Instead of Western Emperors In the year 476, the Roman emperor in the West was deposed by a barbarian leader who was also the Roman army commander. For the next several centuries, the West would have no Roman emperor. It would be ruled from the East by a variety of barbarian chieftains in the name of the Eastern emperor. (After the fall of the Western empire, the empire in the East was no longer known as "the Eastern empire" but as "the Byzantine Empire." The new name came from the original name of the city of Constantinople, which was *Byzantium*.)

One of the barbarian leaders in the West was Theodoric, the king of a Goth tribe, who took over the rule of Italy around the beginning of the sixth century. He managed to keep peace between the Goths and the Italians despite their mutual dislike and different customs. The Italians were allied to the church of Rome—that is, to Catholic Christianity—but the Goths, including Theodoric, were Arians. Although religious tolerance was unusual in those times, Theodoric granted religious freedom to his subjects; he did not persecute the Catholics. This was because he realized that in Italy the church alone had the organization needed to keep the peace. Even as an Arian he did not hesitate to ask Catholic bishops to help him solve the empire's problems. Thus Italy and the church experienced some years of relative calm and order.

As Clovis Goes, So Go the Barbarians A political development with enormous significance for the church was the rise to power and eventual conversion of Clovis, king of the Franks. The Franks were a pagan tribe in what we now know as northern Europe. After uniting small groups of the Franks into one group with himself as king, Clovis conquered tribes to the south. He ruled at about the same time as Theodoric but held different territory.

Unlike most of the other barbarian tribes, the Franks were pagans, not Arians; they had no Christian connection. But as pagans, Clovis and the Franks were more acceptable to the Catholics than the Arian tribes were, for between the Arians and the Catholics lay a bitter, often violent history.

From Pagan to Christian

Clovis married a Catholic princess, from whom he learned much about the faith and who urged him to accept Christianity. But he was reluctant to convert, because he understood the advantage of having the same religion as his newly conquered subjects, most of whom were pagans. Having religion in common with them would enable him to govern more easily.

According to legend, during one fierce battle that he was losing, Clovis prayed to his wife's God for victory. Suddenly the tide turned in Clovis's favor. With his victory, Clovis decided that the Christian God was more powerful than the old pagan gods. But before he would convert, he wanted to be assured that his subjects would also convert. The story goes that his three thousand soldiers yelled out that they would convert with him, and so Clovis, in 496, and gradually all the Franks became Christian. (You may recall from chapter 4 the legend that Emperor Constantine had a similar conversion experience.)

Arianism on the Wane, Christendom on the Rise

As Clovis worked his way south, conquering more of Gaul (what is now France, named for the Franks), Catholic Christianity spread throughout the tribes that had been Arian. Consequently, because of Clovis, Arianism began to die out in the Western part of the empire. Like rulers before him, Clovis used the church to help him bring stability to his kingdom. A common religion gave his subjects a unifying moral code and set of religious rituals to follow.

The conversion of Clovis and the Franks had monumental significance for the rise of what is called Christendom, that is, Christianity as the dominant organizational and cultural force in society. This was because in the centuries after Clovis, the Frankish kings so enmeshed the church in governmental affairs that church and state were hardly distinguishable from each other. This arrangement enabled the church to grow in number, but it often compromised the church as well.

The development of Christendom will be covered in the next chapter. Briefly, however, the rise of Christendom can be seen in a changed way of counting the years of the calendar. At about the time of Clovis's conversion, a new calendar was devised at the direction of the pope. Eventually it replaced the calendar that had been used in the Roman Empire for more than a thousand years. Instead of counting the years from the founding of Rome, the new calendar began counting years from the presumed year of Christ's birth (the estimate was off by a few years but is nonetheless the dating system we use today). Christians accepted this calendar as a reminder that, for them, Jesus Christ was the center of all time and history.

Justinian   The Last Strong Emperor

Justinian, who ruled over the Byzantine Empire from 527 to 565, was its last strong emperor. He is famous for setting up a uniform code of law throughout the empire and for constructing one of the grandest church buildings of all time, in Constantinople. During his rule, Justinian kept the Eastern empire strong enough to withstand barbarian invasion, and the church reached a pinnacle of influence in the East, covering the regions of Syria, Greece, Iraq, Lebanon, Jordan, Egypt, Albania, Turkey, and southern Russia.

The Justinian Code

Justinian's most significant achievement was the reform of the civil law. Most of the existing laws in the empire had been written in pre-Christian times and did not reflect Christian values. So a committee worked for seven years to produce a collection of laws, the Justinian Code, which were stated clearly in Latin and later became the basis of European law.

The new legal system did manifest a more Christian orientation. For example, Justinian's law took away much of the arbitrary power that a man had over his wife and children. A father could no longer send his children into slavery to pay his debts. Women could hold property in their own name. Women were protected from being easily divorced by their husbands. Admittedly, some of the punishments specified by the code for certain crimes were dreadful—not what we would consider Christian—such as the cutting off of hands and ears. Like all law, the Justinian Code was based in part on the customs of the time. Despite its problems, however, it better reflected Christian ethics than the old laws had.

Persecution of Jews and Others

Although based in Christianity, Justinian's rule was not without ruthless elements. The emperor, like many rulers in the pre-Christian era, believed he was responsible for the religion of his subjects. He believed in Christianity, so everyone else should too; thus all would go to heaven. Because of this conviction, Justinian persecuted Jews, other non-Christians, and heretics.

Prejudice toward Jews and persecution of them was common throughout Christianity at the time. Justinian and the Frankish kings demanded that Jews convert. But the rulers also depended on the Jews to provide to Christians those services that Christians were forbidden to provide, such as usury, which is the lending of money with a charge for interest. Jews were forced into moneylending as an occupation because it was illegal for them to own land or participate in many other professions. Besides, Christians needed and wanted loans. But at the same time, Jews were scorned for participating in financial professions and were subjected to torture and sometimes death by the society that benefited from their financial services.

An Emperor in Control of the Church

Justinian thought that in addition to persecuting non-Christians, it was his duty to tell the church what to do and what to believe. Once he even kept the pope under arrest in Constantinople. Justinian made regulations for electing bishops and ordered them to supervise public works projects, enforce laws related to morals, and take care of orphans. In some districts, the bishops, given so many secular responsibilities, had more authority than the governors.

Justinian is especially well known for rebuilding the Hagia Sophia (Holy Wisdom) Church, which had been destroyed by fire. With a labor force of ten thousand people working for more than five years, a magnificent structure for Christian worship was built. It still stands today in Constantinople, as a museum. For many centuries it functioned as a mosque, or place of public worship for Muslims.

After Justinian, the successors to the imperial throne were weak. New barbarian invasions began. The Western empire had crumbled some years before; the East began to disintegrate too.

We have considered the political context in which the church found itself during the fifth and sixth centuries. Now we will turn to a most remarkable and enriching development in the church's life, one that brought about tremendous "church growth in a crumbling empire"—the rise of the monasteries.

The Monasteries   Islands of Culture, Foundries of Faith

One of the most remarkable achievements of the church over the centuries has been the development of monasticism. Chapter 5 explained that monasticism began primarily as a solitary way of life. Hermits such as Antony of Egypt went into the desert to find God. Communal forms of monasticism then gradually started up, with the Rule of Basil being the first attempt to create a regular way of life for a monastic community.

As the Roman Empire deteriorated and political and economic chaos prevailed in the wider society, monasticism rose as a constructive, orderly form of social organization and a means of spreading the faith. We will trace its development during the Dark Ages by using the stories of three great monastic leaders: Patrick, Brigid, and Benedict. Patrick and Brigid did their work in Ireland, which as an island was insulated from the wars with the barbarians and the social disintegration of the European continent. Benedict, on the other hand, founded his monastery in the middle of Italy.

Patrick   The Monk as Missionary

The son of good Christians, Patrick (389–461) grew up on the western coast of Britain, which was part of the Roman Empire.

A Slave Among the Pagans

One day, when Patrick was about sixteen, pirate ships from pagan Ireland landed near his home, and he was taken captive. For the next six years, Patrick was held as a slave in Ireland, tending sheep. He worked long hours in isolation and had to live among his enemies, separated from family and friends. He had much time to think, and, according to legend, he prayed fervently for rescue.

Gradually Patrick learned the Celtic language of the Irish (who were called the Celts). He learned too that they worshiped gods of the sea and forest. And he became familiar with the Druids, who were pagan priests who also served as judges, teachers, and advisers to tribal kings. The Druids spent many years memorizing the legends of the Celts.

Three Styles of Monasticism by 700

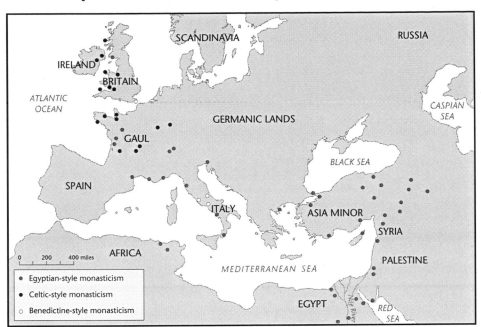

Called Back to Preach Among His Captors

At the end of six years of slavery, Patrick escaped from his master's farm and eventually returned to his home in Britain. In a short time, he decided to enter a monastery in Gaul, on the continent. After twenty years as a monk, however, Patrick felt called to return to Ireland and work among the Celts, who had once held him captive and been his enemies. In 432, Patrick was made a bishop and was sent to the Celts to preach the Good News. Only a handful of people had already converted to Christianity in Ireland, so Patrick had his work cut out for him.

The Monastery as a Missionary Center

Bishop Patrick introduced a new approach to spreading the faith: he established monasteries all over the island of Ireland. He brought monks first from Gaul. Gradually, Irish converts then became monks, swelling the monks' numbers, and more monasteries were built. The monks introduced the people to reading, writing, and Christianity— teaching them Latin first and Celtic later (the Celts had a rich oral tradition but no written tradition until the monks developed the written language). In the centuries that followed, monks and nuns copied books by hand and embellished them with elaborate, colorful designs called illuminations. As one can imagine, books were rare treasures in the days before the printing press.

Because of the ravages of war on the continent of Europe, Irish Christianity became somewhat isolated, and it developed a unique style. In time, though, the Irish monasteries, which were centers of learning and faith, became the roots for the spread of Christianity not only within Ireland but later to Scotland, Germany, Switzerland, and northern France. Without a doubt, the driving force behind the missionary work was Patrick.

The Stuff of Legends

Legends about Patrick abound. If all were believed, he would have to have been a combination of saint and superman. He is pictured as driving throughout Ireland in his chariot, matching magical powers with the Druids. Supposedly they could turn day into night, but only Patrick could bring out the sun. The Druids could produce a snowstorm, but only Patrick could make the snow melt.

Whatever the truth of the legends, after twenty-five years of work, Patrick could rightly claim that Ireland was Christian, and a new hope for the church was blooming.

Brigid   From Servant Girl to Monastic Leader

While a dark age hovered over continental Europe, Irish Christianity was flourishing under the impetus of Patrick's monasteries. One of the most dynamic and remarkable figures of that period was a woman in Ireland named Brigid. She was born around the year 453, toward the end of Patrick's life. Brigid's mother, a slave of Brigid's father, was sold to a Druid and took little Brigid with her. When Brigid grew old enough to work, she returned as a servant to the household of her father, a minor pagan king, and spent her days grinding corn, tending sheep and pigs, and waiting on everyone. She gained a reputation in the household for her annoying habits of feeding hungry wanderers and doing other acts of kindness. Legend has it that one time she even gave away her father's great battle sword to a leper who was begging for alms.

A Calling to Leadership

When Brigid's father decided that Brigid had to marry a certain man, the young Brigid refused. She even found another bride for her would-be fiancé. Brigid had made up her mind to live the single life, dedicated to serving God and humankind. In a culture that oppressed women, Brigid's choice represented great inner liberation and authenticity.

Eventually, Brigid and seven other women made vows and formed a monastic community. Young women flocked to Brigid's community. Soon she was founding monastic communities all over Ireland. By the end of Brigid's life, thirteen thousand women had joined her communities, becoming free nuns and working under her inspiration for their God, their community, and people in need.

The Double Monastery of Kildare

Most remarkably, Brigid founded Kildare, which was unique in Ireland as a double monastery: one for women and one for men. Such was Brigid's authority that she invited a metal craftsman to be ordained as a bishop so that he could say Mass for the communities, lead the men, and assist her in founding other new monasteries. For centuries, until the church placed convents under the jurisdiction of men, Kildare continued to be led by a double line of abbesses and abbot-bishops.

Organized as a self-sufficient little city, Kildare was a thriving center of artisanship and learning. Kildare and other monasteries were the focus of the spread of Christianity in Ireland. The monks and nuns taught people about the faith. Connected to almost every major monastery was a school, with as many as a thousand students. Kildare's school, which offered the liberal arts as well as religious studies, was renowned throughout Europe.

Ireland's monasteries produced scholars, artists, and great missionaries, and Brigid's leadership played a major role in the growth of Christianity. To the Irish she is a beloved household saint.

Benedict   A Balance of Work and Prayer

While Clovis was building the kingdom of the Franks in Gaul and Theodoric the Goth was ruling Italy, a young man named Benedict was studying law in Rome. Before he finished his studies, he became disgusted with the sin, crime, and confusion that seemed to exist everywhere. Like Antony and others who had gone to the desert two centuries earlier, Benedict wanted to seek God in the silence of the countryside.

After some time living as a hermit in a cave, Benedict began to draw around himself monks who wanted help ordering their life. They longed for a more balanced life, so that they could combine prayer, meditation, work, and service. A group of these men formed the nucleus of what would be Benedict's famous monastery at Monte Cassino.

In the year 529, on the top of a mountain about halfway between Rome and Naples, Benedict and his monks built their monastery. The community within the monastery was nearly a complete economic unit, supplying itself with food, clothing, and shelter. In its quiet scriptorium, monks copied sacred books and preserved secular books containing the writings of famous authors.

By the 1100s, the world of a typical BENEDICTINE-STYLE MONASTERY included: (A) the church, where the monks prayed and sang in the choir; (B) the dormitory, where they slept; (C) the refectory, where they ate meals; (D) the cloisters, the secluded square courtyard surrounded by covered walkways; (E) the infirmary, where the monks cared for poor and sick people from both inside and outside the monastery; (F) the kitchen and bake house; (G) the workshops and library; (H) vineyards, fields, and orchards, where the monks grew their own food.

Eventually, a group of women seeking the monastic life formed a community with Benedict's sister Scholastica, not far from Monte Cassino. The two communities were composed of ordinary people, converted Goths and Romans. Benedict and Scholastica taught the monks and nuns how to read so they could understand the Scriptures and the daily prayers. Life for the monks and nuns was simple and well ordered, balanced between "prayer and work"—in Latin, *ora et labora.*

At Monte Cassino, Benedict wrote what came to be called the Rule of Saint Benedict. This rule eventually became the basic guide for life and discipline in religious communities throughout the Western world. Though the points of the rule (stressing a balanced life of prayer and work) came from his own experience and great common sense, Benedict realized that he was building on a tradition that was centuries old—a tradition begun by Antony and carried through by Jerome, Basil, and others. Benedict advocated a style of life that was less severe than the early monastics from the East had lived. Benedict's Rule became recognized as the most inspired description of monastic life in the West, and today Benedict is known as the father of Western monasticism.

As a response to the needs of an empire in chaos, monasticism would bring harmony and order to Christian life, encourage growth in holiness, and ensure the passing on of knowledge.

Gregory the Great: A Pope Engaged with the World

While monasticism was enabling settlements of peace and order to spring up throughout the Roman Empire, a parallel development was focusing on the church's role in the wider world. The man who exemplified this development was Pope Gregory I, later called Gregory the Great (who lived from about 540 to about 604).

From Government Official to Reluctant Pope During a time when the city of Rome was in shambles and people needed to move away even to find food and drinking water, young Gregory was named prefect of Rome, serving as governor, chief of police, and chief justice. Despite his organizational talent and leadership skills, Gregory struggled to feed Rome and maintain basic services, and Rome was only part of Gregory's responsibilities. In charge of a large part of southern Italy, Gregory had to figure out ways to distribute grain and generally take care of the poor.

Gregory was not entirely happy with the prestige and importance of his public office. When his father died, he resigned his position and started giving away much of his money and land. He turned the family mansion into a monastery and lived in it as a monk. Refusing to be the abbot of the monastery, he simply adopted the lifestyle of the rest of the monks who came to live there. This quiet, contemplative life was broken, however, by a command from the pope that Gregory go to Constantinople to keep the emperor informed about the needs of impoverished Rome. The people had once again looked to the church for leadership and mediation.

After seven years at the corrupt imperial court in Constantinople, Gregory gladly returned to Rome. But the conditions in Rome degenerated further when the Tiber River flooded the city, destroying food supplies and homes, and breeding fatal sicknesses. When the pope himself died from the plague, the people of Rome elected Gregory as pope, trusting that his experience and abilities would save them. Like the reluctant Ambrose of Milan two hundred years earlier, Gregory did not want the job. He hid for three days, hoping that the people would choose someone else. They did not. So in the year 590, at age fifty, Gregory became bishop of Rome, or pope.

An Able Leader As pope, Gregory the Great was a social worker, pastor, theologian, educator, administrator, farmer, and builder. He was a rare person who functioned well in all of those roles.

Friend of the Poor

The life of a pope during Gregory's time was far from easy. As the bishop of Rome, he was particularly responsible for the poor; the church was the only welfare agency in existence. Using the profits from farms owned by the church, Gregory fed many poor people. Profits from farms also helped him rebuild crumbling churches and build new ones. He took responsibility for repairing the walls of the city as well, a task that was needed for the defense of Rome.

Church Educator

As the leader of the church at large, Gregory showed concern for the poorly educated clergy. Priests of the time were chosen by local rulers or townsfolk, often for political, rather than spiritual, reasons. Gregory encouraged bishops to open schools for men wanting to become priests. In turn, he expected that the priests would open church schools for children. (The church schools, along with the monastery schools, were the only sources of education for the laity.) Gregory also advocated priestly celibacy, though he did not require it.

Gregory wrote many letters covering topics such as the Bible, the duties of pastors, and the proper way to celebrate the liturgy. Nine hundred of his letters are still preserved in libraries.

Liturgical Music Innovator

One of Gregory's great contributions to the church and to Western culture was his emphasis on keeping a written record of music for liturgy. The earliest Christians had learned Jewish hymns by heart; later Christians had learned Greek and Roman hymns. But without sheet music, melodies could not easily be passed on for future generations or wider distribution. Gregory ordered that church music be organized into a system covering the liturgies of all the feast days as well as the daily prayer of psalms and hymns sung in the monasteries. The result was a type of written music that later evolved into Gregorian chant, a beautiful, haunting style that would nourish the faith of the church's people in the West for centuries.

Diplomat

Like Pope Leo the Great, who restrained Attila the Hun through persuasion, Gregory had to be a diplomat. In effect, the pope had to take the place of the government. Accordingly, Gregory negotiated with and sent missionaries to the Lombards and other barbarian tribes. The church had chosen to try to make alliances with the barbarian tribes and convert them, rather than resist them. That decision made all the difference for the development of Christendom in the West, for gradually all the barbarian tribes would be converted and the whole of what is now Europe would be solidly Christian.

The Mission to Britain Gregory's most distinctive work in spreading the faith was his sending of a mission to Britain, or England. Although there were Christians in Britain already, they had been pushed westward by an onslaught of fierce tribes of Angles and Saxons from the continent. In an effort to establish some communication between the Christians and those tribes and possibly convert the tribes, Pope Gregory sent to Britain forty monks from his own Benedictine monastery in Rome. On their journey, the monks were led by their abbot, Augustine of Canterbury. As the monks passed through Gaul, they heard hair-raising tales about the fierce tribes in Britain, but they pushed on, encouraged by letters from Gregory.

Amazingly, when they reached Britain in 597, Augustine and his monks found a peaceful reception by the Anglo-Saxon king, Ethelbert. According to Bede, a noted historian of the English church,

King Ethelbert was so moved by the spirit of the monks that he happily converted to Christianity. Bede described the event as follows:

At length the king himself, among others, edified by the pure lives of these holy men and their gladdening promises, the truth of which they confirmed by many miracles, believed and was baptized. Thenceforward great numbers gathered each day to hear the word of God. . . . It is said that [Ethelbert] would not compel anyone to accept Christianity; for he had learned . . . that the service of Christ must be accepted freely and not under compulsion.

Unlike many of the other barbarian tribes, whose members were baptized under the orders of their kings and chieftains, the "fierce" Anglo-Saxons came voluntarily into the church. However, it took about a hundred years before the whole of Britain was Christian.

Gregory the Great's contributions to the church were enormous and far-reaching in their effects. His leadership solidified the church in a time of tremendous calamity. Even so he humbly saw himself as "Servant of the Servants of God," a title that all popes since him have adopted.

Most of Gregory's efforts were expended on the Western part of the church because the West was more strife-torn than the East. The West was afflicted by nomadic invasions, widespread disease, and a babble of languages that prevented communication. Latin had become virtually unknown by the common people, and dialects were developing that would later become Italian, Spanish, French, and German.

The East was more stable because the Roman Empire there, although weakened, still had a stronger economy, a more hospitable climate, and a common language (Greek). But even the East's relative stability was soon to be shattered by a powerful new force.

A New Threat: The Muslim Conquerors

While Pope Gregory was exercising leadership in the West, a new force was gathering strength in the East, around the Red Sea. The followers of an Arab prophet named Muhammad (570–632) were dedicated to spreading their new religion everywhere. Muhammad's followers became known as Muslims and their religion as Islam, both terms referring to "submission to God."

Conquering the Mediterranean in the Name of Allah   As a young leader of camel caravans, traveling up and down the shores of the Red Sea, Muhammad had learned about the God of the Hebrew and the Christian Scriptures. He recognized those writings as inspired by God. As a prophet, Muhammad taught his fellow Arabs the central belief of Islam—that there is only one God, and Allah is his name. Aspects of Jewish and Christian teachings would later appear in Muhammad's own writings, which became the Islamic scriptures, called the Koran. Muhammad said that the truths he wrote about were revealed to him by the angel Gabriel.

Muhammad taught that Muslims honor Allah by spreading Islam. Thus Arab warriors for Islam, mounted on swift horses and taking over a navy, conquered much of the territory around the Mediterranean Sea: Syria, Palestine, Egypt, and the North African coast. Generally the Muslim conquerors did not force anyone to accept Islam. However, they did collect annual taxes from the infidels, which was what they called those who refused to convert to Islam. Thus, to avoid the taxes, many Christians in the East converted to Islam.

Shortly before the year 700, the Muslims began a five-year siege of Constantinople itself. Although Constantinople was saved for the Christians for a while, the Muslims had control of most of the southern and eastern shores of the Mediterranean Sea. Muslim ships destroyed trade between the West and Constantinople. The Mediterranean was no longer Roman. Christians began to fear, quite realistically, that the Muslims would conquer Europe.

Stopped in Gaul   By the middle of the 700s, Spain came under the rule of the Muslims. In Spain, the Jewish minority had been harassed for years by Christian kings who wanted the Jews' trade profits. Jews were often forced to choose between being baptized Christian and losing their homes and businesses. So they decided to cooperate with the Muslims, and this accounted in part for the success of Islam in Spain. Eventually the Moors (the Muslims who conquered Spain) pressed their way northward into Gaul.

As the Muslims marched to the north, panic spread in Gaul. Since Clovis's death, the sons and grandsons of Clovis had divided and subdivided the Frankish kingdom until there was virtually no central government left. Lawlessness coupled with relentless poverty made Gaul a hard place in which to live, and it was vulnerable to a huge force like the Muslims.

But in 732, Charles Martel, a kind of prime minister of Gaul called a "mayor of the palace," with his army met and defeated the invading Muslim army at the city of Tours, near Paris. The Muslims retreated over the mountains back into Spain. During the next few years Martel had to fight the Muslims several more times, but he lived up to his name—*Martel* means "hammer." His victories prevented Islam from spreading over Europe.

Despite the threat that Islam posed to the West, Christianity owes a great debt to the Muslims. Many of the ancient Greek philosophers, such as Aristotle, were introduced to Europe and Christianity through Muslim scholars, who had learned Greek philosophy while in Egypt. Centuries after the Muslims swept through the Mediterranean region, Aristotle's philosophy would have a major place in the thought of Thomas Aquinas, perhaps the most influential Catholic theologian.

Conclusion The Western part of the Roman Empire became increasingly Christianized as the barbarian tribes converted to Christianity. In the absence of a central, strong government, the church was the one overarching structure that could hold society together in the period known as the Dark Ages. Monasteries provided islands of learning and culture as well as a means of spreading the faith, and the papacy grew in respect and influence in the wider world. In the West, Christendom was on the rise.

In the East, strong emperors tried to control the church. Although emperors like Justinian did some good, such as making the civil law correspond with Christian ethics, the record is mixed. The emperors' persecution of Jews and other non-Christians and their dictating of church policy for political purposes were not consistent with the Gospel.

Islam posed a huge threat to Christianity, taking over much of the Holy Land and North Africa, where Christianity had been dominant. But the Muslims were stopped on their way from Spain into the rest of Europe.

The centuries after the Dark Ages would see more growth for the church—sometimes through heroism and holiness, as with the great missionary efforts, but sometimes via the exercise of sheer power.

Questions for Reflection and Discussion

1. The Jews were persecuted throughout Christendom. What groups or denominations are scorned by mainstream society today? How is prejudice against them expressed?

2. Saint Benedict encouraged a balance of work and prayer. How can people today include time for prayer and meditation in their busy lives?

3. Part of Gregory's role as pope was to minister to poor, hungry, and homeless people. What are ways in which the church and its members continue this legacy of caring for needy people among us?

7

The Challenge of Christendom
Church and Empire in Tension

AS SEEN IN chapter 6, vast territory in the East, North Africa, and Spain fell to the Muslims in the seventh and eighth centuries. In the West (what we now know as Europe), barbarian tribes were converting to Christianity, usually at the orders of their leaders. Also in the West, monasticism was flowering under Benedict's Rule, and the role of the papacy was growing under Pope Gregory the Great. These were all signs of a church on the rise. But until Charles Martel halted the march of Islam in Gaul in 732, it appeared that Christianity could be blotted out. That was not to be the case, however.

Even as the Muslims threatened to overtake Europe, the church continued to spread into new territories and to grow intellectually in places where it was already established. Irish missionaries had been at work on the European continent since the 500s. The monasteries they founded throughout Europe proved to be indispensable to converting the peasant population. The missionary monks helped the peasants put the land, which had been devastated by barbarian wars, back into cultivation, and the missionaries also found ways to Christianize the peasant culture.

England, which had been Christianized during the 600s largely under the inspiration of Gregory the Great, was becoming a source of new light for the church.

Two English Sources of Light

Two sources of new light for the church were two Benedictine monks who lived at approximately the same time: Boniface and Bede. Boniface, an untiring traveler, is remembered as "the Apostle of Germany." Bede, who spent his childhood and entire adult life in one monastery, is known for his contribution to Christian scholarship and history. Their lives, whose details could hardly have differed more, represent two of the great gifts of the monasteries—missionary work and scholarship.

Boniface: The Apostle to the Germans

Boniface (675–754) was a Benedictine monk in England when he left his monastery to do missionary work in what is now the Netherlands. Even after two years of hard work by Boniface, though, the people of the Netherlands would have no part of Christianity, so the discouraged Boniface went to Rome to see the pope. The pope sent him to preach in the Germanic regions, where he did meet with success.

Timeline . . .

700
- Boniface begins missionary work in Germany.
- Charles Martel stops Muslim advance in Gaul.

- Boniface crowns Pepin king of Franks.
- Pepin gives pope Papal States in Italy.

- Iconoclast controversy rages in Byzantine Empire.

800
- Charlemagne unifies Western empire, is crowned by Pope Leo III.
- Charlemagne dies; Vikings invade Europe; feudalism grows.

- Ansgar evangelizes Scandinavia.
- Cyril and Methodius preach to Slavs in Slavic.

900
- Cluny monastery is founded, becomes center of reform.

- Pope John XII crowns Otto I Holy Roman Emperor.

- Vladimir I of Russia joins Byzantine church.

1000
- Stephen I of Hungary spreads Christianity among subjects.

Four years later, Boniface was made a bishop. He then recruited English monks and nuns to work with him in German territory. Like Patrick, he built monasteries and used them as the base of his missionary work. Christianity was soon flourishing in German lands.

A wandering bishop. During the next twenty years, Boniface became a sort of wandering bishop with a few monks for company. He was a convincing witness to the faith, and apparently he followed the advice of an English bishop who wrote to him on how best to talk with nonbelievers: "Thou shouldst propose to them in no irritating or offensive manner, but with the greatest calmness and moderation." Boniface's friend also advised him to approach the pagans with this logic: If the gods of the pagans are so powerful, why are those gods not striking down Christians who are converting pagans away from their old-time religion?

A famous story about Boniface illustrates that he used that logic with the pagans. One time Boniface, with great boldness and courage, chopped down an oak tree that a pagan tribe worshiped as the sacred tree dedicated to Thor, their principal god. When the people saw that Boniface was not instantly struck down by Thor, many asked for baptism. The missionary proceeded to build a chapel with the wood from the tree, "converting" the tree as well as the people to Christianity!

Boniface and his fellow monks lived a hard life, always on the move, preaching where there were no priests, visiting the small congregations. That life made Boniface rugged physically—but then such a life also took a very rugged soul. Another example of Boniface's bravery was that he dared to send a letter to a promiscuous tribal king, confronting the king about his lustful behavior. The monk declared, "Such conduct must be regarded as criminal in the sight of God."

Working with the Frankish government. Boniface also brought the church into a close working relationship with the Frankish government under Charles Martel and then under Charles Martel's son Pepin the Short. (Recall that the Franks were the tribe that had converted to Christianity under their king Clovis, more than two hundred years earlier, and that they occupied most of Gaul.) In fact, when Pepin assumed for himself the title "King of the Franks" in 751, Boniface, as the pope's representative, crowned Pepin. This act symbolized that the church was getting more and more entangled with the government, a trend that will be taken up later in this chapter.

Despite Boniface's success in church relations, however, his first love was not for administration but for preaching the word of God.

As an old man, he resigned his position as bishop and headed off with a few monks for mission territory in the Netherlands, where he had started out unsuccessfully many years before. Boniface and his companions were martyred there.

Bede: The Historian-Monk

An English monk who made a different kind of contribution to the church was Bede, known after his death as "the Venerable Bede." As a child he was taught by monks in a Benedictine monastery close to his home. After he grew up, Bede himself became a monk and spent his entire life in the same monastery, studying, teaching, and writing. He seems never to have traveled, and in his lifetime he was probably never heard of by anyone outside his little village. Yet he is still remembered today as a great historian of the English people.

The library of the monastery where Bede lived contained immensely valuable books from Gaul, Spain, Rome, and the rest of what had been the Roman Empire. By studying these works, Bede became acquainted with the great minds of Europe. He wrote explanations of the Scriptures as well as sermons on religious topics. His greatest work is *A History of the English Church and People*, which is still read today, more than twelve hundred years after he wrote it in about 731. Vivid and detailed, Bede's history brings alive the people and events of his time.

Bede's work points to the important role of the monasteries in fostering the scholarship that went on despite the violent times in the West. While Muslim scholars in the East, North Africa, and Spain were making great strides in mathematics, astronomy, architecture, and the translation of ancient Greek writings, learning was extremely hampered in Europe; it relied almost totally on the work of the monasteries. Not only did the monks teach children to read and write, but they also hand-copied important manuscripts. Great books from ancient times would likely not have survived the violence of that era in the West without the work of the silently persistent monks. Then, too, a small group of monks like Bede wrote original works on history, theology, and philosophy.

Church and State Entangled

As the residents of the monasteries pursued missionary work and scholarship, another major development was going on for the church. This was the increased entanglement of church and state, with a constant competition between the two for dominance. This enmeshment continued the trend that had started when Boniface, as the pope's representative, crowned Pepin as king of the Franks in 751.

From Adult Baptism to Infant Baptism

By the time of the early Middle Ages (the years 500 to 800), infant baptism became common practice. As the nomadic tribes were converted, whole families were baptized together. Eventually, most Europeans were Christian and were used to the notion that baptism was administered to infants. Sometimes midwives baptized children who were only minutes old. Confirmation was separate from the rite of baptism because it seemed appropriate only for adults. Frequently people went through their entire life without being confirmed.

Another factor prompting the baptism of newborn infants was the high mortality rate among children. Fearing for the souls of their children, parents sought early baptism for them to wipe away the original sin inherited from Adam and Eve, a sin that they believed would keep their children from heaven.

From Public Penance to Private Confession

The Christians of the early Middle Ages had a dilemma: If baptism, traditionally a source of forgiveness of sins, was generally for infants, how could adults be absolved from their sins? How could sinners be forgiven?

For Christians in the first centuries of the church, the opportunity to be forgiven of one's serious sins had come either at baptism as an adult or once in a lifetime in a public ritual of penance. The latter was used only in cases of the most serious sins—murder, for example. The penances were very harsh. Consequently, not many people took the opportunity to be reconciled with God through such severe and public means.

The Irish monks, in response to the need they felt for regular forgiveness of sins, developed the practice of private confession of their sins. Gradually, the practice spread beyond the monasteries into the rest of the church. With private confession, adults could return repeatedly to be forgiven of even minor sins and receive spiritual direction to make their life better. By the 900s, even though public penance was still the official means of forgiveness in the church, private confession had almost completely erased that practice.

The privacy of confession symbolized an unfortunate loss of a communal sense in the forgiveness of sins—the sense that sin is not private but affects the whole community. In addition, an erroneous attitude developed that frequent confession could substitute for a virtuous life.

The private rite also gave rise to the development of penitential books. Most priests found it difficult to select suitable penances, especially when the penitent might be the castle lord who fed and clothed them. Priests needed some outside authority for the penances they assigned. So the penitential books guided the priests in selecting the proper penance for each sin, with the sins listed on one side of the page and corresponding penalties listed across from them. For instance, if a person were gluttonous, she or he had to do one day's penance of going without food. Most of the penalties were strict but seemed lighter than the old public penances. More importantly, people at the time saw their life as a struggle toward God and away from the devil; so the stakes in the struggle were high, and they felt the penalties for sin should be high too. ■

Changes in Baptism and Penance:
How Can Sin Be Forgiven?

The Donation of Pepin: The Papal States After the pope gave his blessing to Pepin's assumption of kingly power, the relationship between the king and the papacy was, of course, cooperative.

An opportunity to strengthen the ties between Pepin and the pope occurred in 753 when Rome was threatened with being overrun by the Lombards, a Germanic tribe. The Byzantine emperor, who at least in theory ruled both the Eastern and the Western empires from Constantinople, was supposed to protect Rome from a distance. But he was ineffective in the West and could not be depended on. Besides, much tension lay between the papacy and the Byzantine ruler.

With Rome under threat, in desperation the pope crossed the Alps on horseback to appeal to Pepin in Gaul. Pepin assured the pope that the Franks would protect Rome.

Not only did Pepin drive off the Lombards, who had begun to march on Rome, but he went one major step further. Pepin decided that the pope needed his own territory. So in 756, in a formal deed called the Donation of Pepin, he gave the pope a wide strip of Italy in the middle of the Italian "boot," or peninsula. The territory became known as the Papal States, with the pope as ruler or king, and its safety was guaranteed by Pepin.

The Papal States remained an independent country under the rule of the papacy for more than eleven hundred years, until 1870. Though the existence of the Papal States was useful to the church for financial and other purposes, it had some negative effects. For one, it infuriated the Byzantines, who claimed some of the pope's territory as their own. Also, it created built-in tension with Western imperial rulers who were supposedly protecting the territory for the pope; many of them saw the states as really theirs, not the pope's.

The papacy, however, had political claim to its own lands. Establishing the pope as a territorial ruler like a king forced him and the church into a more material, less spiritual role in the world. We will see in the discussion of feudalism in this chapter that the attempt to combine land-based and spiritual leadership was going on all across Christendom as bishops and abbots were made lords of feudal estates. The combination of the two types of leadership was an uneasy mix. An emphasis on political power, material wealth, and property was to create serious dilemmas for the church over the centuries.

Charlemagne   A Return to the Roman Empire

After Pepin's death, one of Pepin's sons, Charles, organized a good part of Western Europe into a Frankish kingdom. Charles, a powerful general and a powerful king, became known as Charlemagne (which is French for "Charles the Great").

Conversion by the Sword

First Charlemagne conquered the Saxons, a Germanic tribe, and forced them to receive baptism. Here are some of the rules he imposed:

Anyone who kills a bishop, a priest, or a deacon, shall be put to death. . . .

Any unbaptized Saxon who attempts to hide himself among his own people and refuses to accept baptism shall be put to death.

Anyone who plots with the pagans against the Christians shall be put to death.

In one day Charlemagne put to death 4,500 resisting Saxons. He saw forced conversion as a way of strengthening his kingdom while increasing the membership of the church. As discussed previously, forced conversion was a traditional way of unifying a kingdom. In order to keep his huge kingdom in order, Charlemagne moved constantly, living in the saddle except during the coldest months.

An Emperor Again

Like Pepin, Charlemagne promised protection of the papal lands. He crushed the Lombards, who were threatening Rome again, and took over their territory in the northern half of Italy. Charlemagne soon began to act more like the pope's ruler than his protector, issuing orders to the pope and telling him how to administer the Papal States. Being indebted to Charlemagne, the pope was compliant.

By the year 800, Charlemagne had brought together under his rule the lands that had constituted the long-gone Roman Empire of the West. A surprising event in 800 began a new era, supposedly a return to the "glory days" of the old empire: At the Christmas Mass at Saint Peter's Basilica in Rome, Pope Leo III unexpectedly crowned Charlemagne "Emperor of the Romans." The crowning by Leo implied that God was acting through the pope. This arrangement conferred "holy" status on the new empire and emperor, with church and state seen almost as one.

The creation of this empire and the new role of emperor aggravated conflicts with the Byzantine Empire. For more than three hundred years there had been no emperor in the West, with the Byzantine emperor in Constantinople supposedly in charge of the East and the West. Even though the Byzantine emperor had not had much power in the West, the pope had still been his subject and the Western territory had still been his. Clearly the pope's crowning Charlemagne as emperor of the Roman Empire signaled a church breakaway from the East, while it also further entangled the church with the political governance of Europe.

An Emphasis on Education

Charlemagne appointed educated men—mostly priests, monks, and bishops—to government positions. At his palace in Aachen, Charlemagne started a school headed by a monk who had been a pupil of Bede in England. The school attracted the best teachers from all parts of the empire. The books used were copies made by monks. Valuing the work of the monks in education, Charlemagne encouraged the building of Benedictine monasteries throughout the empire.

Direction for the Church

Charlemagne felt a strong responsibility for the faith of his Christian subjects. Consequently, he directed the church's activities, appointing bishops, sending the bishops out across the empire, and attempting to educate and reform the native clergy, who were prone to moral corruption.

The emperor also got involved in how Christians worshiped. He promoted, throughout the empire, the adoption of the Latin liturgy used in Rome. Charlemagne thought that using Latin gave dignity to the celebration of Mass. And because it was the language of all educated people in Europe, he believed it would unify liturgical practice. But the vast majority of Europeans were illiterate and did not know Latin. Many of them were barbarians who had come into the church at Charlemagne's orders. For them the Latin perhaps added a sense of mystery to the liturgy, but it did not help them understand.

The Fate of the Empire

Charlemagne's great Roman Empire, which was really more a Frankish empire than a Roman one, was not to be long-lived. It disappeared only decades after his death. By 870, it consisted of two parts, Western and Eastern, ruled ineffectively by Charlemagne's grandsons. Many centuries later, these territories became the nations of France and Germany.

A Feudal Way of Life

Charlemagne's vision of a strong empire evaporated in the 800s, due partly to ineffective leaders and partly to attacks all over Europe by new invaders from the north: the seafaring Vikings. With no central imperial authority to deal with the constant threat of attack, people relied on the system of feudalism to protect them. After Charlemagne, in fact, feudalism grew as the dominant social, political, and economic way of life of Europe.

A System
for Defense

The Pyramid of Feudalism

Feudalism was a political and economic system based on a pyramid structure. At the bottom of the pyramid were the serfs, or peasants, who worked a piece of land in return for food and housing. The vast majority of people in Europe were serfs, whose status was little above that of a slave. Next above the serfs was their immediate landlord and boss. This middle-level boss was considered a lord to his serfs but a vassal to his own higher lord (a vassal was one who pledged loyalty to a higher lord, or overlord). The higher lord, who owned the whole feudal estate (fief or manor), protected his vassals in return for their military service in his small army of fighting horsemen. Further up, at the top of the feudalism pyramid, was the king, who was the grand landlord of his region.

Regional kings warred against one another, and within any one region, rival lords and knights waged their own private wars. Roads were mere paths, and travelers were frequently held up by robbers. Many lords demanded payment of tolls from people passing through their lands. Then, too, the seacoasts, areas near rivers, and border territories were being invaded by waves of Vikings. The situation was chaotic and dangerous.

Living Conditions

Lords and wealthy vassals lived in castles on their estates; in the early years of feudalism, these castles were simple stone structures, but eventually they became elaborate. With a lord and his vassals would live the lord's lady; the lord and lady's children; some knights, who served the lord militarily; the personal servants of the family; and maybe a priest who functioned as chaplain for the estate. Paid by the lord, the priest was usually poorly educated and of low status.

Serfs generally lived on the same piece of land all their life, in a hut near the castle; they could seek safety in the castle in case of attack. Knowing that serfs had to be kept strong and healthy if they were to serve their master well, the lord usually took fairly good care of them—although serfs generally lived only a bit better than the lord's horses. Living conditions during the early feudal times took a heavy toll on serfs. Hard work, unsanitary living conditions, primitive health care, scarce food, and frequent warfare accounted for many deaths at an early age.

Life was not really luxurious for anyone on the estate. The lord and lady supervised all operations on their land: farming, making lumber, shepherding, and so on. After all, the manor—the entire estate of the lord—was a self-sufficient unit that could not depend on help from any central government. The manor was involved in a political unit larger than itself only in times of war when a king, his lords, and their vassals would band together for mutual protection.

The Feudal Monastery The church had a major role in the feudal system. Bishops and abbots of monasteries were often powerful lords of feudal estates. Most bishops and monasteries had large landholdings, usually given to them by lords or kings over long periods of time. Many bishops and some abbots and

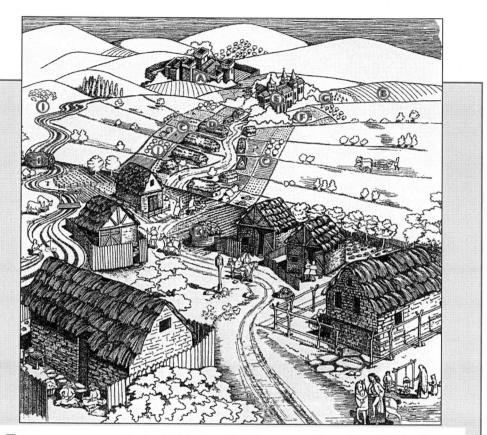

THE FEUDAL MANOR in the Middle Ages had features such as these: (A) lord's castle; (B) cultivated land of the lord's manor; (C) peasants' small plots for gardens; (D) peasants' dwellings, shared with animals; (E) church of the manor; (F) priests' house; (G) cemetery; (H) water mill; (I) grazing land; (J) fruit trees; (K) coal cellar.

abbesses were appointed to their church offices by kings. During the feudal period, the church actually became the largest landowner in Europe. One monastery in Germany had enough land to support fifteen thousand manors, and a French bishop at Tours ruled about twenty thousand serfs.

A landholding bishop, or the abbot of a monastery with lands, had vassals who looked after most of the property. Monks spent their time praying, studying, and educating—unlike in the earlier days of monasticism, when monks themselves worked the fields.

When the king of a region went to war, bishops and the abbots of major monasteries were expected to raise and fund soldiers. Some bishops actually led their troops into battle, even though the church had a ban on doing so.

Many monasteries were small, and in those the monks continued the tradition of work and prayer. But again, the monastery had to be a self-sufficient unit, both to feed and clothe its members and to ensure its own protection.

In the perilous world of feudal times, people had a keen sense that their destiny lay with God. With no control over diseases and plagues, when marauding bands could attack at any time, when one bad harvest could mean starvation, when the local lord could march men off to war at will, people looked to God for mercy and help. Serfs and vassals could only hope that their rulers, who had absolute authority over them, would take seriously Jesus' commands to act justly and charitably. And at a time when the rate of infant mortality was high and life spans were short, salvation in the afterlife, which was promised by the church, gave Christians some measure of hope.

Other Peoples Turn Christian

The Vikings: Invaders from the Sea As mentioned earlier, feudalism became the dominant organizing system in Europe, to create some structure for defense in the midst of a chaotic political situation. The empire had weakened after the death of Charlemagne because it lacked a powerful central authority to hold it together and protect the people in times of danger.

The invasions of the Vikings all over Europe in the 800s spurred the growth of feudalism. These "sea rovers" (the meaning of the word *vikings*) swooped down from Scandinavia in their long, narrow boats, attacking seacoasts and traveling inland on rivers. The first of these Norsemen ("men from the north") came as pirates, looting and then disappearing. Later Vikings took up residence.

Norwegian and Danish Vikings landed in Scotland, England, and Ireland. Attracted by the prosperous monasteries, Vikings raided and destroyed many of them, along with their libraries and works of art. In the aftermath of the invasions, the Norsemen controlled territory in England, Ireland, and a part of France called Normandy, which was named after them. Gradually, however, through intermarriage and treaties with the Christians, the Norsemen adopted the Christian religion.

Swedish Vikings, in the meantime, roved the Eastern European rivers from north to south, and they quickly controlled towns in what is now Russia (named for the tribe of the Rus).

While the Vikings were invading Europe, some daring Christian missionaries, led by the bishop Ansgar, voyaged to the Vikings' homelands. The kings of Denmark and Sweden, amazingly, welcomed the missionaries. Eventually all of the Scandinavian countries became Christian.

The Slavs Line Up   Eastern Europe was populated by the Slavs, the ancestors of today's Czechs, Slovaks, Croatians, Serbians, Bulgarians, Poles, and Russians. Because of a variety of political factors, some of the Slavs converted to Christianity through the Western (Latin) church, and some through the Eastern (Byzantine or Greek) church. Even though the Western and Eastern churches did not finally break with each other until the eleventh century, for many centuries before then their relationship was marked by tension and rivalry. The break between the churches will be covered in the next chapter.

A Need for Worship in Their Own Language

In the 800s, a Slav state called Greater Moravia developed. The first Christian missionaries to Moravia were German, from the Latin church of the West. Not knowing the Slavic language, they had limited success converting the Moravians.

Then the Byzantine emperor at Constantinople, with his influence over the Byzantine church, sent two Greek brothers to try missionary work among the Slavs in Moravia. Cyril and Methodius, the brothers, lived with the Slavs and devised a Slavic alphabet (still called *Cyrillic*) because there was no written Slavic language. Subsequently, the brothers translated the Gospels into their newly developed written Slavic. When the Slavs in Moravia heard the Good News preached by Cyril and Methodius in Slavic, many conversions followed, and soon congregations of Slavs were worshiping in their own language.

Some German bishops heard about the Mass being offered in Slavic and raised objections to the pope. The bishops argued that Catholics for many years had celebrated Mass either in Greek, the first language used, or in Latin, but never in Slavic. Cyril and Methodius were called to Rome to explain what they were doing. After some hesitation, the pope agreed that the Slavs in Moravia could continue celebrating the Mass and the sacraments in their own language. But a few years later, another pope, under the influence of the German

The following excerpt from the novel *Lion of Ireland*, by Morgan Llywelyn, provides a vivid image of the horrors of the Viking invasions. In this story, Norsemen leave their boats and attack a sleeping Irish village, whose inhabitants then seek refuge in the local monastery.

[The Norsemen] came up from the river in a wave of ferocity, guided by the hospitality fire lit near the gate each night to welcome chance travelers. They poured into the compound unchecked, swords waving, axes slashing, pagan war cries ripping across the nerves of the sleeping Irish. Every obstacle they encountered they battered down or put to the torch. People stumbled from their homes, disoriented with sleep, to find hideous death blotting out the stars. (Page 38)

[After murder, pillage, and the abduction of the young women, the hamlet's few survivors fled to the closest place of help: the monastery of Killaloe.]

[The survivors] came at a pitifully slow pace, leaning on one another, emerging painfully from the shelter of the trees into the light of the rising sun. Even at a distance it was obvious that few among them were uninjured. . . .

When the refugees neared the gates, Brother Cael hurried ahead to give the news to the abbot. As the monastery was primarily devoted to prayer and contemplation rather than education and religious ministration to pilgrims, it had only one small guest house. The abbot was hard pressed to accommodate the sudden influx of people, though fortunately the good brothers included in their number several who were skilled in the healing arts and could tend the wounded.

Brother Cael gladly offered his own tiny, beehive-shaped cell for [an injured tribal] chieftain. There was no bed or pallet, as the monks slept on bare earth, but the abbot brought a mattress of straw and feathers that had been made in hopes of luring a bishop to Killaloe. (Pages 45–47) ■

Safe Haven from the Terror of the Norsemen

bishops, condemned the Slavic liturgy, claiming that the Mass could be offered only in Latin or Greek. Cyril and Methodius's followers went south to Bulgaria, where they had great success under the protection of the Greek church.

Other Slavic Peoples

Poland was a new independent nation whose king decided to promote Christianity and make the country a vassal state of the pope. Thus Poland lined up with the Latin church.

Invasions and Empires, 600s to 900s

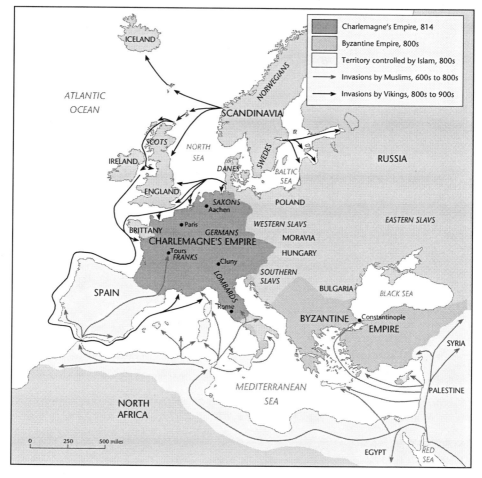

Russia had received Christian missionaries from the Western and Eastern churches for some time, but it was not until the time of the Russian ruler Vladimir I that Russia adopted Christianity. Vladimir decided on a religion for his people by conversing with representatives of the pope, the patriarch of Constantinople (head of the Byzantine church), Muslims, and Jews. Finally, in 988, he chose to be baptized in the Byzantine church. Vladimir encouraged the Byzantine missionaries to preach among his people, at least in part because they taught people how to read and write in the newly developed Slavic language. Thus Russia became part of the Byzantine church.

By the year 1000, most of the Slavs in Europe were Christian. To the Byzantine, or Greek, church came the Russians, Bulgarians, and Serbians. To the Latin church came the Croatians, Czechs, Slovaks, Moravians, and Poles. In addition, another people besides the Slavs—the Magyars, who settled in Hungary—joined the Latin church when their king Stephen I converted and was crowned king of Hungary by the pope. (Later Stephen would be acknowledged as a saint.)

At this time in history, Christians celebrated the liturgy in three official languages: Latin in the Western part of Europe, from Ireland to Poland; Slavic in East-Central Europe; and Greek in the countries on the northeastern coast of the Mediterranean Sea.

Royal Pains for the Church

Conflicts of Church and State The rulers in both the East and the West often treated the church as a department of their government. This kind of interference led to misunderstandings between the Eastern and Western parts of the church; the problems continued off and on through several centuries.

East-Versus-West Tensions

In the East, the Byzantine emperor typically controlled the patriarch of Constantinople. The patriarch was the spiritual leader of Eastern Christians, though he was considered second to the pope in the church as a whole. One of the most serious problems between the East and the West occurred during the late 800s when the patriarch of Constantinople refused Communion to an important official of the Byzantine government. The Byzantine emperor replaced the "unruly" patriarch with a layman who became an instant patriarch by being ordained, right up to bishop, within a few days. When the pope, in Rome, ruled that the newly installed patriarch was not legitimate, the Byzantine emperor excommunicated the pope—in effect throwing him out of the church, at least as far as the emperor was concerned! A few years later, another Byzantine emperor put the original patriarch back into office, so Rome and Constantinople were on speaking terms again, if only for a while.

The Papacy Up for Grabs

The pope's control of far-flung churches was limited by the information he had about them. Messages took months to reach Rome—if they made it there at all. Also, during the 900s especially, the popes had enormous problems in Rome itself. Roman barons sought to control the appointment of the pope. As a result, the rich Roman families did more harm to the church than outside enemies ever did. In their family feuds they did not hesitate to use force to get their candidates on the papal throne, disregarding the Roman people and clergy, who had been electing popes since the time of Peter. On one occasion, the losers in such a struggle over the papacy opened the gates of Rome to allow the Saracens (Arab nomads) to come into the city and rob the sacred places—even the tombs of Peter and Paul. In the period from 896 to 900, there were six different popes. The body of one of these popes was thrown into the Tiber River by his enemies, who had dug up the corpse.

Calling on the power of the state seemed to be the only way to end the feuding over the papal office. In 962, Pope John XII, who has been rated by some as the most unworthy pope of all time, begged King Otto I, ruler of the East Frankish (German) section of Charlemagne's old territory, for help against the Roman nobles. When Otto arrived with his army, Pope John crowned him emperor of the Holy Roman Empire, thus reviving, in name if not reality, the empire of Charlemagne. The pope and the nobles pledged their loyalty to the new emperor. But Pope John soon joined a conspiracy against Otto, who then responded by having John deposed and having one of his own assistants elected pope. The emperor had proven who was in charge.

For almost a hundred years after this, the popes were usually chosen by the German (Holy Roman) emperors. Most of these popes were improvements over past ones, but few of them were suitable spiritual leaders.

Bishops and Abbots Indebted to Counts and Dukes

In the feudal West, other forms of secular control of the church were common. The civil rulers at various levels usually had the final word in the appointment of bishops, though these civil rulers seldom interfered with church teachings. Under the feudal system, bishops and abbots often served as government officials because they were educated and had charge of church lands. Local dukes or counts were naturally interested in putting loyal supporters in as bishops. And a bishop chosen for his ability to manage a farm or lead an army would not be expected to be especially concerned about preaching the Gospel.

Worse, a rich man could buy himself the office of bishop, even though the church condemned this as the sin of simony (named after Simon the Magician, who had tried to buy the power of healing from the Apostle Peter). Some bishops passed on their religious offices to relatives, regardless of the relatives' fitness for the work.

Cluny A Creative Response to the Church-State Dilemma

With abbots and bishops answering to local secular powers such as dukes and counts, corruption among church officials ran rampant. However, in the 900s, a breakthrough in how monasteries were organized led the way to a renewed spirit in the church. A duke began a new Benedictine monastery in Cluny, France. It was unusual in that the charter specified that the monastery at Cluny had to be independent of any control by a local lord or secular ruler. The monks were to select their abbot, who would answer only to the pope. By coming under the authority of the pope, who was outside the feudal system, Cluny broke with the feudal tradition and opened the way for the church to liberate itself from civil control.

A succession of holy and wise abbots at Cluny brought about a renewal of the original Benedictine spirit. The monks at Cluny lived simply, prayed long and devoutly, gave food to the poor, and inspired others to take the message of Jesus seriously. Soon hundreds of other monasteries across Europe adopted the Cluny reforms and asked to be governed, through their own superiors, by the abbot of Cluny. This spiritual renewal was possible because Cluny was free from feudalism, governed not by a secular outsider but by a monk.

Enthusiasm for a better Christian life spread beyond the monasteries as students who were educated at Cluny monastery schools grew up to become priests and bishops. Eventually, Cluny monasteries themselves needed reform, and spiritual leaders arose to call for that renewal. But in its time the Cluny movement did offer a creative solution to a difficult dilemma that characterized feudalism: the entanglement of church and state.

Conclusion   The period described in this chapter saw a convergence of church and civil affairs into the phenomenon called Christendom. The pope took on ownership of the Papal States, popes crowned emperors and then found that they were beholden to them, and bishops and abbots were appointed by civil rulers.

Missionaries such as Boniface and Cyril and Methodius spread the Gospel into new territory, converting Germanic peoples, Slavs, and Magyars. Eventually the church even managed to incorporate the invading Vikings into Christendom.

After the reign of the forceful emperor Charlemagne, feudalism grew as a way to provide some economic and political order in a weakening empire. However, feudalism also promoted its own chaos, because every estate was, in a sense, a kingdom. Regional kings and lords warred against one another. At the bottom of society were the serfs, whose lives were at the mercy of warring overlords.

The church brought some comfort and meaning to people in the midst of bloody wars, devastation of crops, rampant disease, and the injustice of overlords. The monasteries offered examples of prayer and service. But too many church leaders, concerned with land and privilege, led scandalous lives. Powerful, wealthy interests corrupted even the papacy. All the while, the tension between the Eastern and Western churches, complicated by imperial meddling, was building.

The church desperately needed renewal, to find again its roots in the Gospel. The Cluny monastery and the widespread renewal it inspired gave hope to the church in the feudal age.

At the close of the eleventh century, the church and society in the West were heading into a period of relative stability in which the church would take the lead in the patronage of the arts, in architecture, and in scholarship. But the period would also be a tragic time, for Christians would be led into misguided wars, and the Eastern and Western churches would make their final break with each other.

1. What is your reaction to Charlemagne's practice of forcing people to convert and be baptized? How do religious groups go about converting others to their beliefs today, using television and other media? Are these methods any less coercive?

2. Up until the liturgical reforms of Vatican Council II, Latin was the language used in Western Catholic churches for liturgy. How would your experience of liturgy be different if done in Latin?

3. Do tensions between Eastern and Western Christians still exist? What have been the tragic results?

8

The High Middle Ages

High Times, Low Times

AS THE FIRST thousand years of Christian history came to a close, the church was in a time of transition. The renewal begun at the monastery of Cluny in the 900s was slowly dislodging the church from the feudal system, whereby bishops and abbots did the bidding of secular lords and kings. The papacy had suffered mightily from being at the whim of Roman nobles, but by the year 1000 it was faring a little better under the more enlightened control of the Holy Roman emperors. Still, the pope was hardly an independent spiritual leader at that point.

Powerful forces were reshaping the West, creating a European world that would look quite different from the relatively disorganized, lawless world of feudal Europe's Dark Ages. The period from about 1000 to 1300, when the major features of a new world were taking shape, later came to be known as the High Middle Ages. The church had a key role in shaping that world.

A New World in the Making: Cities and Powerful Kings

Two features emerging in Europe were the growth of cities and the increasing power of kings.

Urban Culture on the Rise

For centuries, ever since the old Roman Empire collapsed under the assault of the barbarians, the civilization we recognize as Western Europe had been basically rural. The region had few cities and towns, little significant trade, and only poor methods of communication and travel. Feudal Europe was economically depressed, and people could barely eke out a living on the land.

The monastic spur to urban growth. The monasteries had done a great service by preserving and passing on learning and by offering models of social organization and service. In many respects they enabled the West to pull through the Dark Ages with some sense of order and tradition. Oddly enough, the monasteries, which were rural and agricultural, provided the impetus for the growth of cities and towns, partly because of their innovative farming practices. For instance, the order called the Cistercians, founded in 1098 as a reformed offshoot of the Benedictines, developed new agricultural techniques—ways of draining swamps and the use of crop rotation. Soon these methods were being employed all over Europe. More and better agricultural

Timeline . . .

750
- Iconoclast controversy rages in Byzantine Empire.

1050
- Latin and Greek churches split.
- Papal elections are entrusted to College of Cardinals.
- Investiture controversy.
- Pope Urban II launches First Crusade.
- Crusaders take Jerusalem.
- Concordat of Worms ends lay investiture.

1150
- Second Crusade begins.
- Third Crusade makes only minor gains.
- Gothic cathedrals, universities, and guilds multiply.
- Fourth Crusaders sack Constantinople.
- Franciscan Rule established.
- Dominicans founded.
- Papal Inquisition initiated.

1250
- Thomas Aquinas writes his *Summa Theologiae*.

products in turn improved the quality of life just enough so that the population grew slightly.

The growth of trade and crafts. With the surplus of people, towns began to spring up throughout Europe. People migrated to population centers, looking for a livelihood. Because towns were markets for goods and centers of administration for both church and state, they provided jobs for the people who were not needed in agriculture. Most towns grew around castles or the cathedrals that were under construction; others developed along the roads traveled by merchants. Skilled workers came to live and labor where there were enough employers to hire them or people to buy the goods they produced, such as farming tools, shoes, clothing, spinning wheels, and swords.

As the towns grew, these craft workers formed guilds, which were forerunners of the trade unions we have today. The guilds regulated the training of those who were learning a trade and, at the same time, got a fair price for the guild members' work. Guilds usually chose patron saints and took part in church liturgies with displays of banners and statues. A chief employer of the guildsmen was the church. In building the great cathedrals, the church needed skilled workers: stonemasons, stonecarvers, carpenters, stained-glass makers, sculptors, and painters. Thus, the church encouraged and supported the guilds, from which a whole new class of free citizens evolved.

With the rise of trade in Europe, the supply of money began to increase, and a basic banking system was established. Recall that early Christian teaching forbade usury, which is the charging of interest on loans of money. Because Jews were not allowed to own land, the occupation of banking and moneylending fell to them. Ironically, as in the time of the Emperor Justinian, which was back in the 500s, Jews would again be persecuted for being too successful in roles that they were pushed into by Christians.

Kings and Nations on the Rise

After the year 1000, kings grew stronger, and the shape of government in Europe gradually changed. Power became more centralized and stabilized in the hands of kings. Eventually this rise of kingly power would profoundly influence the church. Though local nobles still held much power, feudalism was slowly being weakened. Kings became strongest in England and France, which were emerging as nations—large territories having independent status and government.

In the twelfth century, the king of England added to his rule the western half of France, from Normandy down to Spain. This ruling of part of France by the monarch of England set the stage for conflict between the two nations—a conflict that would cause much strife between English and French Christians over the years.

Meanwhile, in eastern France, the French king was strengthening his authority. Until this time, the king of France had been more of a regional leader, controlling only a small area around Paris. Each king of France was crowned with great ceremony in the cathedral at Reims. However, not having much land, the king also did not have much power. King Philip Augustus changed all that by conquering small areas one at a time. Then, as towns flourished in areas he had not conquered, he made treaties with these other towns, by which he garnered both men and money. The king of France was becoming a powerful national leader, rather than being just a regional chief.

Since 962, when the pope crowned the German emperor Otto I, each German ruler considered himself the successor to Charlemagne as emperor of the Holy Roman Empire. In that role, the German king was expected to protect the pope. But the special relationship between empire and papacy was problematic and soon came to a head.

Church Institutions Flourish

As we have seen, in the feudal period the appointment of popes, bishops, and abbots was largely controlled by civil rulers. The reform of Cluny changed some of that, but the pope's position in feudal times was still relatively weak with respect to the German emperor. However, the High Middle Ages saw the popes asserting power and influence as never before. In addition, major church institutions were flourishing—namely, cathedrals and the universities that grew from them. Thus, the High Middle Ages brought growth for both church and society.

A Reforming Papacy and Clergy

The Battle over Lay Investiture

When Gregory VII, also called Hildebrand, became pope in 1073, he wanted to free the church from secular control. As a monk of the Cluny movement, he saw the clergy's independence from civil powers as crucial to any reform in the church. Thus, he ruled against lay investiture—the practice by which a high-ranking layperson such as an emperor, a king, a count, or a lord could appoint bishops or abbots, "investing" them with power and requiring their loyalty.

The German emperor Henry IV objected to the pope's ruling. The argument worsened until Pope Gregory excommunicated Henry and declared that Henry's subjects did not need to obey him any longer. Knowing that the German nobles would take advantage of the situation, the emperor went to ask forgiveness of the pope. According to the story, Henry dressed in penitential garb and stood barefoot in the winter snow outside the castle where Gregory was staying. He stood there for three days, until the pope received him back into the church. But Henry's repentance was short-lived. Soon he set up a pope of his own choosing and marched on Rome to depose Gregory. Though Gregory was rescued from the attack, he died a short time later. For a number of years trouble continued between the German emperors and the popes. Finally, in 1122, the controversy over lay investiture was resolved with the Concordat of Worms (Worms, Germany), whereby the emperor agreed that rulers would no longer have the right to appoint bishops; all bishops would be elected and consecrated by church authority.

A Strong Papacy

Gregory had staked out a strong position for the papacy, and it carried over after he was gone. Succeeding popes assumed more authority over the church. Innocent III, who took office in 1198, was the most powerful of the medieval popes (those of the Middle Ages). He had a great intellect and a legal mind, and he was dedicated to eliminating corrupt practices in the church. Power centralized in the papacy ensured unity of action on the part of the church—a unity that the popes would need when facing kings who were more powerful than ever.

Papal Elections

Another important reform put in place during the High Middle Ages was the establishment of the College of Cardinals. For centuries the popes had been elected by the people of Rome—although too frequently the elections were controlled by kings, emperors, or competing noble Roman families. To protect the papacy from corrupt influence and thereby allow reform to continue, the College of Cardinals, a group of bishops from the area around Rome, would meet to elect the pope by a two-thirds vote. (In the modern era, the College of Cardinals is composed of selected men, almost always bishops, from all over the world.)

Reform for Priests

Though earlier attempts at reforming the priesthood had been made, the clergy still were quite uneducated and subject to secular control. Three church councils required celibacy—that is, not marrying—of priests in the West. Celibacy was required so that priests could be more available to God and also, among other factors, because of the way sexuality was understood at the time. The extreme position was that sexual intercourse was incompatible with the sacred character of the clerical state.

The church councils tried to institute other reforms as well. For example, the official sacraments of the church were limited to the seven that the Catholic church celebrates today: baptism, confirmation, the Eucharist, reconciliation, anointing of the sick, marriage, and holy orders. Priests were to be trained in the cathedral schools before ordination and were to dedicate themselves to the ordained ministry rather than take up secular occupations. These decrees were intended to reform an unhealthy situation among the clergy, but many years would pass before the ordinances would be fully followed.

Although arguments continued between civil rulers and the popes, the reforms begun by Gregory VII helped break the stranglehold that secular rulers had on the church.

Beauty and Inspiration in the Cathedrals   Another important development in the church's life was the building of cathedrals. These magnificent structures rose up in towns across Europe among the small wooden houses that most people lived in. The cathedrals were created partly because of the growth of towns and cities with their surplus population from the countryside, but these buildings in turn spurred the growth of the towns by providing focal points for people's lives and work.

The cathedrals were the works of master artisans who knew how to carve images and designs in stone, how to hoist huge blocks three or four hundred feet into the air, and how to fit the pieces together—without power tools, engines, or cranes. Thus, the building of cathedrals made significant contributions to architecture and engineering. Decades, even centuries, were required to construct a cathedral, and even longer to furnish it completely. Money often ran out; new revenues had to be raised from the bishop, the king, and lords. The common people contributed chickens or pigs to sustain the workers.

Two very distinct types of cathedrals—called the Romanesque and the Gothic—were built during the years from 1000 to 1300. The first type, named after the Roman style, employed massive pillars with rounded arches to hold up stone roofs, replacing the flammable wood-beamed ceilings commonly found in earlier churches. Romanesque cathedrals have a more horizontal, solid appearance than do Gothic cathedrals, which, with their tall, slim towers, pointed arches, and tall stained-glass windows appear airy, light, even delicate. A major architectural innovation that enabled the Gothic cathedrals to reach new heights was the use of flying buttresses to balance and support the weight of the tall structures.

Features of the CATHEDRAL OF NOTRE DAME DE CHARTRES include (A) wood rafters, covered with a copper roof (the original covering was lead); (B) ribbed vaults or arched ceilings, made of stone; (C) flying buttresses, which supported and balanced the tall structure; (D) the aisles along the sides of the (E) nave, the open area where people stood for worship; (F) the rose window of stained glass; (G) the Royal Portal; (H) the north spire built in the 1500s after fire destroyed the original one; (I) the south spire; (J) the north transept; (K) the south transept; (L) the area for the choir, the main altar, and the side chapels; (M) the south porch.

The cathedrals were meant to be physical expressions of Christian faith, inspiring the people with the beauty of God. The front enclosure—the choir or chancel—was reserved for the priests and monks who, several times each day, sang and recited the Divine Office (the series of psalms and prayers organized for use during each liturgical season). Along the side walls of the cathedral were small chapels for Mass; in some of these chapels, saints and kings were buried beneath the stone floors. The main room, called the nave, was used for the common people's Mass, and in a section of the nave was the font for baptisms. Most cathedrals also had high pulpits from which long Sunday sermons were given—one of the few sources of religious education for the people.

Though the cathedrals were intended primarily for worship, the people, especially those belonging to guilds, frequently used them for meeting places or hiring halls. Often pilgrims and poor travelers slept on the floors. There was no disrespect in these uses of a cathedral; indeed, using God's house in these ways helped people see God as a loving parent. In addition, the cathedral was a pictorial Bible for the illiterate folk. Wealthy people usually could read, although even they might possess only one or two books. But every poor peasant could visit a cathedral and see the carvings and stained-glass windows that told stories from the Bible.

Universities   While the cathedrals were rising toward the sky, a parallel movement was just beginning—one that is still very alive today. This movement was the development of education, with the first great universities.

From the Cathedral Schools

By about 1200, the schools that were attached to the cathedrals became more numerous, surpassing in number the monastery schools, which were found in rural areas. In Italy and France, teachers and students at the cathedral schools began to group together to study some of the classical subjects, such as rhetoric, logic, literature, and mathematics, as well as theology, philosophy, law, and medicine. Such a group of students and teachers became known as a university, with an organizational structure modeled on the guilds of craftsmen: teachers had to have earned a license, such as a master architect had, and students were given degrees that recognized the steps they had reached in their studies.

At the University of Paris, probably the most famous university in Europe at the time, the students and teachers overflowed from their rooms near the cathedral onto the left bank of the Seine River, gathering wherever they could find a large enough space. Because Latin was the language of the University of Paris, as it was at every other university at the time, the left bank was soon known as the Latin Quarter (as it still is today).

University Life, Medieval-Style

A lecturer at a university would announce a series of classes on a particular subject. Then students would come or not. If they came, they paid a fee to the lecturer; if no students wanted to listen to the lecturer, he was out of a job. Books were rare and expensive, as each one had to be copied by hand. Teachers lectured, and students listened, taking a few notes but depending mostly on their memory (paper was expensive too). Examinations were taken orally, each student being expected to give reasons for accepting or rejecting the teachers' statements about the subjects studied. Outside of study time, students were on their own and frequently ran into trouble because of their rowdy behavior. Popes of the period made the universities responsible for their own affairs and, at the same time, freed them from the control of the local police and the resident bishop.

While the University of Paris concentrated on the study of theology and philosophy, the University of Bologna, in central Italy, focused on law and medicine. The University of Oxford began when a group of students left Paris for England. Soon other universities were founded in Europe at Cambridge, Salerno, Prague, Cracow, Vienna, and Heidelberg. The church supported the universities because most of the students were expected to study theology and philosophy and become priests. But the church also recognized that the knowledge gained in almost any field would increase people's understanding of God's creation.

Help from Muslim Scholars

At the centers of study called universities, the scholars' main task was to try to gather together knowledge of all subjects, but particularly theology and philosophy—and especially Greek philosophy—from past centuries. A most unexpected source of help in this immense work came from the Muslims. No matter what region they were from, Muslims learned the Arabic language so that they could understand the Koran, the sacred book of Islam. Muslim scholars began using their common Arabic language to learn what their neighboring countries were thinking and learning—in philosophy, mathematics, medicine, law, and natural sciences. For example, they translated the Greek texts of Aristotle's philosophy into Arabic.

As Christians and Muslims lived side by side in southern Italy and in most of Spain, Europeans gradually learned of Muslim scholarship.

Soon Western scholars translated texts from Arabic into Latin. By the 1200s, scholars in the universities of Europe were learning how to put together the culture of the ancient Greeks, the special learning of the Muslims, and the understanding that their own Christian faith gave them. Often they used Greek writings that had been translated into Arabic by Muslim scholars and then had been preserved and re-translated into Latin by monks in the solitude of monasteries.

A stronger papacy, a reforming clergy, the rise of magnificent cathedrals, and the birth of universities were remarkable achievements for the church in this period. They represent the "high times" of the High Middle Ages for the church. "Low times" were also going on in the same period, however. We will turn to those next.

A Church Divided, Zeal Misguided

The Split Between East and West As we have seen throughout this book, for many centuries, as far back as the Council of Chalcedon in 451, tension had been building between the Eastern, or Greek-speaking, church and the Western, or Latin-speaking, church.

A Buildup of Differences

The Eastern and Western churches differed in their views of how the church should relate to the state. The Eastern church accepted the emperor's dominance over it, and the Western church, in particular the papacy, more and more asserted the church's primacy over government and society. In addition, theological differences had plagued the Eastern and Western churches since the Arian heresy. Disputes sometimes arose over appointments of patriarchs, as we saw in chapter 7.

During the 700s, too, a controversy had raged through the Eastern church, even pulling the pope into the dispute. This was called the iconoclast controversy, in which a Byzantine emperor decided that devotion to, or reverence for, icons—crucifixes, statues, paintings, and mosaics—was actually idolatry, and that all religious images should be destroyed in both the Eastern and the Western churches. Thus the emperor went on a rampage smashing great works of art and persecuting monks who tried to protect these images. Finally, those who wanted to allow the images triumphed, but the issue had put more pressure on an already strained relationship between East and West.

In addition to these problems were differences in language (Greek in the East, Latin in the West), customs, and religious practices.

Troubadour: "Never Give Up War"

One popular song of the Middle Ages almost seems like satire today, but in fact it rather accurately reflects that period's typical glorification of war. These lyrics are by the French troubadour Bertrand de Born:

> My heart is filled with gladness when I see
> Strong castles besieged, stockades broken and overwhelmed,
> Many vassals struck down,
> Horses of the dead and wounded roving at random.
> And when battle is joined, let all men of good lineage
> Think of naught but the breaking of heads and arms,
> For it is better to die than be vanquished and live. . . .
> I tell you I have no such joy as when I hear the shout
> "On! On!" from both sides and the neighing of riderless steeds,
> And groans of "Help me! Help me!"
> And when I see both great and small
> Fall in the ditches and on the grass
> And see the dead transfixed by spear shafts!
> Lords, mortgage your domains, castles, cities,
> But never give up war!

Church: "Avoid War"

Even though many bishops formed armies and sometimes even led them, the church tried to temper the popular enthusiasm for battle. We can argue that the church's record of warmaking in the Crusades was abysmal, but the church's official voice has always cautioned restraint and tried to curb war.

Just-war theory. One of the strongest arguments the church used to curtail warmaking was the just-war theory. Originally formulated by Ambrose and Augustine in the fifth century, the theory was developed further by Thomas Aquinas in the Middle Ages. Thomas taught that for a war to be just, it must meet three criteria:

1. It must be declared by a legitimate authority, not by private groups or individuals.
2. It must be waged for a just cause such as protecting innocent life or preserving conditions necessary for basic human life.
3. It must be waged with the right intention, not for vengeance, cruelty, or power.

In later centuries, church theologians added more criteria to Thomas's three, putting more stringent limits on what could constitute a just war. For instance:

- The war must be a last resort; all other avenues to bring peace must have been tried.
- The means used to win the war must be moral.
- The suffering and damage caused by the war must be proportionate to the good to be accomplished.
- There must be a reasonable chance of success.
- The terms for peace must be fair.

Using these criteria, it is doubtful that many wars in Christian history could be considered "just." With the massive destruction possible in modern warfare, these criteria may never be met in the future.

The Peace and Truce of God. In the feudal period, when Christian lords and kings were attacking one another almost at whim, the church set up two rules to try to restrain the warring tendencies of its members. One rule was called the Peace of God. This prohibited waging war against unarmed pesants, the clergy, women, and other poor or defenseless people. The nobility wee expected to tke an oath committing themselves to the Peace of God. Some did. Many did not. Most ignored the Peace in any case.

The second rule was called the Truce of God. This specified that war could not be made on holy days, other special feast days, or during Lent or Advent. As a result, only eighty days of the year were left for knights to slaughter one another. Anyone who violated the Truce could automatically be excommunicated. Such a threat proved far more effective than the oath of the Peace of God. Many of the small clan wars ended, and random fighting declined. ■

Attitudes Toward War:

Troubadour Versus Church

For instance, the Eastern church allowed married men to become priests, while in the West celibacy for the clergy was becoming the norm.

The Final Break

In 1054, a serious break occurred between the Eastern and Western churches. The patriarch of Constantinople, Michael Cerularius, publicly declared that because of their differences, the two churches could not be in union. The fundamental issue was the authority of the pope. Although the bishop of Rome was considered the successor of Peter, the church in the East believed that the pope had taken far too much power away from the patriarch of Constantinople.

To reach an understanding of the issues, Pope Leo IX sent his representative, Cardinal Humbert, to meet with Patriarch Michael at Constantinople. Unfortunately, Humbert and the patriarch seemed more interested in proving each other wrong than in working for unity. While the two sides were arguing, Pope Leo died. Even though Humbert was then without papal authority, he excommunicated Michael and left Constantinople. Michael called a synod to condemn the action of the pope's representative and to claim that he, Michael, was in complete charge of the Byzantine church. The year 1054 is recorded as the year the Greek and Latin churches finally split; however, the situation was not that clear-cut at the time.

The Folly of the Crusades

Not too many years after the recorded split between the Greek and Latin churches, a request was sent from the Byzantine emperor to Pope Urban II. Despite bitter feelings between East and West, the Byzantines were appealing to the pope for help against the Turkish Muslims who had invaded their territory. Urban responded by calling for a Crusade that would free Byzantine territory from the Turks and then take Jerusalem and the Holy Land from the Saracen Muslims. The pope wanted Christian armies from the West to help the Byzantines. This seemingly worthy cause initiated a series of Crusades that involved Christians in one of the sorriest chapters of their history.

To Save the Holy Land

The Crusades were seen by most Christians at the time as a great act of faith. After all, people reasoned, the Muslims did not believe that Jesus Christ is the Son of God, yet they had gained control of Jerusalem, the historic birthplace of Christianity. Christians believed that the only thing to do was to get back the Holy Land, by force if necessary.

Pentecost, by El Greco (c. 1541–1614). "Divided tongues, as of fire, appeared among them. . . . All of them were filled with the Holy Spirit" (Acts 2:2–4). Read the story of Pentecost on pages 26–27.

Plate 2

A detail from *The Conversion of Saint Paul*, by Michelangelo (1475–1564).
"Saul, Saul, why are you persecuting me?" (Acts 22:7). Read the story of
Paul's conversion on pages 29–30.

Plate 3

To hide from authorities during times of intense persecution, Christians worshiped in underground cemeteries like these, called catacombs. Read about these persecutions on pages 56–65.

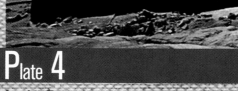

Plate 4

In the Egyptian desert at Mount Sinai, on the spot where tradition says Moses saw the burning bush, the Greek Orthodox monastery of Saint Catherine, one of the world's oldest, stands today. Read about the early monks and nuns on pages 72–77.

uitatem dei siue in hoc temporu cursu
cum inter impios peregrinatur ec fide
uiuens siue in illa stabilitate sedis eter
ne quam nunc expectat per pacientiam
quo adusep iusticia conuertatur in iu
dicium. Deinceps adeptura per excelle
tiam uictoria ultima et pace perfecta. i
hoc opere ad te instituto; et in ea pro
missione debito defendere aduersus
eos qui conditori eius deos suos prefe
... arcelline susce

The monastery church of Hosios Loukas (Saint Luke) in Greece. The architecture and art of the churches in the East added to the sense of mystery surrounding the Eucharist. Read about the church in a crumbling empire, on pages 92–105.

Plate 7

Scenes of the life of Pope Gregory, from fifteenth-century art: As a builder, he supervises church construction. As a friend of the poor and sick, he blesses them, expelling a demon from a possessed man. Read about Pope Gregory the Great on pages 105–108.

Plate 8

Until the Early Middle Ages, baptisms were more commonly performed in adulthood, done by full immersion in a baptismal pool, such as this early one from northern Africa. Read about the changes in the Rite of Baptism on pages 116–117.

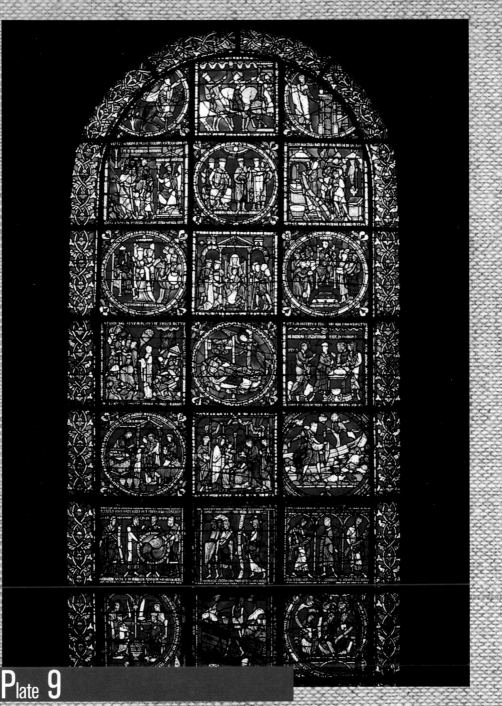

Plate 9

The stained-glass windows of a Gothic cathedral, such as this one in the Canterbury Cathedral, were called the Poor Person's Bible, because they depicted Bible stories for the masses of Christians who could not read. Read about Gothic cathedrals on pages 137–139.

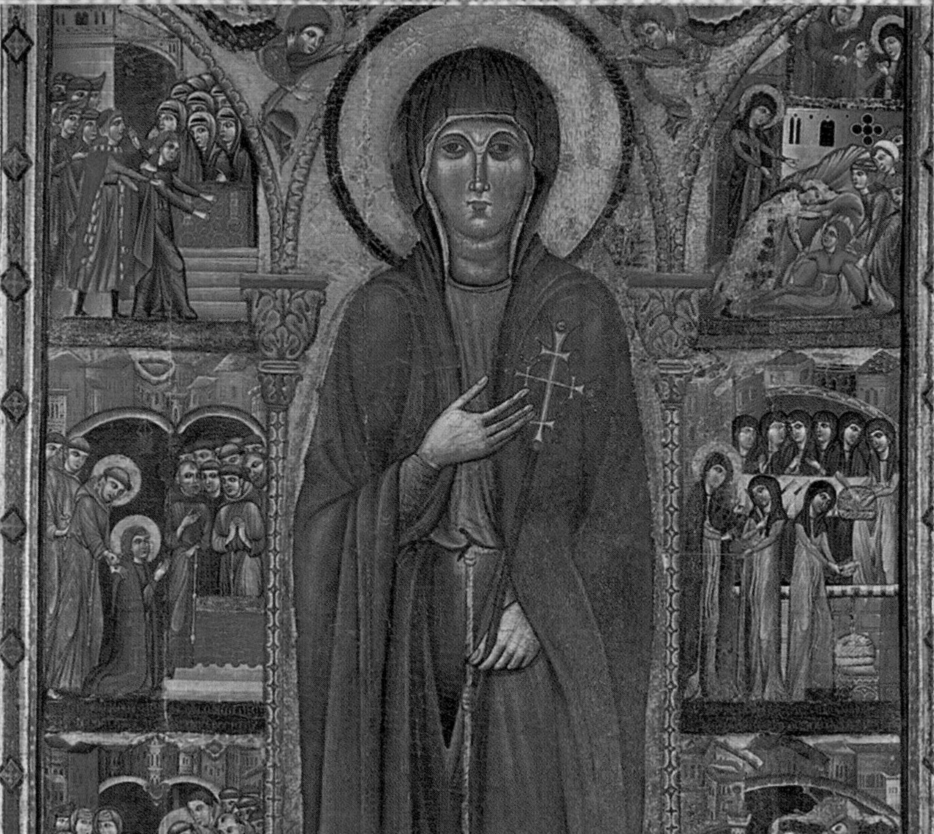

Plate 10

Saint Clare of Assisi is pictured with eight scenes from her life, in a painting from the thirteenth century. "O blessed poverty, / who bestows eternal riches / on those who love and embrace her!" (Armstrong, *Clare of Assisi: Early Documents*, pages 35–36). Read about the lives of Clare and Francis on pages 152–153.

Plate 11

The Black Death killed one-third of Europe's population in the fourteenth century. A fifteenth-century painting depicts the angel of death ravaging the inhabitants of a medieval city. Read about the Black Death and its effects on spirituality on pages 156–158.

Plate 12

Jan Brueghel's paintings, such as this *Visit to a Farmhouse*, convey some of the difficulties of German peasant life. Read about the Peasants' Revolt and the rise of Protestantism on pages 172–183.

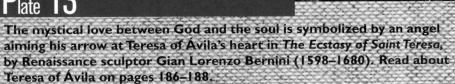

Plate 13

The mystical love between God and the soul is symbolized by an angel aiming his arrow at Teresa of Ávila's heart in *The Ecstasy of Saint Teresa*, by Renaissance sculptor Gian Lorenzo Bernini (1598–1680). Read about Teresa of Ávila on pages 186–188.

Plate 14

Vincent de Paul and the Daughters of Charity responded with compassion and love to poor and sick people by going out to care for them in the streets. Read about revolutionary changes in religious life begun by the Daughters of Charity, on pages 213–214.

Plate 15

Blessed Kateri Tekakwitha, a member of the Mohawk tribe, is depicted in a contemporary icon by Robert Lentz. She holds both the Christian symbol of the cross and the Iroquois symbol of the tree of peace, which can shelter all peoples. The tree rides on the back of a giant turtle, a symbol from a Native American creation story. Read about Kateri Tekakwitha and the spread of Catholicism in the New World on pages 228–247.

Plate 16

Nicaraguans from three villages bring together the statues of their patron saints each year for a big celebration, as shown in the painting *El Tope en Delores*, by Edmundo Arburola. Read more about Catholicism as a world church on pages 248–277.

Controlling the Holy Land and territory around it was a major issue because pilgrimages were an important part of Christian life during the Middle Ages. Some Christians traveled for months under great hardships to visit the shrines of saints and especially the place where Jesus died. In the past, the Arab Muslims had allowed Christians to travel across territory they held, but the Turkish Muslims did not, and Christians on pilgrimage were being attacked.

So for more than two hundred years, armies of knights rode out from their homelands to fight in the Middle East. They knew that many would never return, their bones bleached on a foreign desert. Yet the popes called, and Christians followed.

Although the Crusades did initially express Christian faith, they nevertheless showed the corruptibility of zealous war projects. Interested in grabbing personal power and wealth, the Christian generals of the Crusades often squabbled among themselves. The knights were frequently cruel in their victories. And in one Crusade, Christians made war against other Christians. Now, in retrospect, historians view the Crusades as a case of good intentions turned into disaster.

With All Good Intentions

With the blessing of Pope Urban II, the First Crusade marched off to help the Byzantine church in 1096. The Christian knights recovered Byzantine territory and finally arrived at the walls of Jerusalem. A long siege followed. In 1099 the knights broke through the walls and began to massacre Jews and Muslims alike in a reign of terror that made the Muslims hate the Christians for years to come. But Jerusalem was back in Christian hands, and four Latin kingdoms were set up on the Mediterranean coast, where Latin clergy and monks would settle.

The knights who returned from the First Crusade were honored as defenders of the faith; they were also granted indulgences by the church—that is, their sins were forgiven, and the punishment expected for them in the afterlife was taken away. They received tangible rewards too. Most warriors came back with loot to give their families. Those who stayed on in the conquered territory could create their own feudal estates.

Military and Moral Failure

The Second Crusade was initiated a few decades later, after some of the territory won by the Christians in the First Crusade fell back to the Muslims. This, the Second Crusade, failed calamitously. Before too long the Muslims had recaptured Jerusalem and all the other lands taken by the knights in the First Crusade.

A Third Crusade was launched under the joint leadership of King Richard "the Lion-Hearted," of England, and the kings of France and Germany. Their Crusaders recovered a tiny strip of the coast of Palestine but suffered devastating casualties, many of which were caused by disease and by fighting among the knights themselves. The original fervor of the First Crusade was lost, and many Crusaders were more concerned with booty than with the fate of Jerusalem.

Inevitably, a Fourth Crusade followed. Pope Innocent III rallied a few French nobles to his call. The Crusaders decided to take the Mediterranean Sea route. But to raise the money for transporting themselves in ships, the knights agreed to "stop off" in Constantinople, which was not under Muslim control, on the way to the Holy Land. There they could earn a handsome fee for retrieving the throne by force for a Byzantine emperor who had been deposed by a rival faction.

The Crusaders sailed to Constantinople. After three days of attacks, they took the city and began to loot and pillage it. They broke into churches and destroyed or stole precious shrines. So separated had the Eastern and Western churches become that Christian knights vandalized the most beautiful Christian city in the world.

Back in Rome, Pope Innocent raged with frustration. His army was out of control, even going so far as to set up a Latin kingdom around Constantinople. The Crusaders appointed a Latin patriarch and imported Latin priests and monks, infuriating the Greek Christians against the Christians of the West and the pope who led them. Though later leaders of the Byzantine church would seek reunion with the Western church, the people of the Eastern church themselves would not forget what their fellow Christians had done to their families, homes, and churches in the Fourth Crusade, in 1204. The split of the Christian church seemed irrevocable.

Small Crusades followed. In the notorious and tragic Children's Crusade, thousands of children marched to the Mediterranean coast of Italy, where they thought they would take boats to the Holy Land and win it back for Christianity, by love rather than force. Instead, greedy merchants captured the children and sold them into slavery.

At one point a German emperor actually regained Jerusalem for the West by negotiating with the Muslims, but the pope turned down the agreement because that emperor was under a ban of excommunication. Jerusalem went back to Muslim hands. Eventually, by the end of the 1200s, the "Crusade fever" died. The church had other, even more serious problems back in Europe.

An Opening to Other Cultures

Some good for Western culture did come from the Crusades in spite of the military and, above all, moral failure. For one thing, the Crusades opened Europe to the East, even the Far East, especially China. Crusaders brought back all sorts of new goods and inventions. Through contacts with Muslim scholars, they learned of advances in architecture, astronomy, mathematics, and science. In addition, the Crusaders returned from their travels with volumes of philosophy—especially that of the Greeks—which had been studied and preserved by Islamic scholars. All of these discoveries would bring about profound changes, eventually leading to the period in Western history called the Renaissance, which will be discussed in the next chapter.

Heresy and Inquisition

The Albigensian Heresy   As the Crusaders battled Muslims and each other, the church was battling another foe back in Western Europe, in the south of France. This foe was a sect known as the Albigensians, named after the town Albi, where they were most prominent. Their heresy saw all material things, including the human body, as bad. Among the Albigensians were a strict minority group who called themselves "the Perfect Ones."

One reason that the Albigensians grew in number was that in southern France, many of the Christian clergy and the monks in monasteries were rich, living an easy life and neglecting the preaching of the Gospel. This scandal prompted among Christians a renewed zeal for poverty, simplicity, and self-denial. But the Albigensians took the good impulse for renewal to extremes, teaching that marriage, as well as the body, was evil. Some Albigensians taught that the proper way to be freed from life, which was itself evil, was to commit suicide. Some bishops and priests joined the heretics and took over several local churches.

Heresies throughout Christian history have often begun as correctives for church practices that needed to be challenged. This was certainly the case with the Albigensian heresy. However, a legitimate challenge to church practice or belief sometimes turns into an overreaction. It becomes a heresy when some essential aspect of the faith—in this case, the goodness of creation and the sacredness of human life—is denied.

For more than fifty years church leaders tolerated or ignored the Albigensians. In the early 1200s, however, Pope Innocent III began to act on the policy that had long been accepted in the

In every period of church history, no matter how corrupt or violent, great Christian figures emerge to stand as witnesses to the message of Jesus. Certain holy women of the High Middle Ages, although enclosed within monastic life, had a profound effect on common folk as well as on kings and popes. Among those women was Hildegard of Bingen (Bingen, Germany).

As a child, Hildegard was tutored by a holy woman who lived as a hermit. They concentrated on practical skills, reading and writing in Latin, and religious studies. Hildegard later joined her hermit mentor in a Benedictine nuns' community and eventually was elected abbess. Soon Hildegard's reputation for wisdom and charity attracted many women to the community.

Hildegard's reputation as an herbalist and healer drew sick people from all over Europe. Her monastery had a large herb garden. Several nuns worked in it, and Hildegard studied the plants and their curative powers. She wrote texts on medicine, dietary prescriptions, gynecological cures, and what would today be recognized as homeopathic principles. In the monastery, Hildegard advocated regular warm baths, and she installed plumbing—both of which were unheard of in Europe in the Middle Ages.

As a preacher, Hildegard drew enormous crowds to hear her condemn church corruption and call people to conversion. Kings and bishops, abbots and ordinary people, sought her guidance. Upset about corruption in Rome, Hildegard prodded Pope Anastasius IV to clean up the city. She wrote these blunt, fearless words to the pope:

> Why do you not cut out the roots of the evil which chokes out the good, useful, fine-tasting, sweet-smelling plants? You are neglecting justice. . . .
>
> . . . You who sit on the papal throne, you despise God when you don't hurl from yourself the evil but, even worse, embrace it and kiss it by silently tolerating corrupt men. . . . And you, O Rome, are like one in the throes of death.

Hildegard had the courage of one who tries to do God's will. Once the local church authorities placed Hildegard, then in her eighties, and her monastery under an interdict for burying the body of a revolutionary youth in their cemetery. (An interdict forbids those under it from receiving most of the sacraments and being given a Christian burial.) Still, Hildegard refused to dig up the youth's body and eject it from her monastery grounds, insisting that the youth had made a good confession before he died. In one of her letters to the archbishop, protesting the interdict, Hildegard argued:

> [In prayer] God ordered me: the corpse must never be removed . . .
> for God has taken this man from the bosom of the Church as someone
> for whom the joy of the redeemed has been prepared. To do anything
> contrary to this would . . . be contrary to the will of truth.

In the end, Hildegard won the argument. The interdict was lifted.

This astounding woman also wrote musical compositions that are still being recorded, as well as accounts of her mystical experiences of God, scores of letters, and even morality plays. But most important, Hildegard showed people God's love by her words and actions. ■

Hildegard of Bingen:
Healer, Preacher, Visionary

church: "Heretics are to be overcome by reasoning, not by force." He sent a new kind of monk among the Albigensians to convert by preaching and by the example of a poor, holy lifestyle. With trust in God's providence, these mendicants, or begging monks, challenged the Albigensians' assumptions that the church was full of materialism and corruption. Still, not many heretics were converted.

When a heretic assassinated a representative of Innocent III, the pope took drastic action. He called for a military crusade against the Albigensians. But even twenty years of struggle did not root them out entirely; the survivors only went underground. In desperation, the pope at the time, Gregory IX, initiated the Papal Inquisition.

The Roots of the Inquisition From peasant farmers to kings, the European Christians of the Middle Ages considered heresy a great evil. People feared that heresy would tear civilization apart and lead to eternal damnation for those people lured astray. Christianity was recognized as the official religion of the European kingdoms, and uniform religious belief created a sense of stability in the state; so anyone who disrupted the harmonious church-state relationship by introducing erroneous beliefs was looked upon as a traitor. Heresy was not just a religious error; it was treason.

Thus civil authorities became involved in punishing heretics, ordering them to be tortured and in some cases put to death by burning at the stake or hanging. Until about the year 1150, all persons suspected of heresy were prosecuted by civil authorities. After that year, local bishops could run their own inquisitions. (The word *inquisition* means "inquiry.") Those whom the bishops found guilty of heresy were turned over to local civil authorities for punishment.

An Inquisition Based in Rome The Papal Inquisition, begun in about 1232 by Pope Gregory IX, was centrally run from Rome in an attempt to be systematic. The purposes of the Inquisition were, first of all, to find out who the heretics were, and second, to persuade them to give up their heresy.

When church officials arrived in a town to hold a local hearing of the Inquisition, they called the known heretics to come in, confess their sins, and receive a penance, such as reciting prayers, fasting, going on a pilgrimage, paying a fine, or being flogged. Then the public was invited to report anyone they suspected of being a heretic. Two witnesses were sufficient to make a charge against an accused person, but the names of the witnesses were kept secret so that the accused would not attack the witnesses' credibility. Inevitably, some people would falsely accuse an enemy just to get him or her "out of the way," often for political or financial reasons. And one pope even authorized torture as a way to extract evidence or confessions from the accused.

The trial of an accused heretic would take place before a papal representative called an inquisitor, sometimes with a jury. If the heretic refused to give up her or his beliefs, the result was severe punishment, such as life imprisonment or death by burning at the stake. The sentence was made publicly, as was the execution of a condemned party. Sometimes an execution was held back for as much as a year in hopes that the heretic would have a change of heart and mind.

The Inquisition threw fear into the hearts of men and women, but many accepted it as a necessary evil. Fearing the effects of heresy on their lives, they were willing to turn in a heretic for trial, and, when the trial was over, they witnessed the punishment. Actually, though, relatively few executions were ordered by the Papal Inquisition. One famous inquisitor known for his severity turned over for punishment just 5 percent of those who were brought to trial. At least with the Papal Inquisition a person came before a jury and had a chance to try to prove his or her innocence. That was not the case with most civil trials, in which a king or lord could condemn a person to death for a rather trivial offense. Neither was the Inquisition used everywhere, but principally in southern France, northern Italy, and parts of northern Spain. By the end of the thirteenth century, the Inquisition was largely discontinued, except in Spain.

Christians today look back on the Inquisition as a terrible, even shameful, episode in their history. Given the Christian belief in human rights and the dignity of the person, the Inquisition appears as a gross distortion of the faith. At the time, of course, it seemed necessary in order to combat heresy. What the Inquisition, like the Crusades, does provide for us today is a lesson in how easily religious zeal and good intentions can be turned into great mistakes with tragic outcomes.

Mendicant Friars:
From the Monasteries to the Streets

As mentioned earlier, the Albigensians set themselves against the materialism and corruption they found in the clergy and the monasteries, and they carried that stand to extremes. But others in the church who were not heretical also saw the need to renew the Gospel spirit of poverty and simplicity, and they responded in creative, prophetic ways to the needs of the church. In particular, the mendicant orders stand out: the Order of Preachers and the Order of Friars Minor (*friars minor* means "little brothers"). These two religious groups were different from the earlier orders whose members usually lived in large country monasteries. These friars stayed on the move, teaching and preaching mostly in the growing towns, and they lived a simple life, dependent primarily on what people gave them for their efforts. Because they were, in effect, beggars, they came to be known as mendicant orders. (The word *mendicant* means "beggar.") They had no farms for food or large monasteries for housing, at least not originally.

Dominic's Preachers and Teachers Dominic de Guzmán (1170–1221) founded the Dominicans (Order of Preachers). As a young priest, he had been sent to convert the Albigensians. Frustrated that he had too little help in that task, Dominic gathered a group of men who were willing to dedicate themselves to preaching. Soon his followers spread throughout Europe teaching and preaching.

The following account of Dominic's efforts to convert the Albigensians gives a picture of his perseverance and sense of humor.

Dominic travelled indefatigably, . . . visiting villages, towns, and châteaux, and setting an example by his way of life, which was more austere than that of the perfecti [Perfect Ones] themselves.

He was not always kindly received; far from it. "The enemies of truth," wrote Jordanus of Saxony, "made mock of him, throwing mud and other disgusting stuff at him, and hanging wisps of straw on him behind his back." Such treatment was not calculated to worry a mind as enthusiastic as Dominic's.

From the same source we learn the reply which the Saint made to those heretics who asked him: "What would you do if we seized you by force?" He told them: "I should beg you not to kill me at one blow, but to tear me limb from limb, that thus my martyrdom might be prolonged; I would like to be a mere limbless trunk. . . ."

The . . . exaggeration of these remarks must have discouraged his adversaries. Even though they persisted in regarding Dominic as an envoy of the Devil, they were forced to realize that with such a madman they could do nothing. He went singing through the villages where men and women pursued him with threats and jeerings; when he was exhausted he would sleep by the roadside. (Oldenbourg, *Massacre at Montségur,* page 93)

Eventually, the Dominicans, or Black Friars (so called because their habit was a white robe covered with a black cloak), lived in communal houses. They fostered excellent scholarship, and consequently many of the great university teachers of the Middle Ages were Dominicans. They believed that through scholarship they would be better able to illustrate the truth of the Gospels and the wisdom of church Tradition.

Francis's Little　**The Franciscans**
Brothers and Sisters　The other great mendicant order was the Order of
Friars Minor, also called the Franciscans. Their founder, Francis of Assisi (1181–1226), is one of the most popular of all saints.

Total Trust in God

As the son of a wealthy silk merchant in Assisi, Italy, the young Francis squandered money and occasionally fought in one of the small wars between his town and its neighbors. Then, at age twenty-five, Francis twice had visions of Christ. After a pilgrimage to Rome, he decided to live as a poor man and to take care of needy and sick people. Francis's father angrily disapproved of such a life for his son, but Francis was unswerving in his decision and even publicly discarded the clothes on his back as a sign of putting off the old life. Francis declared that God was his only father. Thus he began his life of wandering the countryside speaking of God, repairing run-down churches, and serving persons who were lame, blind, poor, or afflicted with leprosy.

With this living trust in God, Francis drew men and women to Christ. He also attracted followers to himself. After much coaxing from them, he wrote a very simple rule of life for his first band of friars. Within ten years, five thousand friars had fanned out across Italy.

A Poor Lifestyle

The severe poverty of lifestyle that Francis followed was not easy for his friars. So at times Francis was at odds with some of his brothers. Likewise, his rejection of wealth, because he saw it as a source of corruption for the Christian—especially when so many poor people existed in the world—did not sit well with some rich church officials. The story below shows Francis's attitude toward poverty.

One day the Bishop of Assisi said to St. Francis: Your way of life without possessions of any kind seems to me very harsh and difficult. My Lord, Francis answered, If we had possessions we should need arms for their defence. They are the source of quarrels and lawsuits, and are usually a great obstacle to the love of God and one's neighbour. That is why we have no desire for temporal goods. (Clissold, *The Wisdom of St. Francis and His Companions,* page 32)

Despite misunderstandings, the pope approved the Franciscan Rule with its ideals of simple living and total trust in God.

The Poor Clares

Men were not the only ones attracted to Francis's life and Gospel witness. Soon after Francis began his mendicant life, Clare, a rich young woman of Assisi, asked to join him. Women religious of the time, however, lived only in the seclusion of convents and were not allowed to roam. Accordingly, Clare founded the first of many women's orders that would try, from within convent walls, to follow the ideals of Francis. For years after Francis's death, Clare kept among her sisters the inspiration of his total trust in God. The Poor Clares, as the sisters came to be known, depended on gifts from those outside their convent walls. They spent their lives in prayer and meditation, relying completely on God's providence. As the power of this kind of life became known, the order spread to several other countries in a short time. Confident that Clare's closeness to God gave her a clear vision of what should be done, bishops and even a few popes came to ask Clare's advice on important matters.

Thomas Aquinas   Mendicant Scholar

As time went on, the new mendicant orders moved increasingly into scholarship and university teaching. Some of the brightest intellectual lights in the church came from the Dominicans and the Franciscans of the Middle Ages. Bonaventure stands out among the Franciscans, but the greatest scholar to emerge out of the period was the Dominican Thomas Aquinas (1224–1274).

The son of an Italian count, Thomas was educated as a child at the Benedictine monastery at Monte Cassino. He finished his formal studies at the University of Naples and joined the Dominicans, in spite of the protests of his rich family. To try to force him to change his mind, his family kidnapped him and kept him a prisoner in the family castle for more than a year. However, Thomas remained firm in his religious vocation and eventually went to Paris, where the brilliant Dominican scholar Albert the Great was his teacher. Thomas taught at Paris and later at several Italian universities. Ironically, the young man who had been nicknamed the "Dumb Ox" because he was considered slow moving and too serious became well known for his intelligence even in his own time.

Thomas had many new ideas inspired by his study of Greek and Arabic thinkers. His innovations prompted his bishop in Paris as well as some of the other professors at the university to oppose his use of Greek and Arabic thinking in theology. However, Thomas was able to show that God's revelation is not contrary to reason, that in fact we can know some truths about God by using our mind. He took his method for doing theology from the Greek philosopher Aristotle but tried to base much of his thinking on the Bible. Thomas's writings, summarized in his four-volume *Summa Theologiae,* were debated vigorously during his life and right after his death. However, by the time of the Council of Trent (held from 1545 to 1563), Thomas's *Summa* was the inspiration behind most of the official decrees coming from the church.

In a sense, Thomas was the right person at the right time; that is, his genius brought together much of the scattered thinking from various sources and gave it method—philosophical reasoning. Certainly Thomas was a genius, but he was also a simple person—a Dominican friar who never held any high positions outside the university and who loved to compose lyrics and music for religious feasts.

Conclusion   In the High Middle Ages, the church rose to some of its greatest heights of achievement: a strong papacy, the building of the cathedrals, and the creation of the great European universities. The church also experienced the depths of human misjudgment and folly: in the breakup of the Eastern and Western churches, in the disastrous Crusades, and in the excesses of the Inquisition. The period of the High Middle Ages illustrates how graced the church has been but also how subject it is to human weakness and how much it is constantly in need of conversion and reform. The mendicant orders, with their emphasis on poverty, simplicity, trust in God, and an active reaching out to the common people, offered an opportunity for that very conversion.

The church in the centuries after the High Middle Ages was to face a world devastated by a terrible plague, a crisis in the papacy, and more wars. In the midst of the hard times, the church would again rely on the guidance of the Spirit to keep a genuine faith alive.

Questions for Reflection and Discussion

1. The church committed enormous amounts of its resources to learning, art, architecture, and the professions during the High Middle Ages. Should the church maintain these commitments today? How is it doing so?

2. As a faith community, how can the modern church address disputes, disagreements, and differences in religious practice and theology? What methods of conflict resolution will build up the Body of Christ?

3. What role do saints, especially saints like Francis of Assisi and Hildegard, still play in the spirituality of contemporary Christians? Is it an important role?

9

The Late Middle Ages

Public Turmoil, Personal Piety

THE PERIOD OF the Late Middle Ages was filled
with calamities for both Europe and the church. A war
between England and France over English claims to
French territory lasted for a century. The papacy,
which had been strong and reform-minded under
Pope Innocent III, stumbled into corruption and chaos. At one time, three men claimed the title of pope.

Even in the midst of war and a crisis in the papacy, however, a rebirth was beginning in Europe, and it would spur on great advances in science, literature, and the arts. These advances, partly created by the church, would in turn influence the church profoundly. Despite the turmoil and corruption, and amidst these conditions, great saints and humble Christian folk worked faithfully for reform and peace in the church. Popular piety, or acts of religious devotion, flourished in towns and villages.

The whole period must be seen against the backdrop of the Black Death, a horrible plague that affected all of Europe. The arrival of this plague (also called the bubonic plague) in 1347 set the scene for years of strife and heroism. The specter, or phantom, of death became a subject of art, music, and folklore, and it influenced the whole consciousness of the people. Naturally, a sense of impending death permeated people's religious sense too.

The bacteria of the plague was brought to Italy and North Africa on merchant ships that had been trading with the East; most likely, fleas infected the shipboard rats. The plague spread rapidly, reaching even as far as the northern areas of Scandinavia and Russia. In his novel *Narcissus and Goldmund*, Hermann Hesse, a German Nobel Prize winner, describes the horror of the plague through the eyes of Goldmund, a vagabond artist:

The whole vast land lay under a cloud of death, under a veil of horror, fear, and darkening of the soul. And the empty houses, the farm dogs starved on their chains and rotting, the scattered unburied corpses, the begging children, the death pits at the city gates were not the worst. The worst were the survivors, who seemed to have lost their eyes and souls under the weight of horror and the fear of death. Everywhere the wanderer came upon strange, dreadful things. Parents had abandoned their children, husbands their wives, when they had fallen ill. The ghouls reigned like hangmen; they pillaged the empty houses, left corpses unburied or, following their whims, tore the dying from their beds before they had breathed their last and tossed them on the death carts. Frightened

Timeline . . .

1300

- King Philip IV of France attempts to arrest pope.
- Pope Clement V moves papacy to Avignon.
- Hundred Years' War begins.
- Bubonic plague arrives in Europe.
- John Wycliffe attacks clerical wealth, papal authority.
- Pope Gregory XI receives Catherine of Siena, returns papacy to Rome.
- Election of rival popes begins Great Papal Schism.

1400

- Election of Martin V ends Papal Schism.
- John Hus is burned at the stake.
- Hundred Years' War ends.
- Constantinople falls to Ottoman Turks.
- Johannes Gutenberg invents movable type, printing press. Bible is first large book printed.
- Columbus reaches the New World.

1500

- Michelangelo paints ceiling of Sistine Chapel.

fugitives wandered about alone, turned primitive . . . hounded by fear of death. Others were grouped together by an excited, terrified lust for life, drinking and dancing and fornicating while death played the fiddle. Still others cowered outside cemeteries, unkempt, mourning or cursing, with insane eyes, or sat outside their empty houses. And, worst of all, everybody looked for a scapegoat for his unbearable misery; everybody swore that he knew the criminal who had brought on the disease, who had intentionally caused it. . . . Whoever was suspected of these horrors was lost. . . . The rich blamed the poor, or vice versa; both blamed the Jews, or the French, or the doctors. In one town, Goldmund watched with grim heart while the entire ghetto was burned, house after house, with the howling mob standing around, driving screaming fugitives back into the fire. . . .

In a cloister he came upon a recently painted fresco. . . . A dance of death had been painted on a wall: pale bony death, dancing people out of life, king and bishop . . . peasant . . . everyone he took along with him. . . . It was a good picture, and a good sermon. . . . It was the obligation to die that was painted here, the stern and merciless end. (Pages 218–220)

In only a few years, one-third of Europe's entire population died in the plague. Over a thousand deserted towns dotted the map.

When the plague subsided, many towns were left without priests. Those priests who had not fled but ministered to the dying during the plague were constantly exposed to the disease; many died. Consequently, new priests were often ordained without adequate training, and frequently the selection of priestly candidates was hasty and ill-advised, thus reducing the esteem people had for the church.

The Black Death plunged Europe into disaster when the English and the French were fighting the Hundred Years' War (1338 to 1453) and when the papacy was deeply discredited by corruption and political wrangling. Left by church and state to fend for themselves, common folk sometimes devoutly turned to God, sometimes gave themselves over to desperate wickedness, too often relied on superstition for explanations of the way things were, and found scapegoats such as Jews and witches to blame for the evil in the world.

The Popes in Political Turmoil

During the 1300s, the stable center of European life—the church—was in precarious shape. The Christians of Europe suffered from a decline in the power and prestige of the popes. Older people remembered hearing their parents talk about the power of Pope Innocent III, who had not allowed kings to do what they wanted regarding the church. But the papacy was weakening in influence. With two Catholic nations, England and France, at war over territory, national identity was exerting more of a hold on people than was their Catholic identity and affiliation with the pope. Nations and kings were growing stronger in their ability to command loyalty.

The Avignon Papacy: The Popes Abandon Rome

King Versus Pope—Again

In 1303, the king of France felt so secure in his power that he sent troops to Italy and put the pope under arrest. This violent action came about because the pope had asserted papal supremacy over the king's decisions to tax the French clergy and to put a French bishop on trial in a French civil court. The king had been trying to make the French church a national church instead of one loyal to the pope. Though the people of Rome rescued the pope from the French troops and drove the soldiers out, the pope died a month later, humiliated and shamed. This manhandling signaled that the papacy was becoming captive to nationalism. The situation would only get worse.

Two years later, a Frenchman was elected pope by the College of Cardinals, which by that time included some French cardinals. Pope Clement V was completely under the sway of the king of France and the nationalized French church. In 1309, the pope moved the papal headquarters to the south of France, to the town of Avignon. This first pope of the Avignon Papacy appointed some new cardinals—all of them French. He changed several church policies to suit the French king's liking. Pope Clement, suffering from cancer and living in France, was in no position to oppose royal wishes.

Corruption and Cooperation

Clement's successor, also French, decided to make Avignon his papacy's permanent city by moving there all the officials needed to run the church government. In all, seven French popes lived at Avignon from 1309 to 1377, and they were largely cooperative servants of the French kings. Furthermore, the popes of the period established a luxurious, corrupt papal court. Such a show of wealth and vice scandalized many Christians across Europe. Some even interpreted the devastating plague as a sign of God's wrath at the papacy.

Why Not Avignon?

Besides being concerned about the lavish, corrupt lifestyle of the Avignon popes, Christians in Europe, especially outside of France, had other reasons to believe that the pope should be in Rome. For one, in the early church Peter had been bishop of Rome, and it was fitting that his successor should live there too. During the Hundred

Years' War, it also seemed politically unwise and morally unjust to have the pope allied with the French cause.

The situation was aggravated by the fact that the Avignon popes asked the dioceses for increased taxes, as well as donations for indulgences (see pages 167–168) and for spiritual services. Living away from the Papal States, the popes could not collect the usual revenues from that territory.

Catherine of Siena: "Pope, Come Back Home"

The memory of Roman popes stayed alive, and the impetus for the popes to return to Rome increased. Gregory XI, the seventh Avignon pope, had been thinking about Rome for five years or more when, in 1376, an unexpected visitor came to see him. She was Catherine of Siena (Siena, Italy), a thirty-year-old member of a Dominican lay order. Few of the French clergy at the corrupt papal palace were impressed by her; she seemed too naive.

Catherine's message was indeed simple: While in prayer, she had perceived that God wanted the pope back in Rome. The people of Europe, still recovering from the devastation of the Black Death, needed to be reassured by a pope in Rome. Moreover, only in Rome could the pope bring peace between France and England and among the warring Italian city-states.

The following plea is from a letter that Catherine wrote to Pope Gregory about her concerns over a papacy that had gotten off track.

Alas, what confusion is this, to see those who ought to be a mirror of voluntary poverty, meek as lambs, distributing the possessions of Holy Church to the poor: and they appear in such luxury and state and pomp and worldly vanity, more than if they had turned them to the world a thousand times! Nay, many seculars put them to shame who live a good and holy life. . . . Holy Church should return to her first condition, poor, humble, and meek as she was in that holy time when men took note of nothing but the honour of God and the salvation of souls. . . . For ever since [the church] has aimed more at temporal than at spiritual, things have gone from bad to worse. . . .

. . . Return to Rome. . . . Let not your holy desire fail on account of any scandal or rebellion of cities which you might see or hear. . . .

. . . Be manly in my sight, and not timorous.

We cannot be sure how much Catherine's impassioned plea played a role in Gregory's decision, but shortly thereafter, in 1377, a year before his death, the pope brought the papacy back to Rome.

Catherine is well known for intervening with the pope, but her short life was remarkable in many other respects as well. In her teenage years she lived a contemplative life alone, but at age twenty-one she became active serving Siena's many poor and sick people, especially victims of the bubonic plague. Gradually Catherine became recognized as an uncommonly holy person, a woman of great conviction and forceful personality. Consequently, while still in her twenties, she was asked to mediate disputes between city-states and between the city-state of Florence and the pope. Equally amazing is the fact that in an era when few women were allowed real rights, nobles and generals looked to Catherine for advice. She also authored a book on her mystical experiences and a book of prayers.

Not long after the papacy returned from Avignon to Rome, Catherine started a monastic convent near Siena. But soon she moved to Rome with some of her followers to advise a new pope who needed her help. At age thirty-three she died, having made large contributions to the church.

Who Is the Real Pope? The pope who succeeded Gregory in 1378 was Urban VI, an Italian. He was a compromise candidate: the cardinals probably would have elected another Frenchman, but the people of Rome were rioting in demand of an Italian or a Roman.

Double Trouble, Triple Trouble

The new pope saw that the top level of church government needed to be cleaned up. However, Urban had a hot temper, and he went about making changes in a way that turned people against him. The French cardinals slipped quietly out of Rome and met to see what could be done about him. They claimed that Urban was not a real pope, because they had elected him in fear of the Roman mob howling outside. Accordingly, they elected a French cardinal as pope. Naturally the French pope went to live at Avignon. So now the church had two rival popes and two church governments.

Who was the real pope? Christians had to make a choice, and they based their choice primarily on national and personal loyalties. Those in England, Scandinavia, and parts of northern France chose to support the pope at Rome, while those in the rest of France, Spain, and southern Italy obeyed the pope at Avignon; the Christians in Germany and northern Italy were divided. This situation continued for about thirty years in what became known as the Great Papal Schism (a *schism* is a split). At one point, some cardinals representing the two rival popes called a council to try to solve the problem, but they only made it worse. They elected a new pope. Neither of the other popes would resign. This meant there were three popes!

During the 1300s, French and English soldiers were butchering one another in the Hundred Years' War, the Black Death was wiping out millions of people, and the church was dithering at Avignon. Meanwhile, an uncommon woman—Julian of Norwich—was living in England. Even though she lived as an anchoress (a woman hermit dwelling in a room attached to a church), her reputation for wise counsel and goodness spread. Fish dealers, merchants, and many other common folk came to talk to Julian through a window looking out on a street from her tiny room, or anchorhold, in the church at Norwich.

At age thirty, Julian experienced sixteen powerful revelations from God. She recorded these in a book entitled *Showings*. Many people today read Julian's writings because of her unique perspective on Jesus. In the passage that follows, she gives a startling, but comforting, picture of Christ's love for us.

> Though our earthly mother may suffer her child to perish, our heavenly Mother Jesus may never suffer us who are his children to perish, for he is almighty, all wisdom and all love. . . .
>
> And if we do not then feel ourselves eased, let us at once be sure that he is behaving as a wise Mother. For if he sees that it is profitable to us to mourn and to weep, with compassion and pity he suffers that until the right time has come, out of his love. . . .
>
> It is his office to save us, it is his glory to do it, and it is his will that we know it; for he wants us to love him sweetly and trust in him meekly and greatly. And he revealed this in these gracious words: I protect you very safely. ■

Julian of Norwich:
Revelations of a Comforting God

Back to One Pope, but a Weakened Papacy

Finally, to deal with the intolerable situation, a Holy Roman emperor called together a general church council, which settled the matter by electing a Roman, Martin V, as the one and only pope. Thus the scandalous papal schism ended in 1417, and the church regained its stability.

However, the papacy as an institution had been weakened by a century of scandal associated with the Avignon Papacy and the Great Papal Schism. After the church council ended the schism, a movement known as conciliarism was started, in an effort to recognize general church councils as having more authority over the church than the pope had. Ultimately, the movement was unsuccessful; nevertheless, the prestige and power of the papacy had been weakened.

National and monarchical power continued to grow and to challenge popes as well. For instance, Spain was united under the monarchs Ferdinand and Isabella, and they accomplished this unity partly by stamping out all possible sources of opposition. Thus, the Spanish Inquisition, a holdover from the Papal Inquisition of almost two centuries earlier, began under the control of these two forceful rulers. The methods of the Spanish Inquisition were notoriously cruel, and the chief targets of this inquisition were Jews and Muslims who had converted to Christianity but were nonetheless suspected of heresy. The pope at the time protested the cruelty of the Spanish Inquisition, but to no avail. Papal power was weak in the face of strong monarchs.

The Renaissance Begins

During the Late Middle Ages, many educated Europeans, especially in Italy, studied the literature and art of the ancient Greeks and Romans. This cultural movement came to be known among the educated as the Renaissance, which means "rebirth."

Popes as Patrons of the Arts The popes of the late 1400s took an interest in the artistic trends of the day, and most of them encouraged writers and artists who were inspired by the classical past. Indeed, some popes became patrons, paying artists to do projects for them. For instance, the great artists Michelangelo and Botticelli were sponsored by popes; some of the greatest creations of Christian art were done under papal sponsorship. One pope started the renowned Vatican library, where thousands of priceless manuscripts could be stored, cataloged, and studied. He also began plans for rebuilding the basilica of Saint Peter's in Rome, into the new style inspired by the ancient Greek and Roman temples.

Inventions Remake Society A tremendous boost to the rebirth in literature came from the work of Johannes Gutenberg, a German printer who cast letters of the alphabet in lead, making it possible to arrange them into words. This movable type could be used repeatedly. Gutenberg then invented the printing press, modeling it on the presses used by vintners and papermakers. The first large book produced on the printing press, around 1456, was the Bible. Within a few years, most of the larger cities in Europe had busy printing presses. Literature of the past as well as new writings could be multiplied relatively quickly and easily. Soon almost everyone could own books; literacy increased.

The printing press enabled many people to possess Bibles. (This factor, in the next century, would be a catalyst for the spread of the Protestant Reformation, which emphasized individual interpretation of the Scriptures.) But most new literature was in Italian, French, Spanish, English, or other national languages—not in Latin, the language of the Bible version available at the time. Soon people were demanding Bibles in different languages as well.

In the midst of the Renaissance, which was a revival of the past, some scholars concentrated also on the future—that is, on practical scientific inventions. Mathematics was used to help sailors navigate the Mediterranean as well as to make more accurate cannons. Reading glasses came into use with the invention of ground lenses. The horrible experiences of the Black Death helped doctors learn about the spread of infection. And the printing press made it possible to disperse all of this information widely.

The emphasis on the importance of *this world,* and on making human life more fulfilling by way of the classical arts and literature and through scientific innovations, came to be called humanism. Although humanism was a welcome relief from the Black Death, this concentration on the human sometimes became distorted into a glorification of human pleasures.

Popes with Double Lives   Some popes of the Renaissance, remembered today as humanists for sponsoring the work of great artists, fell into the exaggerated form of humanism. They indulged in a lifestyle of excessive pleasure seeking rather than the Gospel way of simple living and charity. Because the popes were supposed to be spiritual leaders, their failure seems all the worse to us, just as it did to people under their authority at the time. Christians were ashamed of some of their popes.

Of the ten men who are usually called Renaissance popes, most lived double lives. On the one hand, they were officially the leaders of Christendom, with all the spiritual authority that role entails. But on the other hand, many had landed the papal office through bribery and vote buying. Once in power, they appointed loyal followers, often their own relatives, to important positions in the church. Surrounded by pleasure and ease, they lived decadent lives.

For two of the Renaissance popes, this meant violating the rule of celibacy. Alexander VI, the most notorious of the Renaissance popes, had six children—although they were born before he became pope. Further, Alexander did not hesitate to give his children high positions in the church. Such bad examples by the popes became excuses for other clergy and religious to live contrary to their vocations.

Most of the popes knew that the church needed reform. The leadership of the church was teetering on the point of crisis.

Meanwhile, Back in the Pews . . .

Surprising as it may be, neither the Avignon Papacy, the Great Papal Schism, nor the corruption of the papal court at Rome destroyed the faith of the common people "in the pews." They believed in God, they worshiped in the cathedrals, they prayed fervently for God's protection from more outbreaks of the plague, and they found comfort in belief in heaven. Though some high-ranking clergy were not the examples of Christian service and love that they should have been, many priests cared for their parishioners with patience and trust. Many of these priests lost their life ministering to the sick during the plague; these faithful ones were not forgotten by the common folk.

Countryside and Towns Life in the countryside had changed little for the serfs who remained on the feudal estates. Primarily they hoped for fair treatment and enough to eat. At noon and 6:00 P.M., when the church bells rang out, they said special prayers in the fields. They walked to Mass every Sunday, and, like everyone else, they enjoyed the celebrations of religious feasts.

The towns grew larger, with a new banking class able to make loans to people in business. In each town a rich family or two had most of the money, but a whole merchant class (a forerunner of the modern middle class) was developing. In the next century, this rising class would challenge corrupt officials in the church.

The guilds of merchants and of craftsmen grew stronger, not only protecting their members but also becoming prominent organizations in the towns. Some of the crafts guilds, for example, put on religious plays in front of the church or in the village square. They also took part in the liturgy, standing out as special groups with their banners and uniforms. At times, strikes and violence disturbed the towns as the craftsmen demanded more money for their work.

Worship at a Distance   The theology of the Eucharist during the Late Middle Ages emphasized, above all, the real presence of Christ in the consecrated elements of bread and wine. (The doctrine of the transubstantiation, defined at a church council in 1215, holds that the bread and wine are changed in substance, though not in appearance, into Christ's body and blood at the consecration of the Mass.)

Awareness of the transubstantiation and the real presence generated a great sense of reverence in the presence of the Eucharist, especially the consecrated host. But it also inhibited laypeople from participating in the Mass; they watched from afar and received Communion rarely. Even the physical structure of a beautiful cathedral, inspiring awe as it did, tended to distance the laity from the action of the Mass, to make the Eucharist more remote. The laity were separated by a screen from the priest, who celebrated Mass behind the screen with his back to the people. People longed merely to get a glimpse of the host when it was lifted up after the consecration. Consuming the host was more and more for the clergy, and the laity were never allowed to drink from the cup. Increasingly, priests would say several Masses daily for the private intentions of individuals who donated fees, and no congregation at all was present for such Masses. Cathedrals had many small altars besides the main one, just for this purpose.

Gazing with adoration at the host—in rituals besides Mass, such as Forty Hours Devotion and Benediction—became the laity's main way of relating to the Eucharist. One church council, recognizing this imbalance, mandated that the faithful had to receive Communion at least once a year, as well as confess their sins to a priest once a year.

Besides the physical problem of distance, the Latin language of the Mass made it impossible for most laypeople, and many priests as well, to understand what was going on. In addition, over the centuries, many gestures, adornments, and prayers had been added that reflected the practices of a royal court. This created an added sense of remoteness for the laity.

Devotion to Saints   Although the Mass did not involve the laity much, people found a way to express their faith through popular forms of piety and devotion to the saints. Believing that Jesus and God were distant, many Christians turned to the saints to intercede for them in heaven, to plead their cause. The Blessed Mother, Mary, was particularly honored with devotion; shrines, feasts, and special titles were created to revere her.

Nothing was or is wrong with devotion to saints. Such devotion is basically an awareness of the holy examples of those who have gone before us. It is an attempt to unite ourselves consciously with them, for encouragement, in the community of all the living and the dead who have tried to do God's will. But devotion to the saints can become distorted if the saints become more significant to people than God is.

In the Middle Ages, devotion to the saints led to the collecting of relics, things such as small pieces of bone from a saint's body or bits of clothing a saint wore. In the 1400s and 1500s, devotion to relics became exaggerated. It became a kind of hobby so interesting in itself that the collectors forgot the original intention of the relics, which was to remind people of what the saints' lives meant as expressions of love for God.

Indulgences   Another exaggerated element of medieval Christian faith was the preoccupation with obtaining indulgences. These privileges offered release from the punishment that would otherwise have to be suffered in purgatory, the afterlife condition of being purified of all traces of sin before one could enter heaven. The church practice of granting indulgences had begun several centuries before, when people were allowed to build a chapel or create a stained-glass window for a church instead of doing some penance for their sins. As seen in the last chapter, indulgences were also given as rewards to those who served in the Crusades. The idea behind indulgences was that a just and loving God would surely reward people for doing good. So actions like going on a Crusade or praying at a certain church on particular days were seen as meritorious in the eyes of God, and the merit gained from such actions could be stored up as indulgences. Thus, a person could use indulgences to reduce the punishment owed for sins he or she committed.

The sincere seeking of indulgences had a positive side; that is, it required a person to be genuinely sorry for her or his sins. However, individuals often forgot the sincerity in their anxiety about avoiding God's punishment. Eventually, true penance gave way to the buying and selling of indulgences—as though God could be bribed into forgiving sins. Many people saw indulgences as automatic: "If I give x amount of gold to the church, the indulgence I gain will automatically reduce my suffering time in purgatory by y."

The buying and selling of indulgences led people to believe erroneously that they could buy their way into heaven. Some church officials, including a couple of popes, did little to discourage this error of belief. Popes endorsed the selling of indulgences to support the artworks that they commissioned for the Vatican and, eventually, to complete Saint Peter's Basilica in Rome. Unscrupulous sellers of indulgences scattered throughout Europe. They used all sorts of pious threats and arguments to sell the indulgences to unsuspecting people and usually raised the prices to take an additional cut of the profits.

In contrast with the corruption in parts of the church, a revival of meditation and prayer was going on in pockets all over Europe. Several of the great works of the spiritual life were written during this period. The most famous of these works was *The Imitation of Christ,* by Thomas à Kempis (1380–1471). In books like this, many Christians found the necessary inspiration and support to be faithful—a help that Rome did not always provide.

A Fracturing Church: Divisions Deepen

Calls for Church Reform Demands to reverse corrupt practices in the church came from many sources. Some of the reformers denied key aspects of Catholicism, so even their legitimate criticisms of the church were ignored. Two men lost their life for persisting in their beliefs.

In England, about the year 1375, John Wycliffe, a zealous priest and teacher at Oxford, attacked unworthy clerics. He declared that all church property should be confiscated so that clergy and monks would be forced to lead a simple life. Wycliffe went further when he preached that the Bible was the sole source of belief (which excluded the church's Tradition as a source) and when he denied the doctrine of the transubstantiation. Disgusted with the corruption in the church, many devout believers followed Wycliffe, even though his teachings were condemned by an English synod of bishops.

One of the most avid readers of Wycliffe's ideas was John Hus, a young Czech priest and influential preacher in Prague. Hus began calling for many of the same changes in the church that Wycliffe had. In addition, Hus taught that people should receive Communion under both forms, bread and wine. Recall that in that period, nationalism was becoming even more significant than church loyalty. Many Czech nationalists rallied to Hus, seeing his cause as representing Czech people generally. Hus decided to defend his ideas at a church council, the same one that ended the Great Papal Schism. When he refused to recant his beliefs, the council had him burned at the stake. His execution in 1415 spurred the movement for Czech nationalism and demands for reform of the church.

In Italy, another reformer was at work: a Dominican friar named Savonarola began preaching publicly against injustice and against dirty Florentine politics, which were controlled by the powerful Medici family. The common people rallied behind Savonarola. Many people did penance for their sins. Savonarola was so popular that for a few months he ruled the city of Florence. However, his sermons against corruption antagonized Pope Alexander VI, who was an ally of the Medici family. In 1497, Savonarola attacked the pope verbally and directly, declaring, "To say nothing of his most wicked crime of simony, I affirm that he is not a Christian and does not believe in the existence of God." Next, Savonarola called for a church council to depose the pope.

The conflict escalated until finally even the people of Florence turned against Savonarola. After a trial held by the government of Florence, Savonarola was burned at the stake. The Medici family returned to power. The pope, instead of supporting reform, had supported the continuation of corruption.

A Widening East-West Split   While calls for reform were rumbling and erupting throughout Europe, a chance to reunite the fragmented churches of the East and the West presented itself. Again, as in the Crusades, the opportunity came through an alliance of military forces.

Hopes for Unity Dashed

The Muslim Ottoman Turks had been steadily advancing westward through Asia Minor, breaking off pieces of Byzantine territory. By 1400, the Turks had conquered almost the entire Byzantine Empire. Constantinople stood alone, a capital without a country.

The Byzantine emperor asked the Christians of the West for help in defending Constantinople against the Turks. To sweeten the request, he and many Eastern bishops signed an agreement accepting the pope as head of the church. Officially, all Christians were again united under the pope at Rome. However, the common people of the Eastern church and the clergy who had not signed the agreement refused to accept the pope or unity with Rome. Surely the memory that Western Christians had savagely attacked their beautiful city during the Crusades was a factor in their bitterness against the West and the pope. Despite the Eastern Christians' rejection of unity, the pope called for a crusade to help them fight off the Turks. But after initial success, the crusaders were soundly defeated near the Black Sea. This left Constantinople wide open to the Turks.

The Fall of the Byzantine Empire,
the Creation of the Orthodox Church

The Turks assaulted Constantinople. The last Byzantine emperor was killed in battle, and for three days the Turks looted the rich city and slaughtered or enslaved the inhabitants. Thus, in 1453, after more than one thousand years, "the second Rome" and capital of a once great empire fell. The Turks renamed the city Istanbul. Many Byzantine scholars escaped to the new town of Moscow in the newly united and independent Christian country of Russia.

Ivan the Great, the leader of the Russian people, saw himself as the successor of the fallen Byzantine emperor and considered Moscow to be "the third Rome." Ivan ruled the Russian church through his appointed patriarchs, just as the emperors at Constantinople had ruled the Greek church. In Istanbul, the Turkish sultan appointed a new patriarch to govern the Greek church and allowed a certain amount of religious freedom to Christians.

At this point the Christian church was divided into two parts: the Roman Catholic church in the West and the Orthodox church in Russia, Bulgaria, Greece, and Asia Minor. The two churches remain separated to this day.

A New World and a New Old World The lure of adventure and the desire for new sources of trade spurred several explorations by Europeans in the mid-1400s. Portuguese navigators explored the western coast of Africa. In an effort to reach the lucrative land of India, one navigator went around the southern tip of Africa—or the Cape of Good Hope—and another sailed on into the Indian Ocean. On hand during all the explorations were some hardy missionary friars ready to spread the word of God. Franciscans began preaching in Africa as early as 1484. To the church, exploration meant new fields for conversion.

In 1492, sponsored by Ferdinand and Isabella (of Spanish Inquisition infamy), the Italian explorer Christopher Columbus sought a shortcut to India. In the process he made an unplanned discovery: he stumbled upon several islands and then a continent of a New World, as yet unknown to Europeans. Further explorations of the Western Hemisphere followed under the English flag.

The prospects of adventure, of conquering land for royalty, and of making converts for Christianity were sources of optimism in a Europe beset by so many problems—corruption in church and state, fear of the Black Death, poverty, and high taxes. But even as a New World was opening up to Europeans, the Old World was continuing to reshape itself. The old Holy Roman Empire, which had supposedly brought together church and state, was breaking apart into many smaller, independent states. In the 1500s, the autonomy of these states would greatly influence a tremendous movement of revolt and reform in the church.

Conclusion Much of the history of the Late Middle Ages has been cause for scandal to Christians and non-Christians alike. The age was characterized by corrupt and competing papacies, war between Christian nations, superstitious religious practices, rigid responses to challenges to reform the church, and a further tearing of Christianity into Roman Catholic and Orthodox churches.

The Bible reminds us in many passages that the ways of God are not the ways of humans. The Spirit of God can work everywhere and through all things, even in the midst of human sin and corruption. The truth of this reminder is seen all throughout church history, but perhaps especially in the scandalous centuries of the Late Middle Ages. Unfortunately, the church of the fourteenth and fifteenth centuries did not seriously hear and respond to the challenges until later. Reformers' discontent with the church simmered from 1300 to 1500, when it came to a furious boil.

Questions for Reflection and Discussion

1. Given the exaggerated, often faulty, understanding of indulgences in the Late Middle Ages, what must have been believers' image of God at that time? What do you believe about indulgences?
2. What conditions within the church permitted the rise of so many corrupt, immoral popes? Could the papacy fall into such disrepute today?
3. Is the reverence with which people approach the Eucharist today different than it was during the Late Middle Ages? If you think so, try to describe any differences.
4. What were the positive contributions that reformers like Wycliffe, Hus, and Savonarola made to the church? Would they have cause to take today's church to task?
5. How did the rise of humanism during the Renaissance change the church? Do you see a similar rebirth taking place today?

10

Revolt and Reform
Divisions in the Body of Christ

EVERY AGE SINCE the beginning of the church has seen great changes in the church and society. The changes that came about during the 1500s, however, were some of the most radical the Western world has ever experienced. In less than a century, the cultural and religious unity of Europe was shattered. Conflicts emerged within the Roman Catholic church, and as dissenting groups broke off, they took entire nations with them. The intellectual and emotional turmoil of those years would eventually lead to national revolutions and the overthrow of monarchies in Europe.

At the start of the 1500s, the church and the political situation were powder kegs waiting to explode; the forces of nationalism were in great tension with a church that was seen as corrupt. A scandal over indulgences proved to be the fuse, and a then-unknown German friar, Martin Luther, unwittingly put a match to that fuse. Before we look at the religious revolution that Luther began, though, let's consider the matter of indulgences as they were being promoted in Luther's time.

The original intent of indulgences was to offer Christians a way of doing good as penance for their sins. For instance, service in the Crusades could merit a special indulgence, which took away punishment that would otherwise have to be suffered in purgatory, after death. But indulgences became regarded as a kind of magic cleanser that purified people without really requiring them to convert to a more Christian life. Some Christians believed that they could sin all they wanted to, as long as they had purchased enough indulgences to cover their sins. The selling of indulgences seemed to make a mockery of God's saving power.

The most famous seller of indulgences was the Dominican friar John Tetzel. His selling campaigns raised money for the pope to complete construction of Saint Peter's Basilica, and they also generated revenues for the German prince-archbishop who had hired Tetzel. The Dominican friar held the attention of huge crowds wherever he went. A campaign began with a procession, complete with banners, drums and flutes, a huge crucifix, and the pope's coat of arms. After attracting a crowd, Tetzel would preach his sermon, trying to scare his listeners into purchasing his indulgences. Here is a sample from one of his sales pitches:

How many mortal sins are committed in a day, how many in a week, how many in a month, how many in a year,

Timeline . . .

1500
- Martin Luther's Ninety-five Theses spark theological debate.
- Luther responds to heresy charges.
- Luther excommunicated.
- Peasants' Revolt.
- Augsburg Confession written.
- Henry VIII declares himself head of Church of England.
- Society of Jesus (Jesuits) founded.
- English Parliament passes Act of Supremacy.
- John Calvin establishes strict theocracy in Geneva.
- Council of Trent.

1550
- Peace of Augsburg: local rulers can choose religion for their domain.

- Teresa of Ávila establishes reformed Carmelite order.
- Council of Trent closes, achieves reform but not unity.

- Revival of Inquisition continues, especially in Spain.

1600
- Puritans flee religious persecution in England.

173

how many in the whole course of life! They are well-nigh numberless, and those that commit them must needs suffer endless punishment in the burning pains of Purgatory.

But with these confessional [certificates] you will be able at any time in life to obtain full indulgence for all penalties imposed upon you, in all cases. . . . [And] at the hour of death, [you will obtain] a full indulgence as to all penalties and sins, and your share of all spiritual blessings that exist in the church militant and its members.

. . . Are you not willing, then, . . . to obtain these letters, by virtue of which you may bring, not your money, but your divine and immortal soul safe and sound into the land of Paradise?

After such a sermon, people who feared for their soul purchased certificates with a blank space in which to write their name. Tetzel declared that the purchaser, upon presenting the certificate to a priest at any time in the future, would be granted immediate absolution from all sins and punishments.

This disgraceful situation with indulgences prompted Luther to "light the match" of the Protestant Reformation.

Martin Luther's Call for Reform

Martin Luther (1483–1546) was a serious Augustinian priest and monk who held an important position in his order. He was also a scholar who had studied the church fathers and the Bible. Luther's monastery, in Wittenberg, Germany, was known for its strict religious life, which he adhered to faithfully.

The Protestant Reformation began undramatically in 1517 when Luther mailed a letter to Prince-Archbishop Albert of the neighboring diocese of Mainz. (Albert was the one who had hired Tetzel to sell indulgences.) The respectfully worded letter contained Luther's famous Ninety-five Theses, and it initiated a radical change of history.

The Problems with Indulgences Luther's theses were statements about sin and its forgiveness, the meaning of indulgences, and the pope's power to grant indulgences. Luther wanted to discuss these issues with Albert. The letter did not attack the whole idea of indulgences. Rather, it bemoaned the misunderstanding promoted by the sellers of indulgences, who claimed that the indulgences offered or guaranteed salvation. Luther correctly asserted that this claim was contrary to Catholic theology. Before long, everyone in the German state of Saxony, where Luther lived and taught, seemed to be talking excitedly about his ideas.

Overrelying on External Practices

Luther recognized that profound faith and trust in God is necessary for salvation, but he also believed that faith is given by the grace of God. He was convinced that people relied too heavily on external practices to guarantee salvation. Long prayers in church, accompanied by hymns and processions, were common, and indulgences were granted for these kinds of practices. To receive indulgences, people visited shrines of the saints, and they collected relics. Duke Frederick of Saxony himself had thousands of relics in his palace in Wittenberg. Despite these practices, though, going to confession and Communion was rare, even among those in religious orders. Somehow, people's priorities had gotten mixed up; they had forgotten the message of Jesus that is found in the Bible.

Resenting Rome and the Pope

As people in Luther's area discussed the Ninety-five Theses, they naturally began to take sides. While many people were concerned about the theological issues involved, more than a few were concerned about how the church used the money it received from indulgences. Why, they asked, should their German money go to build Saint Peter's Basilica for the pope in Rome? For a long time, money had been a recurring issue between various countries and the church in Rome.

Besides the people's concern about the outflow of money, there was another problem: some people wondered whether the pope actually could grant indulgences. Did he have the authority to do such a thing? In any case, wasn't faith enough for salvation? Wasn't the Bible the only authentic source of Christian truth?

Failed Attempts to Reconcile with Rome The pope at the time, Leo X, did not initially become involved in the matter of Luther's Ninety-five Theses. Leo saw the situation as an argument among monks. Being a Renaissance pope with a lavish lifestyle, he was too busy with other pursuits to worry about what went on in a small German town. Duke Frederick of Saxony protected Luther, while trying to remain neutral on theology. Frederick was pleased about the publicity Luther was giving to Saxony and the University of Wittenberg.

Luther attracted a large following in Saxony, and his support spread. However, some people accused him of heresy for supposedly denying the pope's authority. Such accusations disturbed Luther, who had never intended to start a breakaway movement from the church. So he decided to write directly to Pope Leo X to deny any heresy. Luther said that he merely wanted to do what other theology professors were always allowed to do—which was to discuss Christian teachings. He wanted to assure the pope of his loyalty: "I acknowledge your voice as the voice of Christ, who reigns and speaks through you."

Although the pope seemed rather unconcerned about the controversy at that point, the Curia—the cardinals and bishops around the pope—were alarmed. Soon Luther was summoned to Rome to answer to the charges of heresy. The German emperor publicly said that Luther should be excommunicated. Luther appealed to Duke Frederick of Saxony for continued protection. Then Luther wrote an answer to the charges against him.

Theses Become Hardened Convictions

On Papal Authority

Luther's theses were hardening into convictions. In his response to the charges of heresy, Luther said that the pope and his councils were not the final authorities on matters of faith—that only the Scriptures were authoritative. To Luther, popes had authority, but only by human agreement; their authority was not given by God. Jesus did give Peter and the Apostles special authority, but Luther claimed that this authority could not be handed down. His assertion struck at the heart of Catholic claims of papal authority.

On Grace Versus Works

Moreover, Luther said that people are saved *solely* by the grace of Jesus Christ, which gives people faith. His point was that people cannot merit or earn salvation by doing good works; salvation comes as a sheer gift. In Luther's developing theology, he put indulgences in the same category as all other human efforts to secure God's grace, calling them all "works."

Luther was right in reacting negatively to the abuses of indulgences. Incidentally, several other Catholics, such as the humanists Erasmus and Thomas More, were also critical of church abuses; but unlike Luther, they remained with the church. Eventually a document went out from Pope Leo X clarifying the meaning and purpose of indulgences, and as a result, the selling of indulgences declined and even stopped in some areas. Most of Luther's early concerns about the abuse of indulgences were incorporated into Catholic teaching at the Council of Trent, held later in the sixteenth century.

On the Bible as the Sole Supreme Authority

Living in Wittenberg, Luther continued writing, preaching, and teaching at the university. More and more, he reaffirmed that the

Bible was the sole supreme authority in the life of a Christian. This belief stood in contrast with the Catholic position. Rome emphasized that the Bible and church Tradition have equivalent authority.

Luther Excommunicated While Martin Luther was wrestling with religious questions, Charles V was elected to the throne of the Holy Roman Empire. In 1520, the Roman Curia, who were sure of the new emperor's support, produced a document excommunicating Luther. Pope Leo X signed the paper. Luther had sixty days to reverse his teaching or be excommunicated.

In the 1500s, excommunication orders were posted in the public squares of as many towns as possible. The officials from Rome had a difficult time posting them in Luther's case; many Germans stood with Luther. In a few towns, however, his writings were burned according to the instructions of the excommunication notice. Luther gave no signs of changing his stand, so the excommunication became final in January 1521. According to the European law of the time, a secular ruler—in this case, Charles V—had to arrest and punish heretics, which usually meant burning them at the stake if they would not recant.

With only three weeks left before he had to recant or be arrested, Luther was "kidnapped" by his friend Duke Frederick and was hidden in a castle at Wartburg. Safe in the castle, Luther wrote and completed a translation of the Bible from Latin to German. This enabled more people to read the Bible—which, of course, Luther and his followers saw as the supreme authority for Christians. After about ten months, Luther returned to Wittenberg, where he had strong support.

Still a Catholic? Luther still considered himself to be a Catholic. He had originally intended to reform the church, not to divide or replace it. He believed in the sacraments. However, he said that only two, possibly three, sacraments—baptism, the Eucharist, and perhaps penance—were justified in the Scriptures. Luther believed in Christ's real presence in the Eucharist, but he denied that the Mass was a sacrifice in the sense popular in his day. Emphasizing that people did not need intercessors with God, Luther discredited relics, indulgences, prayers to saints, the rosary, and other religious customs that were not biblically inspired. He encouraged greater emphasis on preaching, because people had to hear the word of God to believe in it.

Luther stressed the priesthood of all believers—that all Christians, not just specially ordained ministers, can communicate directly with God and are responsible for the growth of the Christian church.

Luther did not agree that pastors should be required to remain unmarried. Luther saw all of his beliefs as reforms, not as innovations. Yet as far as the church authorities in Rome were concerned, Luther was no longer a member of the Catholic faith. By 1525, Luther was married and still teaching at the university; he preached and wrote vigorously. His home was often the scene of lively discussion, or "table talk," with his friends and colleagues in the reform movement.

Five years later, Luther's good friend Philipp Melanchthon composed a document for the German national assembly in Augsburg. He was trying to show that Catholics and Luther's followers still agreed on the most important truths of faith and that a basis for compromise existed between the two groups. The document, known as the Augsburg Confession, summarized the teaching of those who followed Luther, claiming that "nothing in it is discordant with the Scripture, or the teaching of the Catholic Church. . . . We are therefore judged unfairly if we are held to be heretics." The document also outlined the reforms proposed by Luther to correct the abuses in the church. Catholic theologians greeted the Augsburg Confession with condemnation, and thus a new religious body—the Lutheran church—emerged.

The Augsburg Confession is still used by Lutherans today as a statement of their faith, and the year 1530 is considered the beginning of the Protestant churches.

Luther's Impact on the Political Scene

The Peasants' Revolt

Luther's ideas had widespread effects on German politics and society, and some of the effects were opposed vociferously, even by Luther himself. Luther's notions of social justice led the peasants to question the feudal system.

The German peasants, who were still trapped in the feudal structure, wanted freedom from lords who mistreated them. The peasants took Luther's teaching about the priesthood seriously. They reasoned that if all people had dignity and were priests, why should a class structure oppress certain groups in society? For instance, they stated:

It has been the custom hitherto for men to hold us as their own property, which is pitiable enough, considering that Christ has delivered and redeemed us all, without exception, by the shedding of his precious blood, the lowly as well as the great. Accordingly, it is consistent with Scripture that we should be free and wish to be so. . . .

. . . We will not hereafter allow ourselves to be farther oppressed by our lords, but will let them demand only what is just and proper according to the word of the agreement.

The peasants' demands seem reasonable and even mild to us today, but at the time they were viewed with fear and trembling by the powers of Europe. The peasants' ideas upset the order of society.

At first, Luther took the peasants' side, urging nobles to reform the conditions of German working people. Little changed, and as a result, the Peasants' Revolt erupted, lasting from 1524 to 1525. When the open revolt began, Luther was alarmed at the violence and became very conservative; he condemned the peasants and broke from their cause. In the ensuing battles, the nobles' armies slaughtered 130,000 peasants and blamed Luther for having stirred up the peasants to rebel. The peasants criticized him for abandoning them. Luther's theology led to results that he had never dreamed of. Such consequences of his reforms shook him profoundly.

Rulers Choose the Religion for Their Region

Gradually, Lutheranism grew into a popular movement in northern Germany. Many Catholic pastors became Lutheran, and some new Lutheran ministers took over Catholic churches. They began holding Reformed religious services, which at first were much like the Catholic Mass but in the German language. Eventually Charles V agreed with the German national assembly's decision that gave Catholicism freedom to be practiced everywhere, while restricting Lutheranism to places where it was already in existence. Because the Lutherans protested that decision, they became known as Protestants. Armed conflict broke out between Lutherans and Catholics.

By 1555, an assembly of German Catholics and Lutherans agreed to the Peace of Augsburg, which said that local rulers could choose the religion of their domain. From then on, the various German provinces generally followed the beliefs of the local duke or prince, whether Lutheran or Catholic.

The Protestant movement spread from the German lands to other parts of Europe. People heard of it from articles printed in booklets and from Protestant preachers who traveled from one region to another. For some rulers, accepting the new religion meant independence from Roman church taxes and from the Holy Roman emperor. For other rulers, whose subjects were quite loyal to Catholicism, staying with the Catholic church secured their throne by ensuring uniformity of belief. In short, whether a leader chose to remain Roman Catholic or to join the Protestant movement often depended as much on political motives as on religious ones.

Sweden, Denmark, Iceland, and Holland joined the Reform. Luther's ideas were also taking hold in Scotland, Finland, Switzerland, and Moravia.

Italy, France, Spain, southern Germany, and Poland maintained their ties to Rome. Russia, Greece, and some other Eastern European areas remained firmly in the Orthodox tradition.

Other Protestant Movements

Calvinism Beyond Luther

As with most periods of change, one change in the religious makeup of sixteenth-century Western Europe led to another. Luther demanded reforms that were not too far from traditional Catholic thought and practice. Then another reformer, the Frenchman John Calvin (1509–1564), took Luther's ideas much further, creating his own version of Protestantism, which became known as Calvinism. Like Luther, Calvin believed in the supreme authority of the Scriptures alone. Unlike Luther, he rejected the Catholic form of the Mass as well as the belief in Christ's real presence in the Eucharist. Calvin advocated very simple church worship, with none of the elaborate rituals, ornamentation, or statues of the medieval tradition. Under the threat of the French king's terrible persecution of Protestants, Calvin fled France for Switzerland. There he wrote *The Institutes of the Christian Religion,* clearly outlining his understanding of Christian faith and practice.

The Reform in Switzerland

When Calvin arrived in Switzerland, that country already had a religious revolution of its own in progress, led by Ulrich Zwingli (1484–1531). Zwingli, like Calvin, departed significantly from Luther's theology. Protestants in the city of Geneva asked Calvin to help them implement Calvinist reforms.

Calvin proved to be an able administrator. He founded a university at Geneva to train the ministers of his churches. He encouraged the work of hospitals and favored laws that promoted the economy, especially through the wool and silk industries. He preached almost daily and wrote approximately six thousand letters. Protestants came from all over to consult with him. He worked constantly in spite of chronically poor health.

A Strict, Intolerant Theocracy

Calvin established a theocracy—a complete integration of church and state—in Geneva, just as Zwingli had done in the Swiss city of Zurich. It was clear to Calvin that the church should dominate all civil affairs. Thus the Geneva council, under Calvin's influence, passed extremely strict laws for the city. For example, a woman who wore a fancy hairdo could be fined. Jail sentences were given for activities such as dancing in public, drinking in taverns, playing cards, or even reading certain books. Adultery and fornication were punishable by death. On one occasion, a child was even executed for disrespect to parents. A rigid adherence to moral principles was the duty of every citizen.

Besides enforcing moral strictness, Calvin came to stand for complete intolerance of any religion other than his variety of Protestantism. To practice any beliefs opposed to Calvin's was punishable by death. Blasphemers and "witches" were burned in public. Torture was a policy of the government in such cases. When a Spaniard, Michael Servetus, strongly differed with Calvin's theology, the man was tried for heresy in Geneva and burned at the stake. The intolerance that had characterized the Catholic church's treatment of heretics in the Middle Ages was continued by Calvin's intolerant demand for conformity.

Predestination as a Central Belief

A belief in predestination was central to Calvin's form of Protestantism. According to Calvin, God had complete foreknowledge of events and marked certain people for heaven and the rest for hell. In other words, God not only knew the destiny of individuals but *willed* it for them. Calvin believed that each person's fate was predetermined, or predestined, by God and that no one could do anything to change it.

Calvinism would be the guiding theology for a number of Protestant denominations that were growing up on the continent of Europe and later in England and Scotland. It would become the dominant form of European Protestantism.

The Church of England

A Political Breakaway

About the time Lutheranism was becoming well established and Calvinism was just beginning, another religious revolt occurred—this one in England. The revolt, however, had more to do with politics than with theological differences.

Henry's Dilemma

King Henry VIII, who reigned from 1509 to 1547, had been given the title "Defender of the Faith" by Pope Leo X. This was because Henry had condemned Luther and his theology early on in Luther's revolt. But now Henry was facing a serious problem: he had no son to succeed him on the English throne. In fact, the English considered this a major crisis, because each time the royal succession was unclear, contenders for the throne went to war with each other and turned England into a battleground. Henry saw it as his duty to

England to have a son. Carrying this rationale to an extreme, he assumed that he was morally justified in taking almost any measure to get a son. Because his wife, Queen Catherine of Aragon (Aragon, Spain), had borne him a daughter, Mary, but not a son, he wanted the pope to grant an annulment of the marriage. In other words, Henry wanted the pope to declare the marriage invalid.

Clement VII, who was pope at the time, refused to grant the annulment. This was partly because the church was convinced that the marriage was valid, but it was also because of political considerations involving the Holy Roman emperor Charles V, who was a nephew of Catherine.

A State-Sponsored Church

Henry rebelled against the pope. Capitalizing on the popular sentiment against Rome, Henry declared himself the supreme head of the state-sponsored Church of England. The conflict over annulling Henry's marriage had severed the ties between England and the Roman Catholic church.

The king required that all English clergy give their loyalty to him, which by and large the bishops did. Then he ordered the archbishop of Canterbury to annul the marriage to Catherine so that he could marry Anne Boleyn. For various reasons—including the fact that Henry and Anne's child, Elizabeth, was not a boy—Henry ordered Anne beheaded a few years later. He married six times in all: One wife, Jane Seymour, died giving birth to the long-awaited son, Edward. Two wives (including Catherine) were divorced, two (including Anne) were beheaded, and the last was scheduled for execution when Henry himself died, in 1547.

Consequences for Resisting the Oath of Loyalty

Henry dissolved the monasteries in England and gave the monastery lands to helpful nobles. In 1534, Parliament passed the Act of Supremacy, which declared the English monarch the head of the Church of England. Naturally, Henry appointed bishops who were loyal to him. Every important person in England's public life was required to take an oath acknowledging the king's supremacy. Some courageous Catholics dissented and faced severe consequences.

Among the Catholics executed was Sir Thomas More, who had been the chancellor of England—the highest government official under the king—until he resigned in protest over the king's actions. More was a lawyer and a writer. He invented the term *utopia* (meaning "an ideal world"), and his novel by that name is still studied. Arrested and imprisoned in the Tower of London, More refused to take the oath that negated the pope's authority—although he did not renounce the king. After a long prison stay, during which Henry tried to change More's mind, More stood trial in Parliament. He openly proclaimed his support of the pope. Soon after, More was beheaded.

Rejecting Henry as head of the Church of England was considered an act of treason punishable by death. Henry's approach to dissenters, both Catholic and Protestant, was not terribly different from Ferdinand and Isabella's approach to Jews and Muslims who had converted to Christianity in Spain. Nor was it much different from Calvin's approach to nonconformists in Switzerland.

Henry's Spiritual and Political Descendants

Ironically, the statements of faith and practice Henry approved for his church were very Catholic in theology. The one exception, of course, was that these statements rejected the pope's authority over the Church of England, also called the Anglican church. Henry rejected Lutheran teachings and never considered himself a Protestant. Later developments in Anglican theology brought it somewhat closer to Luther's and Calvin's thinking, although it remained remarkably similar to Catholicism. In the United States today, spiritual descendants of the Anglican church are called Episcopalians.

Edward VI, the son Henry had longed for, was a sickly young man, and he reigned only briefly. After a short reign by the Catholic Queen Mary (called "Bloody Mary" because she executed hundreds of Anglicans), Queen Elizabeth I took the throne. Elizabeth reigned for forty-five years and solidified the dominance of the Anglican church. Nevertheless, English dissenters sprang up, wanting to follow a Calvinist, "purist" religion. Thus the Puritan movement began, and its members soon became subject to persecution, which drove them to found the Massachusetts Bay Colony in the New World.

Over the next two centuries, many Protestant denominations were founded across Europe. Almost all of them were derived from or related to the three main movements of Lutheranism, Calvinism, and the Church of England.

The Catholic Response: Reform and Renewal

The Council of Trent   **The Catholics Turn to Reform**

About the time Henry VIII assumed headship of the Church of England, Pope Paul III took office in Rome. Interested in reform within the Catholic church, he arranged for meetings between Lutherans and Catholics in southern Germany. The meetings began cordially enough, but they broke off over the issue of the meaning of the Eucharist.

Nonetheless, Pope Paul decided to hold a general church council, to which Protestants would be invited. The city of Trent, in the southern Alps, was to be the site. The council was to have two purposes: (1) to bring Protestants and Catholics back together again and (2) to state clearly the principal teachings of the Catholic church. The first purpose had to be dropped, however, when the Lutherans declined to attend the council.

Defining Catholic Faith and Practice

The meetings at Trent concentrated on defining Catholic teachings and on setting new rules for establishing order and eliminating corruption in the church. The Council of Trent (held from 1545 to 1563) was responsible for what is now called the Catholic Reformation. No essentials of the faith were rejected by the council, but traditional Catholic faith and practice, which had become corrupted, was spelled out and restored.

The Council of Trent reaffirmed the following teachings:
- Christian faith is based in the Bible but also in the Tradition of the Catholic church.
- The church has the final word on interpretation of the Bible.
- Salvation comes through both having faith and doing good works inspired by that faith.
- All seven sacraments are valid.
- Christ is really present in the Eucharist.
- The Mass is a sacrifice, not simply a memorial meal.

In addition, the Council of Trent imposed new discipline on the church:
- Bishops who lived outside their dioceses were ordered to return. (One problem had been that bishops of rural dioceses sometimes lived in big cities, where life was more pleasant.)
- Celibacy for priests was upheld.
- Bishops were ordered to eliminate abuses surrounding the granting of indulgences in their dioceses.
- Each diocese that did not have a university was told to set up a seminary for training priests.
- The pope was to follow up the Council of Trent meetings with the publication of a number of new books: a catechism, or summary of church teachings; a book of official daily prayers for priests, called the Breviary; and an index, or list, of forbidden books that contradicted the faith or moral teachings of Catholicism.
- A commission composed a missal that standardized the prayers and rituals of the Mass. (The missal remained unaltered until the 1960s and the liturgical changes of Vatican Council II.)

Reform, but Not Unity, Achieved

Despite its many innovative responses to the church corruption that caused the Protestant Reformation, the Council of Trent failed to reunite the followers of Luther, Calvin, or Henry VIII with the Catholic church. The decisions for reform came too late, and most of the decisions supported traditional Catholic teachings. Additionally, the era of the Council of Trent was marred by a revival of the Inquisition, especially in Spain, where the pursuit and punishment of suspected heretics was fanatical and cruel.

The Council of Trent had many positive outcomes: It did reform many of the church abuses that had scandalized Christians. Religious orders returned to their rules, and new orders were founded to undertake the reforms started by the council. The standardized practices and well-defined decisions of the Council of Trent guided the church steadily until Vatican Council II, in the 1960s.

Ignatius and the Jesuits

Spirituality and Education

Among the new religious orders founded in the sixteenth century was the Society of Jesus, or the Jesuits, founded by Ignatius of Loyola (Loyola, Spain), who lived from 1491 to 1556.

From War Soldier to "Soldier for Christ"

When Ignatius was a young swashbuckling soldier, he hardly seemed a likely candidate to work for the church. Only when a cannonball injured both of his legs during battle did Ignatius begin to look at life differently. Lacking other books during his months of recovery, Ignatius read the life stories of saints such as Dominic and Francis. Gradually, Ignatius recognized that only a life lived according to the Gospels had any meaning for him. As soon as he recovered sufficiently, he vowed to become a soldier for Christ. He gave away his armor, went off to the mountains to pray, and eventually made a dangerous pilgrimage to the Holy Land, begging along the way to purchase food and passage. Upon returning from his pilgrimage, he studied in Spain and then went to Paris become a priest.

The Society of Jesus

In the 1530s, Ignatius organized six of his fellow students at the University of Paris into a kind of religious club. He began to lead them in a process of deeper conversion to Christ that he had developed, called the Spiritual Exercises. In a chapel on a hill overlooking Paris, the group made a vow to go to Palestine to convert the Turks to Christianity. When war prevented the group members from going, though, they offered their services to the pope. Their main purpose was to spread the Christian faith by teaching and preaching the Gospel message. They even took a vow of absolute obedience to the pope, going beyond the usual religious vows of poverty and chastity. The Society of Jesus, as they were known, grew rapidly.

Ignatius placed great emphasis on the training of members of his society; most went through at least fifteen years of study. Soon Jesuits were on the faculties of most of the major European universities in Catholic regions. In addition, Jesuits opened colleges and schools wherever they went. They were convinced that a good Catholic education would ensure loyalty to the church. Jesuits ran many seminaries, so the level of education among the clergy rose.

Jesuits spearheaded other religious activities for the church, too. Many of the important theological works of the church's Reformation were written by Jesuits. Through the peaceful means of studying and teaching, the Jesuits helped promote the Catholic reform and stop the spread of Protestantism in Europe. In addition, Jesuit missionaries fanned out to carry the Good News all over the world.

Today, besides treasuring the great heritage of Jesuit universities and scholarship, many Catholics value Ignatius's thirty-day program of spiritual exercises as a powerful method of growing in spiritual maturity and love of God.

Teresa of Ávila   A Return to Simplicity

Another great spiritual light for the church also came from Spain. Teresa of Ávila (1515–1582), a Carmelite nun, aided in the reform of monastic life.

A Renewed Kind of Carmelite

The huge convent Teresa entered as a young woman was a busy place filled with activity—too much activity for her. The monastic life was supposed to provide an atmosphere of prayer, study, work, and meditation. But Teresa recognized that her convent, like many in the years before the Catholic Reformation, had lost the spirit of quiet focus on God. So in 1562, after more than twenty-five years as a Carmelite, Teresa established a small convent, called Saint Joseph's, in Ávila, Spain.

The Saint Joseph's community of thirteen nuns wanted to live very simply, pray regularly, and concentrate on meditation. To do so, the women gave up the material comforts of the larger convent. Teresa's group of Carmelites were called discalced, that is, "without shoes," because they wore sandals instead of shoes. The main Carmelite order objected strongly to Teresa's reforms and tried to close down the new convent. Teresa, however, was not politically naive; she managed to have her convent placed under the direct protection of the king.

After five years, Teresa was requested to open Discalced Carmelite convents all over Spain, so the contemplative but exuberant Teresa traveled throughout the country founding new houses. Most of the trips were made on foot, or bouncing along in a rough cart. These travels kept Teresa away from the silent life of prayer that she desired. Nevertheless, convinced that her reformed convents would help restore the spiritual life of the church, she carried on. Her down-to-earth good humor came to her assistance many times.

Once when she was traveling from one part of Spain to another with some other nuns and a priest to start a convent, and their way took them over a stream, she was thrown from her donkey. The story goes that our Lord said to her, "That is how I treat my friends." And she replied, "And that is why You have so few of them." (Dorothy Day, *The Long Loneliness*, page 140)

Hard times tested Teresa's good humor, but she quipped, "God deliver us from sullen saints!"

In the midst of founding numerous new convents, Teresa was still being challenged by the main order of Carmelites. They did not approve of what she was doing, nor did they like being confronted with their own lack of serious commitment. Finally, after several years of dispute, the king made Teresa's Discalced Carmelites a separate religious order.

A Renowned Spiritual Writer

Another major commitment of Teresa's time and energy was the correspondence she kept up. She wrote thousands of letters in her lifetime—some to instruct and inspire, others to discharge business. She was a spiritual guide to many, including another great Spanish Carmelite, John of the Cross, who was trying to bring reform like Teresa's to the Carmelite friars.

Teresa's most famous piece of writing, a book still read avidly today, is *The Interior Castle*. In it she describes how one can come to God through prayer and love. Teresa says that at the center of every person's soul is God: "In the center and the middle is the main dwelling place where the very secret exchanges between God and the soul take place."

Many of Teresa's poems are well known today too. Here is one of them:

Nada te turbe,	Let nothing trouble you,
Nada te espante,	Let nothing scare you,
Toda se pasa,	All is fleeting,
Dios no se muda,	God alone is unchanging.
La Paciencia	Patience
Toda la alcanza;	Everything obtains.
Quien a Dios tiene	Who possesses God
Nada le falta.	Nothing wants.
Sólo Dios basta.	God alone suffices.

Christian Denominations in 1560

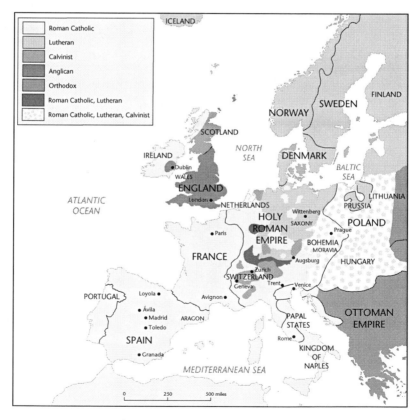

Conclusion   In the momentous century described in this chapter, the church—the sign of Christ's presence as the unified Body of Christ—was split into factions and was almost beyond hope of reunion. Reform was needed in the church, and in some ways the Protestant challengers did Catholicism a favor by highlighting that need. The Council of Trent began the reform process for the Catholic church by clarifying beliefs, setting up seminaries, disciplining the clergy, and defining standards for religious practices so that the practices would not be corrupted.

Tragically, fighting and mutual persecution between Catholics, Protestants, and Anglicans made religious dialog impossible. The Christian church was splintered badly, into Catholic, Orthodox, Lutheran, Calvinist, and Anglican churches and many offshoots of the Protestant denominations. These divisions remain today, though much progress has been made since Vatican Council II in healing wounds between Catholicism and the other Christian churches. Perhaps saints like Ignatius and Teresa shone so brightly during the Reformation because the era was so dark for the church.

Despite the revolutions that rocked Europe and the tragedy of divisions in Christianity, the zeal to convert people to Christ soared in the century after the Protestant and Catholic reformations and beyond. Other new worlds were awaiting the Gospel, and Catholic missionaries stood ready to take up the banner of the cross.

Questions for Reflection and Discussion

1. Since Vatican Council II, ecumenical dialogs have been steadily moving Christian communities toward some common understanding of theological agreement and differences. In what ways has this new openness to dialog helped heal the Body of Christ? How can Christians help in this healing?
2. Politics played a significant role in the Protestant Reformation. What are some contemporary issues in which religion and politics have become intimately intertwined?
3. During the Reformation both Catholics and Protestants had their martyrs. What would you be willing to give up your life for?
4. Who are modern Teresa of Ávilas—women who have exercised dynamic leadership to bring about the Reign of God despite strong opposition?

11

A Missionary Church

Carrying the Gospel Around the World

WHILE THE PROTESTANT Reformation was revolutionizing Europe's political and religious life and the Catholic church was trying to respond with its own reform, yet another movement was shaking the world as the Europeans had known it. Daring voyages by Europeans to lands they had previously not imagined, such as Christopher Columbus's journey to the New

World, spread excitement through Europe and the church. Europeans imagined the wealth that could be claimed. The church saw souls to be saved. Wherever the European explorers went, missionaries followed.

In the fifteenth and sixteenth centuries, Portugal and Spain were the two greatest exploring nations. To justify not only exploration but conquest of new lands, these two countries declared that they would plant the faith wherever they landed. Pope Alexander VI tried to eliminate conflict between Portugal and Spain by dividing the globe in half, granting all lands on one side to Spain and all those on the other side to Portugal. The pope's hope, of course, was that the Europeans would evangelize other lands—that is, bring the inhabitants of the new lands to Christ and the Catholic faith. For this reason, he allowed the crown heads of Portugal and Spain to appoint bishops and priests in their spheres of influence. All too often, this arrangement meant that the church became an agent of the state, focusing more on controlling the native peoples than on spreading the Gospel.

Certainly, however, most missionaries who took off for the new lands saw themselves as following in the steps of the Apostles, risking their life and security to bring souls to Christ. Although some missionaries fell prey to greed and corruption, most sincerely believed that without baptism, the inhabitants of the new realms had no chance of salvation.

Soon missionaries crowded ships heading to the four corners of the earth. They knew next to nothing about their destinations, such as the people's languages and customs or the geography. They did know what they wanted to do—preach the Gospel and bring souls to the church. They thought they would establish a village and church when they landed, encourage natives to move into the village, and set up a school to teach religion and perhaps a clinic and an orphanage. That was the vision.

However, the first challenge facing a missionary was a long and dangerous voyage. Then at the end of such a voyage, a missionary did not have any idea what lay ahead—success in converting the native people or rejection and cruel death.

Timeline...

1500
- Pope Alexander VI divides globe between Portugal and Spain.
- Franciscans begin work in New World.
- Cortés conquers Mexico.
- Pizarro overthrows Inca empire (Peru).
- Francis Xavier in India and Japan.
- Spain seizes the Philippines.
- Slavery banned in the Philippines.

1600
- Matteo Ricci enters Chinese royal court.
- Japan's shogun bans Christianity.
- Vatican creates Congregation for the Propagation of the Faith for missions.
- Jesuits establish missions in Africa.
- In China, Mass said in Chinese.

1700
- Pope bans Chinese Mass or any Christian accommodations to local customs.

- First Christians arrive in Australia.

1800
- First Catholic chaplain settles in Australia.
- Latin American countries, native clergy, throw off European rule.
- David Livingstone opens African interior.
- Colonial governments forbid slavery.

191

Between 1500 and 1900, the church spread to most areas of the globe, vastly changing the world and the church itself. This chapter will look at the church's missionary reach into Latin America, Asia, Africa, and Australia. Missionary work in North America will be covered in chapter 13.

The Church in Latin America

Explorers and Conquerors Arrive First In the 1500s, Spanish missionaries went in great numbers to the New World, following the explorers and soldiers whose purpose was conquest. Columbus claimed many of the Caribbean Islands for Spain and touched land on northern South America. If he had explored further into the continent and into Mexico, he would have found three advanced cultures: the Mayas, of Mexico and Guatemala; the Aztecs, of Mexico; and the Incas, of Peru.

By the 1500s the Mayas were overshadowed by the far more powerful Aztecs, whose empire included many other Mexican tribes. The Aztecs' temples were amazing feats of design and construction. Their governmental structure was complex, although ultimately one man ruled as both king and high priest. Also, they had a plentiful supply of gold.

Despite their cultural sophistication, though, the Aztecs were no military match for the Spaniard Hernando Cortés and his small group of soldiers, who were called conquistadors ("conquerors"). The Spaniards' superior weapons, armor, and horses inspired terror in the Aztecs. Cortés and his troops were supposed to barter for gold, but instead, Cortés decided to take the gold and Mexico with it. At first the Aztecs thought that the invaders might be "people of heaven," but Cortés betrayed their trust, killed their king, and massacred the people of what is now Mexico City, looting anything of value.

Further south, Francisco Pizarro found the empire of the Incas in the Andes Mountains. In the Incan mountain cities, the Spaniards saw magnificent pyramid temples where sacrifices were offered to the sun. Of most interest to the Spaniards, however, were the gold and silver ornaments in the temples. After three expeditions against the Incas, Pizarro managed to kill most of them, steal their treasures, and ruin their empire. The Incas who were not killed were enslaved and forced to work in silver mines or on plantations. By 1550, two Spanish colonial empires were established in the New World: one centered in Mexico and the other in Peru.

The Spaniards killed a large portion of the populations of these colonial areas, either by the sword or by the many diseases the explorers and the colonists carried with them—especially smallpox and measles. By the end of the 1500s, after only one hundred years of contact, the indigenous peoples, or native populations, of Mexico and Central America were reduced to 10 percent of what they had been before Columbus arrived. To make matters worse, the Spanish colonizers were generally poor, uneducated, but ambitious men who wanted wealth, no matter what the cost to the Indians, whom they considered to be subhuman anyway.

Conquest and even enslavement were the contexts in which the missionaries would try to preach the Gospel to the natives.

The Missionaries Follow The missionaries who traveled to the Spanish colonies were usually powerless to stop the exploitation of the native peoples. Nevertheless, they preached the Gospel in the new areas. The earliest missionaries were the Franciscans, who in 1500 began work on Santo Domingo, the island in the Caribbean where Columbus had first landed. In 1524, the Franciscans went to Mexico, and they were later joined by the Dominican friars and then the Augustinians. Soon missionaries were in the areas that are now Panama, Colombia, Ecuador, Guatemala, Belize, and Honduras. By 1549, the first Jesuits arrived in the jungles of Brazil, the colony owned by Portugal. The Jesuits fanned out into other areas, including Paraguay, Peru, and Mexico.

Why Convert?

The Indians became Christian for a number of reasons: First, many of the missionaries were good to them. The friars generally took an educational approach; they learned the native languages (which were oral, not written), constructed alphabets, and wrote catechisms to teach the faith. Second, some of the natives believed that the Christian God must be stronger than their own gods, because the Spaniards had conquered the native people. If the Indians converted, they would be on the winning side or at least they would have something in common with the Spaniards. Finally, some Indians no doubt genuinely believed in the Christian faith. These three reasons for converting were similar to the reasons that had motivated the European tribes of Goths, Vandals, and Franks to convert to Christianity many centuries before.

Guadalupe: An Affirmation of the Native Peoples

An important development in the evangelization of Latin America happened in 1531, about ten years after Cortés's victory over the

Aztecs. This was the miracle of Guadalupe, in Mexico. According to the written account of the Guadalupe event, a native peasant, Juan Diego, encountered the Virgin Mary on a hill while he was on his way to church in a rural area near Mexico City. The Virgin told Juan Diego that she wished a temple to be built on that hill, and she directed him to tell the Spanish bishop of Mexico City about her desire.

During visits to the bishop, Juan Diego's claims were dismissed. The peasant asked the Virgin for a sign to give the bishop. So the next time Mary appeared, she told Juan to gather from the hilltop some beautiful roses that were growing (amazingly) out of season and to take them to the bishop as a sign. Juan did as he was told, gathering the flowers in his blanket-cloak, and then Mary rearranged them. Hurrying to show the bishop, Juan opened the cloak in front of him, and the roses spilled out. But a miraculous thing had occurred: on the cloak was a brightly colored image of the Virgin as she had appeared to Juan—an image that has not faded or deteriorated to this day.

Significantly, in appearing to Juan Diego, the Virgin Mary affirmed all indigenous peoples. After all, she chose to communicate not with a Spaniard or a bishop but with a humble Aztec peasant. Her appearance to Juan Diego also helped great numbers of indigenous peoples accept the Gospel; in the seven-year period following her appearance, eight million Indians converted to Christianity.

Since that time, the Virgin of Guadalupe has occupied a beloved place in the hearts of Mexicans and Latin Americans, for whom she is a source of hope, love, and trust. Devotion to Mary is central to the spirituality of Latin American Catholics.

A Mixed Record for the Missionaries   Despite the miracle of Guadalupe, which affirmed native peoples' dignity and faith, in sixteenth-century Latin America, the word *Christian* became equated with *Spanish* or *Portuguese*. In this situation, the missionaries found themselves with conflicting loyalties.

On the Side of the Conquerors

Parish priests in the New World served as government functionaries, working for the Spanish colonial administration. They wrote birth certificates, kept records of deaths and marriages, and often collected taxes and oversaw the church's considerable land-holdings. In some cases, religious communities and parish priests amassed sizable wealth, power, and territorial control. Such wealth and power led to some clerics' losing sight of their mission to serve God's people instead of themselves.

The first protests against enslaving native peoples in the New World came from the Dominican religious community where Bartolomé de Las Casas served, on the island of Santo Domingo. One Sunday morning in 1511, Friar António Montesino mounted the cathedral pulpit and gave a blistering sermon to the shocked and angered congregation of leading Spanish citizens. Las Casas provided this record of the event:

> [Montesino] began to speak of the sterile desert of the consciences of the Spaniards on this isle, and of the blindness in which they lived. . . .
>
> ". . . You are in mortal sin, and live and die therein by reason of the cruelty and tyranny that you practice on these innocent people. Tell me, by what right or justice do you hold these Indians in such cruel and horrible slavery? . . .
>
> "Are they not men? Do they not have rational souls? Are you not bound to love them as you love yourselves? . . . Be sure that in your present state you can no more be saved than the Moors or Turks."

According to Las Casas, none of the listeners were turned against slavery. In fact, Spanish and Portuguese settlers continued to enslave the Indians for decades to come. Friar Montesino had named the crux of the evil: most of the colonizers did not believe, or did not care to believe, that the natives were human beings. ■

Slavery Is a Sin

The missionaries were loyal Spaniards, and even though most of the missionaries wanted to serve the people, some of their policies and practices implied that the indigenous peoples were not as worthy as the Spanish. For example, in most places the Christian Indians were not given Communion. They were allowed only the sacraments of baptism, penance, and marriage, because the missionaries thought that they could understand these sacraments more easily than they could the Eucharist. Also, Indians were not ordained as priests for almost three hundred years, because the king of Spain forbade it. A native clergy having the same status as Spanish priests might have posed a threat to colonial rule.

On the Side of the Native Peoples

Despite the faults of some religious, the friars were frequently the Indians' main defenders. Bartolomé de Las Casas (1474–1566) was especially outspoken in confronting abuses by the colonizers. Since his youth, Las Casas had lived on the island of Santo Domingo (the Dominican Republic and Haiti today) as a landowner, inheriting slaves. Later he gave up his holdings and became a Dominican priest, working among the Indians he so admired. Then he was made a bishop.

Las Casas's respect for the native peoples is apparent in this description he wrote of them: "They cultivate friendship and live in life-giving ways and run their governments according to laws that are often superior to our own." As a pastor, he developed advice for missionaries that is relevant today. He wrote that the only way to draw all peoples to a living faith is the way of neighborly love and peace.

Las Casas, allied with many other friars and the Jesuits, encouraged missionaries to respect native peoples. He countered the centuries-old idea that war and violence were the way to convert people to Christianity. This Dominican bishop's documentation of atrocities by the colonizers and his courageous stance against the slavery of Indians finally caused the Spanish king to prohibit slavery.

In the 1600s, in places such as Paraguay and Brazil, the Jesuits established towns and areas like reservations for Indians. In those places the Indians could live together under Indian authority. The Jesuits set up schools, weaving projects, and communal farming. The Indian settlements were so successful that the Jesuits made enemies among the greedy colonizers. Eventually those enemies forced the Jesuits out of South America.

A Less European Church for Latin America

In the 1700s, Spanish and Portuguese power declined. British and Dutch fleets ruled the seas, and the gold and silver that had fed the initial conquests in Latin America were running low. Hundreds of monasteries and convents dotted the Latin American landscape. A large cathedral served as the focal point of most large towns. Some of the early abuses against native peoples had been eliminated. Native priests were being ordained, but they formed only a small fraction of the clergy in Latin America.

During the 1820s, Latin America threw off the yoke of Spain and Portugal. Native clergy played an active role in the revolution. Long-held grievances against the Spanish and Portuguese clergy surfaced. By 1829, almost all of the Spanish-born bishops had been forced out of Latin America. Only half of the priests and religious brothers and sisters remained. Many dioceses had no bishop, and scores of parishes had no priest. The church in Latin America was less powerful, but it tended to act more in sympathy with the peoples' needs.

The Church in Asia

India and Sri Lanka   **Converting with Respect**

When a Portuguese explorer sailed onto the shores of an island off the eastern coast of India in 1500, eight Franciscans landed with him. Soon the island was claimed as Portugal's, and the missionaries were given an Islamic mosque to use as their first church. Before long the port colony bustled with sailors, adventurers, and those who made their living off of seafarers. The few missionaries living on the island struggled among the hard-bitten seamen and had little chance to preach to the Indian population.

Francis Xavier Reaches Out

As more missionaries arrived, the situation in Asia changed. The Spanish Jesuit Francis Xavier (1506–1552), along with other Jesuits, was a driving force for the spread of the Gospel in India. After arriving on the island off the coast of India, Xavier threw himself into his ministry, cajoling the Portuguese back to the practice of their religion and teaching Indians about Christ.

After some months, Xavier started working among fishing folk on the southern coast of India. Then he moved on to Ceylon, known today as Sri Lanka. Xavier's method of instruction was gentle and enjoyable. He would gather men and women, young and old, and get them to repeat the Ten Commandments, the Lord's Prayer, and the Hail Mary in their own language, with Xavier explaining the meaning. Slowly people converted.

In 1545, Xavier left India and Ceylon for what is now Malaysia. Other missionaries had followed him to India, so by the close of the 1500s, Jesuits ministered in sixteen main villages along the coast of India. Each village had a small church and a school.

Respect for the Traditions of India

After Xavier moved on, the next important missionary figure in India was another Jesuit, Robert de Nobili. De Nobili adopted the dress and manners of a Hindu Brahman, which was the highest caste, or class, of Indian. He lived as a *sanyassi,* or holy man, wearing the distinctive robes and nothing made of leather, eating a strictly vegetarian diet, and speaking in the dialect of the people. De Nobili believed that if he lived as closely as possible to the way that a proper Indian lived, it would add to the credibility of his message.

After all, the Indian culture had ancient and sophisticated roots. By respecting Indian traditions, De Nobili hoped the Indians would listen respectfully to his beliefs about Christ.

Native Indian Clergy Carry On

De Nobili's respectful approach carried over into ordaining and educating native Indians and Ceylonese as priests who would carry on the work of the original missionary Jesuits. By the mid-1700s, the church was well established in one state of India, and scores of churches had been opened in Ceylon.

By 1900, Catholicism had spread throughout India and Sri Lanka. The prevailing religion, Hinduism, was notable for tolerating other religions, and the Catholics were not persecuted. Even so, however, Catholics remained a tiny minority in both countries.

The Vatican looked on the missionary efforts in these areas with avid interest. Beginning in 1622, the Vatican's Congregation for the Propagation of the Faith coordinated the efforts of all missionary groups in the world, and a special college in Rome trained many missionaries for their work.

Japan Steadfast Christians amid Persecution

During Francis Xavier's travels, he met and converted a young Japanese man who persuaded him to bring the Christian faith to Japan. The Japanese people, deeply suspicious of foreigners, did only limited trading with the Portuguese through the port of Nagasaki.

Street Preachers

Arriving in Japan in 1549, Xavier and his companions began their work of spreading the Gospel in a land where Buddhism and Shintoism were the predominant religions. As Xavier entered a town or village, he would ring a bell and invite the inhabitants to come and listen to the truths of Christ. Here is how one of Xavier's companions described their preaching:

We preached in the streets without any licence or permission of the King, taking up our position at crossroads where people thronged. I first read from the book in a loud voice about the creation of the world, and then . . . denounced the . . . chief sins committed by the Japanese. . . . While I harangued in this fashion, [Xavier], standing beside me, gave himself to prayer, begging God to bless my words and my listeners. . . . Some [listened] merely in order to kill time, others to have their ears tickled with novelties, and many just to make sport of us. A few showed us marks of affection and pity.

Gradually the Jesuits constructed small churches and settled in the towns on a southern island of Japan. Later, Xavier urged other Jesuits who were in India to come to Japan to continue the work that he had started. Spanish Franciscans and Dominicans also began arriving in Japan to do missionary work, and by 1582, an estimated two hundred thousand Japanese people had embraced Christianity. But disaster was about to strike.

Christians Banned and Martyred

A crew member of a Spanish ship that had wrecked off the coast of Japan bragged to the Japanese that the missionaries were just forerunners of Spanish colonial power. Dutch and English ships had started trading in Japan too, and their officers had already warned the Japanese about the colonial ambitions of Spain and Portugal.

In 1614, Japan's shogun (ruler) became so concerned that Christianity would divide his subjects' loyalty and eventually overthrow the government that he banned the foreign religion and banished all foreign missionaries. In addition, he closed the ports of Japan to all foreigners. Some of the Jesuits, friars, and secular clergy who were already in Japan went underground. But the shogun's agents systematically sought out and executed them as well as any Japanese Christians who hid the missionaries and still practiced their religion.

Over the next couple of decades, about two thousand Japanese Christians and sixty-two foreign missionaries were martyred, even though the Japanese officials offered Christians the chance to denounce Christianity rather than be killed.

Because of the repression, rebellion simmered among Japanese Christians and other Japanese citizens who suffered under the shogun's policies and the rule of a brutal governor of one region. In 1637, a revolt broke out. Christians joined angry samurai-farmers against the governor and, thus, the shogun. Eventually the rebels were besieged in a castle, where for months they held out. The government commander promised amnesty to the non-Christian rebels, many of whom then surrendered. Finally, the shogun's army took the castle, defended only by the starving Christians. Nearly thirty thousand Christian men, women, and children were put to the sword. Afterward, most people believed that Christianity had been totally destroyed in Japan. But this proved not to be so.

A Hidden Faith Kept Alive

For more than two centuries, Japan's doors remained shut to the outside world. Then, in 1853, the United States commodore Matthew Perry sailed into a bay of Japan and forced the Japanese to sign a treaty of commerce. Soon merchants and government officials from other countries were pushing Japan's doors open even wider. French missionaries started a church in Nagasaki. One Sunday in 1865, a small group of Japanese showed up at the door of the church, declaring that they were Christians.

To the astonishment of the French priests, the faith had stayed alive in Japan since the banning of Christianity in 1614. With no priests in Japan, elders had led prayers every Sunday, baptized, and ministered to the dying. The faith had been passed on from generation to generation for over two hundred years. Gradually, after the French priests opened the church, more Christians emerged from their collective silence. About ten thousand people, concentrated around Nagasaki, had clung to Christianity.

Despite a period of persecution in the 1860s, the Japanese Catholic community slowly grew. Tragically and ironically, Nagasaki, the home of steadfast Japanese Christianity, was one of the two Japanese cities that the United States attacked with nuclear weapons in 1945, at the end of the Second World War.

The Philippines   The Only Christian Country in Asia

In countries like Japan, which were not ruled by a colonial power, conversions to Christianity were limited. The Philippine Islands became a Spanish colony in the 1500s. They were the most successfully evangelized Asian country. Today the islands are still the only predominantly Christian country in Asia.

Early Spanish Missionaries: Advocates for the Philippine People

The Spanish conquerors of the 1500s brought Franciscans, Augustinians, Jesuits, and Dominicans to the Philippines. The islands, with the colonial capital at Manila, were split into regions with different religious orders in charge of each. In 1581, a Spanish Dominican was named the first bishop of the Philippines.

Even though the church was allied with the Spanish colonial powers who had come to conquer and exploit the Philippine people, the church was frequently the only protection the people had from their oppressors. The Spaniards sent parties of troops into the countryside to subdue the natives and help Spanish landowners organize their plantations, using Filipinos as slaves. The friars opposed this and even objected to Spaniards' owning land. In 1574, the friars convinced the king of Spain to prohibit slavery in the Philippines.

Even though the missionaries did not hesitate to criticize colonial abuses, these religious generally assumed that the Spanish king's authority over the Philippines was valid. After all, the pope had empowered the king to have the Gospel preached on the islands. The friars thus accepted that the king was responsible for the spiritual well-being of the Filipino people and that colonial rule was justified.

Missionaries as Bearers of Spanish Culture

With the friars came Spanish culture, and the Filipinos began taking on Spanish religious practices such as fiestas and religious dramas. As the friars moved further and further inland, they frequently were the only presence of Spain in the countryside. There, they preached and taught in the country's native languages, of which there were more than eighty. Spanish missionaries wrote the first grammars for some of these languages. In addition, the friars often helped with new agricultural techniques. Some of them opened small parish schools and clinics. And eventually, some religious orders opened colleges; although these colleges were primarily for Spaniards, Filipinos were being admitted to them by the 1700s.

After the friars converted the leaders of a town or village, the rest of the people usually followed. Then the friars tried to unite the village and create a sense of community around the church, its celebrations, re-enactments of the Passion of Christ, fiestas celebrating the town's patron saint, and the development of lay religious groups.

Danger to Missionaries

The missionaries generally were well received by the native people of the Philippines. However, the missionaries did face the danger of Muslim raiders coming from Mindanao, one of the southern islands. Jesuits working on that island were particularly at risk. A report in 1656 summarized the Jesuits' losses over a fifteen-year period: seven priests had been killed by Muslims, and others had been taken into captivity. Hostilities between Muslims and Christians in the Philippines continue even to the present.

The Issue of Native Priesthood in the Philippines

Because the Spanish king forbade the training of natives as priests, Filipinos saw the church as a foreign institution in which they would always be second-class members. Although Catholicism spread and deepened in the Philippines, the priesthood was denied to Filipinos until the 1700s. Even then, the Spaniards harbored deep reservations about a Filipino clergy. Spanish priests could be counted on to side with the Spanish government in any war or uprising; Filipino priests, on the other hand, were suspect. Nevertheless, by 1750, native priests ministered in nearly 150 parishes.

In the 1800s, under Napoleon's rule of Spain and Portugal, missionaries could not travel to the Philippines. As Spanish friars died and were not replaced, Filipino clergy assumed more control over church life on the islands. The Spanish government grew nervous that these native priests would fan the flames of Filipino nationalism.

Later, after Spain gained its independence from Napoleon, Spanish friars went back to the Philippines to resume control of major parishes. But instead of stabilizing Spanish control of the church and the country, such actions alienated Filipino priests further. Many Spanish priests found that working in parishes was nearly impossible, because parishioners greeted them with suspicion. Filipino priests did contribute to revolutionary activities. Finally, active revolution broke out, and an independent Philippine government was established.

The independence of the Philippines, however, was short-lived. The U.S. government, wanting a base in Asia, used victory in the Spanish-American War as an excuse to take over the Philippines. In 1900, American soldiers found themselves fighting a guerrilla war to snuff out Philippine independence. Thousands of Filipinos lost their life in this little-known war. Not until after World War II would the Philippines become fully independent again. Meanwhile, the American colonial rulers sought to diminish the Spanish presence there. Many Spanish clergy left the country, so the Philippines had far too few priests to minister to a people devoted to Christ and the church. In spite of these hardships, though, today the Catholic church is strong and vital in the Philippines. It is an advocate of justice for the people, most of whom live in desperate poverty.

China   A Question of Cultural Tolerance

Some Franciscan missionaries preached to the Mongols in Beijing, China, as early as the 1200s. After those missionaries died, the Gospel was not heard again in China until the 1500s, when the Chinese gave the Portuguese permission to use an island off the coast of China as a port and trading center. Soon Jesuit, Dominican, Franciscan, and Augustinian missionaries arrived on the island, hoping for entrance to China. Their hoping was to no avail, however. The Chinese hesitated to invite what they saw as foreign intrusion.

Entry to China Through Knowledge and Friendship

Missionaries were not able to make any inroads into China until the Italian Jesuit Matteo Ricci (1552–1610) gained entry into China's imperial court. Ricci's knowledge of astronomy and other sciences provided a way in. He brought European clocks as gifts for the emperor. When these clocks needed repairs, the Chinese had to depend on Ricci. Before long, he became well known in royal circles and began slowly to talk about his religion to the Chinese, whose predominant religion was Confucianism.

Ricci spoke fluent Chinese and dressed as Chinese people did; he respected Chinese civilization and traditions and tried to show how Christianity complemented those traditions. Ricci translated Western books on mathematics and science into Chinese and wrote books about Christianity in terms that were appealing to Chinese scholars. By 1605, two hundred converts to Christianity had been made in Beijing, and Jesuit missionaries worked in three other cities.

Two Approaches to Chinese Culture

Ricci's respect for Chinese culture was wise. The culture was highly sophisticated, in many ways far more advanced than any culture in Europe. This presented immense challenges for any missionary effort. To the Chinese, an acceptance of Christianity seemed to be an acceptance of Western culture, which they looked upon as inferior to their own. And because the missionaries were involved with foreign governments that were clamoring for favorable trade agreements, the Chinese saw the missionaries as foreign agents.

In addition, the missionary approach taken by the Spanish friars—Dominicans, Franciscans, and Augustinians—conflicted sharply with the tolerant approach taken by Ricci and the Jesuits. The Spanish friars tried to get the local people to reject Chinese customs and give up the Chinese language in worship. The Jesuit missionaries, on the other hand, tried to live as the local people did and to use the language of those with whom they worked. For instance, by 1660, the Jesuits in China were saying Mass in Chinese, not Latin—to the Spanish friars' dismay. Conflicts between the missionary groups would prove disastrous.

Trouble over the Jesuit Approach

By 1652, in spite of periods of Chinese hostility against the missionaries, 150,000 Chinese people called themselves Christian. Over succeeding years, Christians increased in some places and suffered persecution in others. The Chinese imperial court suspected that Christianity would cause disunity and political turmoil. But the Jesuits' services to the emperors gave some protection to Christians. In 1692, a Jesuit gave quinine to the emperor, who was nearly dead from malaria. Out of gratitude for his recovery, the emperor issued an edict tolerating Christianity, and the Jesuits' work continued. Among their contributions to Chinese learning, the Jesuits made the first accurate maps of China. But change was coming from the direction of Rome. The source of the trouble was the Jesuits' method of ministry.

At first the Congregation for the Propagation of the Faith endorsed the Jesuits' approach of openness to Chinese culture. However, the Spanish friars could not accept the practice of saying the

Mass in any language but Latin, and they raised objections with various popes. Finally, in 1704, the pope sided with the Spanish friars, banning the Chinese-language Mass and approving the notion that native people in missionary lands should adopt Western customs along with Christian faith.

That decision had far-reaching effects, but the immediate effect was that the emperor outlawed all Christian missionary work and threw most of the missionaries out of China. Understandably, the emperor found the pope's decision to be an insult to Chinese culture. For generations the Chinese had suspected that the missionaries wanted to subject China to the West. The pope's decision seemed to confirm their suspicions. Chinese Catholics felt abandoned by the church; they were persecuted by the Chinese government, and some who did not renounce their Christian faith were executed as traitors.

Later Developments for Chinese Christians

China opened up again in the mid-1800s, forced by Western governments to trade with the West. As a result, both Protestant and Catholic missionaries rushed to this huge field of work. They set up clinics, schools, churches, and orphanages all over China. Among the new flood of Catholic missionaries were communities of women, such as the Daughters of Charity. By the end of the 1800s, nearly a half-million Chinese had been baptized into the church. Besides the missionaries, more than four hundred Chinese priests and hundreds of Chinese religious sisters served the people.

Under the leadership of the People's Republic of China, which has been the communist-led government of China since 1949, religious activity other than that by state-approved organizations has been suppressed. Thus, a Catholic church exists in China today, but its bishops are appointed by the government, so it is not in union with the Roman Catholic church. There is a small underground Roman Catholic church, whose members' identity and worship are hidden from the authorities.

Southeast Asia   **The French Influence**

During the 1600s, the French Jesuit Alexandre de Rhodes worked in Southeast Asia, where Buddhism was predominant. His greatest successes were in Vietnam. De Rhodes put the Vietnamese language into a written form, translated religious materials into Vietnamese, and trained catechists. His catechists also learned simple medical treatments. Thus they spread the word of God and served God's people. De Rhodes and other Jesuits also established a seminary in Thailand.

Christianity spread slowly in Southeast Asia and remained a minority religion. In the early 1800s, Vietnamese emperors submitted Catholics to two periods of persecution. When another outbreak of persecution began in 1862, Napoleon III sent the French army to Vietnam. He used the persecution as an excuse to colonize Vietnam and occupy Laos and Cambodia. Once again, although Catholicism spread, it became identified with European colonial power. Nevertheless, by the start of the twentieth century, there were over a million Vietnamese Catholics. Many Catholics fled that country after all of Vietnam came under communist control in 1975.

The Church in Africa

Christianity took root in African soil in the early centuries of the church. Many of the great theologians and saints of the early church came from Egypt, in northeastern Africa. Monks like Antony of Egypt inhabited the wild places, communing with God. Augustine came from North Africa. However, as Islam swept across North Africa in the seventh and eighth centuries, it replaced Christianity as the major religion there. South of the Sahara Desert, native peoples did not see Christian preachers until the 1600s.

Early Missionary Efforts As Portuguese mariners explored the western coast of Africa in the 1500s, they established small settlements. Soon missionaries followed. A branch of Franciscan friars known as Capuchins started preaching in the settlements, including what is now Angola. Between 1645 and 1700, the missionaries baptized an estimated six hundred thousand Africans.

The large number of converts, though, was not necessarily an indication of a deep commitment to Christianity on the part of those who were baptized. The people merely followed their leader to baptism. Likewise, if a leader rejected Christianity sometime after being baptized, the people would throw it off also. In addition, the friars did not have the resources to provide even a minimum education in the faith.

Mozambique, on the eastern coast of Africa, was an area of significant missionary activity. By 1624, Portuguese Jesuits had established twenty mission stations in the countryside. The Dominicans and Augustinians opened houses too. Like the peoples of Latin America and Asia, the Africans often resisted the missionaries' efforts. The Africans thought, with good reason, that accepting Christianity would indicate that they also accepted Portuguese colonial rule.

Into the Heart of Africa   The rest of Africa did not hear the Gospel until the 1800s. For one thing, no accurate maps of Africa existed, and the Europeans had virtually no knowledge of the languages, customs, values, and history of the continent. Among the first Europeans to enter the heart of Africa were missionaries—both Protestant and Catholic. Perhaps the most notable figure in opening the interior of Africa to missionaries was the Scottish Protestant missionary David Livingstone, who charted courses into the continent in the mid-1800s. Other Protestant and Catholic missionaries followed, as did colonial powers: the French, the British, the Germans, the Belgians—all wanting a share of Africa's richness.

Many new missionary orders were founded, with most sending missionaries into Africa. Among them were the Sisters of Saint Joseph of Cluny, the Missionaries of Africa (which came to be known as the White Fathers), the Society of the Divine Word, and the Maryknoll Missioners. These and dozens of other communities went to preach, teach, heal, and minister in Africa.

The Persistence of Slavery   The missionaries faced many difficulties in Africa. One of the most persistent problems was slavery. From about 1600 to the mid-1800s, millions of Africans were sold into slavery by European and American slave-traders. Slave ships sailed from the coast of Africa to the New World and to Islamic countries in the Middle East. By 1800, ten to fifteen million blacks had been transported to the Americas; millions more had died on the way. Even up to the year 1900, Arab slavetraders raided mission stations, killing missionaries and anyone else who opposed their taking Africans into slavery. The colonial governments forbade slavery in 1850, but they were unable to stop it for decades.

The Catholic missionaries fought slavery as well as they could. They sometimes bought people out of slavery, instructed them, and then gathered them into Christian settlements. Also, missionaries sheltered children who were left behind when their parents were captured into slavery. When the children grew old enough, a group of them, under the supervision of a catechist, would be sent to a village. There they would raise their own food, take care of other abandoned children, and teach local people new agricultural methods.

Rivalry Among the Missionaries   Other difficulties facing the missionaries often arose from within their own ranks. Nationalism was vexing. French priests did not agree with Dutch or British missionaries. Added to this were the conflicts between Catholic and Protestant missionaries.

Sometimes Catholic and Protestant missionaries were working in the same town, and relations between them were not often cordial. Such antagonism between groups who professed belief in the same God confused the non-Christian Africans. Some African rulers took advantage of the divisions among Christians. In Uganda during the late 1800s, the king played one missionary and national group against the other: the Anglican missionaries were British, and the Catholic missionaries were French. Finally, the next king of Uganda turned against both groups, expelling the missionaries and burning alive twenty-two Ugandan Catholics and eleven Ugandan Protestants.

Despite times of persecution, inter-religious fighting, natural dangers, and colonial interference, the church grew steadily throughout sub-Saharan Africa. As in Latin America and Asia, the orders only slowly opened to recruiting natives as priests and members of religious orders. Phenomenal gains were made in the twentieth century, so today more Catholics live in Africa than in North America. Africa is now the fastest-growing part of the worldwide church.

The Church in Australia

When a flotilla of ships sailed into what would be called Sydney Harbor, the first Christians arrived in Australia. The year was 1788, and the first Christians were 750 British and Irish convicts and their overseers. With the independence of the United States, Britain had nowhere to send the criminals and political prisoners it wanted to be rid of. Captain James Cook's discovery of Australia in 1770 came at the right time to provide a distant colony for these undesirables.

Missionary work, minimal as it was, focused on the convict population in the beginning. Later it extended to new nonconvict immigrants. Missionaries did not reach out to the native peoples of Australia until much later.

Minimal Pastoring for Prisoners In the early years of the British in Australia, the Catholic convicts went without the sacraments; the public practice of Catholicism was forbidden, as it was in England and Ireland. Then, in 1803, an Irish convict who was a priest celebrated the first Mass in Australia. Between 1803 and 1810, three convict priests worked among the prisoners. However, when they left Australia at the end of their sentences, ten years elapsed before another Catholic priest was allowed to minister in Australia.

Starting in 1815, a steady flow of Irish political prisoners disembarked in chains from ships in Australian ports. The authorities sent them to work in convict factories or on chain gangs, dispersing them so that they could not organize. The British condemned the most desperate or rebellious men to Norfolk Island, off the coast. About one-third of the men sent there were Irish Catholics, and a large proportion of them died from floggings, malnourishment, madness, or hanging—most often without the consolation of the sacraments.

In 1819, a French ship docked at Australia. For the weeks it stayed in port, its Catholic chaplain stayed constantly busy baptizing, performing marriages, saying Mass, and hearing confessions. Finally, in 1820, the first permanent Catholic chaplain arrived in Australia. Others soon followed, although the number of priests would remain insufficient for years to come.

The Growth of Australian Church Institutions

By the 1840s, the majority of Australians were free immigrants who had come to escape the slums or the landlessness of England or Ireland. The immigration of free settlers and their children spurred Catholics and Protestants to establish their own schools. In a few years, a steady stream of sisters, brothers, and priests arrived to serve the Catholics. The Irish Sisters of Charity ministered to the female convicts who worked at forced labor in government factories. In later years, religious orders set up an extensive network of schools, clinics, orphanages, and parishes. All of these institutions were needed as the population swelled with a gold rush in the 1850s. People called "diggers" poured in from Europe, China, and the Americas.

When the gold rush subsided, former diggers supplied the labor force that built the country. The need for convict labor subsided. Partly due to testimony from the Catholic bishop, the British government moved toward abolishing the transportation of convicts to Australia. The last convict ship unloaded sixty Irish political prisoners in 1868. By 1900, a large percentage of Australians were Catholic.

Conclusion

Between 1500 and 1900, Catholicism extended beyond Europe to the Americas, Asia, Africa, and Australia. Typically, the missionaries followed explorers and conquerors, although in most of the Asian countries that was not the case.

Being linked with European conquerors often caused problems for the church and decreased the possibility that genuine conversions would happen. While receiving the protection and financial support of one of the European governments, the church in a foreign land usually became a representative of the colonial power, with all the negatives that entailed.

In spite of colonial power overlaying missionary work, many missionaries exerted a restraining influence on the colonizers, advocating for the native peoples' rights. Many of the missionaries brought significant improvements to the peoples' lives in the areas of education, health care, and nutrition. Some of the clergy were wise enough to recognize that they needed to understand and appreciate the local culture rather than try to substitute European culture for what was likely an advanced foreign civilization. Of course, many missionaries erred on the side of imposing their own culture on others. But in evaluating that behavior, we need to remember that few people in those days, religious or otherwise, had any ability to see beyond their own cultural perspective.

The missionaries of the sixteenth to nineteenth centuries were a varied group. Some were heroic saints filled with love for the people they served. Some were guilty of reinforcing colonial control, or at least of being insensitive to the cultures and peoples they came to serve. None were perfect, just as the church is not perfect. But the church and humanity owe a great debt to the men and women who bravely went beyond the relatively secure life they knew and faced uncertainty, discomfort, and even death to spread the Gospel of Jesus Christ to the world.

Even as missionaries of the early colonial period were attempting to win souls for Christ, the scene back in Europe was increasingly hostile toward the church. The forces of revolution were gathering strength, and the church was part of the "old guard" that would be thrown off.

Questions for Reflection and Discussion

1. Today's Catholic missionaries have abandoned the practice of requiring people to shun their culture to become Christians. How does the Good News of Jesus Christ transcend any one culture, and how does each culture bring its own richness into Christianity?
2. How is the appearance of Our Lady to Juan Diego still celebrated, and why is Our Lady of Guadalupe still so important in Latin American spirituality?
3. Despite the protestations of people like Las Casas, many clerics actively supported Spanish or Portuguese oppression of native peoples. Cozy relationships still exist in some places between the Catholic hierarchy and the ruling elite, even when the elite perpetrate suppression of basic human rights. Should church officials ever tolerate violations of human rights? Would Christ remain silent in the face of abuses?

12

The Age of "Isms"

Revolutionary Thinking Confronts the Church

AS SEEN IN chapter 11, after the Protestant and Catholic reformations, Catholic missionaries bravely tried to spread the faith beyond Europe. Back in Europe, however, religious persecution and war raged throughout most of the 1600s. That strife created the chaos, misery, and poverty that would form a back-drop for the revolutionary "isms" of the 1700s and 1800s—"isms" such as rationalism, empiricism, skepticism, individualism, secularism, nationalism, capitalism, Marxism, and Darwinism. In these very powerful "isms," the Catholic church, still recovering from the struggles of the Reformation era, faced intellectual and political movements that at times appeared to threaten the church's fundamentals, and even its existence.

Religious Strife and War: Buildup to the "Isms"

Religious differences mixed with political ambitions made Europe a battleground in the 1600s. Protestant countries fought Catholic countries, and Catholics fought non-Catholics within the same country.

England: Persecuting the "Papists"

In England, where the king or queen headed the Anglican church, to practice Catholicism was considered treason. The crown threw all Catholic priests out of the country and enacted harsh laws against "papists," as Catholics were derisively labeled for their loyalty to the pope. When the Gunpowder Plot—an attempt by Catholic fanatics to blow up the king and Parliament—was uncovered in 1605, the monarchy's reaction was swift and brutal: some Catholics were executed; others fled for their life. Catholics who stayed and wanted to avoid execution were forced to take an oath renouncing the pope. To keep the faith alive, Catholic priests were smuggled back into England to minister to Catholics. But even "safe houses" with hiding places could not protect some of these priests from being discovered, tortured, and executed.

A Devastating War

By 1648, the bloody Thirty Years' War, fought over religion and territorial control in Europe, had swept across the continent, leaving dead six million people out of a population of sixteen million. The devastating impact of the war was similar to the impact of the bubonic plague, or Black Death, in the Middle Ages. In the aftermath of the long war, religious lines were

Timeline . . .

1600
- Gunpowder Plot spurs persecution of Catholics in England.
- Thirty Years' War begins.
- Daughters of Charity founded.
- Church brands Galileo's theories heretical.
- Peace of Westphalia ends Thirty Years' War.
- King Louis XIV promotes religious nationalism.

1700
- Christian Brothers founded.

- Rousseau challenges monarchical power with notion of social contract; rationalist philosophies emerge.
- French Revolution begins, Reign of Terror follows.

1800
- France united.
- Catholics granted freedom of religion in England.
- Revolution in Italy.
- Marx publishes *Communist Manifesto*.
- Newman links scholarship and faith.
- Darwin publishes *Origin of Species*.
- Vatican I upholds papal infallibility.
- Bismarck initiates Kulturkampf.

1900
- *Rerum Novarum* promotes social justice.

sharply drawn in Europe: Scandinavia, Prussia, and parts of southern Germany were Lutheran. Switzerland, much of Holland, and Scotland were Calvinist. England had its own church. All the rest of Europe was predominantly Catholic. The Peace of Westphalia, of 1648, largely ended the religious warring among nations.

In 1628, Johannes Junius, a Catholic layman, was charged with practicing witchcraft in Bamberg, Germany. When he denied the charges, the authorities tortured him, but they got no confession from him. The torturer then prepared to use more horrible methods. Junius, knowing that the officials would execute him whether he confessed or not, finally wrote out a confession in order to avoid further torture. He recounted meetings with the devil, curses on people, animal sacrifices at witches' sabbaths, and so on. Under threat, six people witnessed against him. Soon after, Junius was burned at the stake, probably an innocent victim.

In the midst of his tortures, Junius wrote a letter that was secretly carried out of prison to his daughter:

> Many hundred thousand good nights, dearly beloved daughter Veronica. Innocent have I come into prison, innocent have I been tortured, innocent must I die. For whoever comes into the witch prison must become a witch or be tortured until he invents something out of his head—and God pity him—bethinks him of something. . . .
>
> [After sessions of torture,] when at last the executioner led me back into the prison, he said to me: "Sir, I beg you, for God's sake confess something, whether it be true or not. Invent something, for you cannot endure the torture which you will be put to. . . ."
>
> And so I begged . . . to be given one day for thought and a priest. The priest was refused me, but the time for thought was given. . . . And so I made my confession [of witchcraft to the authorities]; but it was all a lie. . . .
>
> . . . Dear child, pay this man [who brought you the letter] a dollar. . . . I have taken several days to write this: my hands are both lame. I am in a sad plight.
>
> Good night, for your father Johannes Junius will never see you more. July 24, 1628. ■

Accused of Witchcraft

Mutual Intolerance

Within nations, religious persecution continued. For example, in France, the Huguenots (French Calvinists) were hounded by Catholic officials; campaigns destroyed Calvinist strongholds. As the 1600s came to an end, harsh acts by government officials against dissenting religions declined, but restrictive laws stayed on the books. Catholics were denied certain rights in Protestant countries, and Protestants were treated as second-class citizens in Catholic countries.

Witch-Hunts

In this seventeenth-century period of religious strife, both Protestants and Catholics commonly launched campaigns to accuse and persecute supposed witches, or persons thought to be the "devil's servants." Given the intensity of death and suffering in Europe, people were glad to find scapegoats to blame for their misery, which seemed to be the devil's doing. Many of the suspected witches were merely unique, or even just odd, persons. Single women proved to be easy marks for accusation. Sometimes officials settled old scores by targeting personal or political enemies and labeling them as practitioners of witchcraft. In the 1600s and 1700s, many innocent people in countries from England to Italy fell victim to people's irrational fears and were executed.

New Styles of Religious Life: A Response to Poverty and Misery

As war and religious strife created poverty and misery, Catholic men and women were fashioning new styles of religious life that would respond compassionately to the great level of human need. Religious orders were founded to serve the poor, the sick, the ignorant, and the homeless—and also to instruct them in the word of God.

The Vincentians and the Daughters of Charity

Ministering with the Poor

One innovative founder of religious orders was Vincent de Paul (1581–1660). Although born of peasant parents in France, he was sent by a rich patron to the seminary and was ordained at age twenty. On a boat trip from Marseilles to another part of France, he was captured by pirates and sold as a slave to a European farmer (an ex-monk who had left the faith) in Algeria, Africa. After converting his master back to Christianity, Vincent de Paul made his way back to France.

For a time he served as chaplain to the French queen, but then he removed himself from the dazzle of the French court to become the pastor of a small country parish. That was where his heart was. Yet he was frustrated that he could not respond to the immense needs of the large poor population in seventeenth-century France. So Vincent de Paul organized the Ladies of Charity, a group of wealthy laywomen who volunteered to feed the hungry and care for the sick.

By 1627, groups of Ladies of Charity had been set up in dozens of French parishes. Vincent also established the Congregation of the Mission, later known as the Vincentians. This band of priests and brothers walked through the countryside teaching and preaching to ordinary folk. So successful were Vincent de Paul's missionaries that the bishops asked him to open a seminary to train diocesan priests.

Supervising the work of the Ladies of Charity was too big a job for Vincent de Paul to do alone. Fortunately a young widow and mother, Louise de Marillac, began helping Vincent and soon directed the spreading movement. She realized that service to poor people was essential to the church's mission. Knowing that volunteers like the Ladies of Charity needed support from full-time sisters, Louise de Marillac took several women into her home, formed a community, and established the religious order called the Daughters of Charity.

The new group of sisters was revolutionary. Up to that point, women religious had been required to live in cloistered, or closed, convents. In other words, they had been hidden from the world. Some women's communities, such as the Ursuline Sisters and the Visitation Sisters, provided schools for girls, but they did so as nuns, within the confines of their convents. Sisters were not allowed to serve as teachers or welfare workers "out in the world."

To get around these restrictions, the Daughters of Charity took private religious vows for one year at a time instead of taking permanent vows as nuns. They went out in the streets among the poor people, and they wore the style of dress of French peasant women. Many of the sisters themselves were peasants, and those they served were too. Soon the Daughters of Charity ran hospitals, hospices, orphanages, and schools. Some of the sisters even ministered to galley slaves when the ships that the slaves were forced to row came into port. With their idealism and compassion, the sisters' numbers increased rapidly.

The spirit of the Daughters of Charity was summarized in this comment by Vincent de Paul: "The love of the Daughters of Charity is not only tender; it is effective, because they serve effectively the poor . . . [giving] oneself to God in order to serve Him in the person of the poor." The Daughters of Charity charted a new course of service for women in the church. Eventually other new congregations of women were founded along similar lines as the Daughters.

The De La Salle Christian Brothers

Teaching the Poor

Another significant development in seventeenth-century religious life was the founding of the first teaching order composed completely of religious brothers. John Baptist de La Salle (1651–1719), a priest at the cathedral of Reims, France, became involved in the educational work with poor boys that was being done by two dedicated friends of his. Like Louise de Marillac, De La Salle realized that to continue such essential work, a group of religious with a common rule of life and proper training was needed. Like Marillac, De La Salle initially formed a home community of religious. These schoolmasters eventually became known as the Brothers of the Christian Schools or the De La Salle Christian Brothers.

In the 1600s, only the rich could afford to educate their children. What De La Salle wanted to do—teach poor children—was revolutionary. His belief was that if poor children were given a practical education, they could better support themselves and their families and climb out of the poverty that spawned so much crime and despair. While receiving an education, the children could also learn religion.

To reach poor children, De La Salle developed much of the methodology that has since become standard in schools worldwide. Before his innovations, students were taught, for the most part, one at a time by tutors; this was practical only for the rich and the few. To accommodate the masses of poor children, De La Salle created classrooms with rows of students. A fixed daily schedule of a variety of courses was required in his schools, and all subjects were taught in the language of the students. (Previously, students had been taught in Latin.) De La Salle also created commercial or business courses, which had not been offered before. Today, De La Salle is considered one of the founders of modern education.

De La Salle told his teachers that they should look at their students in this way:

Consider that it is only too common for the working class and the poor to allow their children to live on their own, roaming all over as if they had no home, until they are able to be put to some work. These parents have no concern to send their children to school because they are too poor to pay teachers, or else they have to go out to look for work and leave their children to fend for themselves.

. . . These unfortunate children . . . have great difficulty when it comes time for them to go to work. In addition, through association with bad companions they learn to commit many sins which later on are very difficult to stop, the bad habits having been contracted over so long a period of time.

God has had the goodness to remedy so great a misfortune by the establishment of the Christian Schools. . . . (Page 50)

. . . Your zeal for the children . . . will only become perfect if you practise yourself what you are teaching them. Example makes a much greater impression on the mind and heart than words. (De La Salle, *Meditations for the Time of Retreat,* page 80)

If you show the firmness of a father in withdrawing [the children] from evil, you should also show the tenderness of a mother in gathering them together, and in doing them all the good in your power. (Battersby, editor, *De La Salle: Meditations,* page 400)

With the founding of the new religious orders, the revival of the church took a great step forward. Although various high-level church officials still involved themselves in the political intrigues of the courts of Europe, hundreds of devoted laypeople as well as women and men religious renewed the church's commitment to service.

The Rise of Rationalist and Scientific Thought

As Europe struggled to recover from the damage done by war and religious persecution in the seventeenth century, a new attitude toward life was beginning to take shape. This attitude countered the traditional beliefs of Christianity and presented the church with a great challenge, at times threatening its very existence. The Age of Reason, or the Enlightenment, was beginning.

Rationalism   **A Universe Without a God**

The philosophy called rationalism held that the universe was regulated completely and reasonably by universal natural laws that could be explained by science. These laws could, in turn, be applied to human behavior. According to the rationalist perspective, people did not need the Bible and religious authority as sources of truth. Even the rationalist philosophers who reasoned that God did exist said that God had created the world but then had abandoned it; after being abandoned, the world simply followed universal laws without God's involvement.

Rationalists were very skeptical of the notion of a personal God who was revealed in Jesus. According to their way of thinking, such a God would have been an interference in the natural order of the universe. The rationalist philosophers who believed in a God that was distant and removed from the world were called deists. Among the deists were the American statesman Benjamin Franklin and the French philosopher and writer Jean-Jacques Rousseau.

Empiricism and the Scientific Attitude

Knowledge Through the Senses

A philosophy related to rationalism that also challenged religion was empiricism. Its proponents were convinced that all knowledge came solely through the senses or experience; that is, they believed that what people saw, heard, tasted, touched, and smelled provided the only basis for knowledge. Religious revelation, which is central to Christian faith, was irrelevant to these philosophers as a source of knowledge. British empiricists such as John Locke tried to show that some Christian teachings were correct only because they could be proven by human experience. For example, the existence of an intelligent God as creator of the world could be proven by observing the obvious order and intelligence built into the universe. But other empiricists, such as David Hume, used their philosophy to try to prove that God could not exist. A new mood, one of doubt and skepticism, arose in intellectual circles.

What gave empiricism great force in the 1700s was the growing field of empirical science, represented by great persons such as the English physicist Sir Isaac Newton. Newton himself did not believe that scientific truth was at odds with religious truth. But philosophers like Hume tried to use Newton's findings in physics to prove that the universe was guided by universal laws that had nothing to do with a divine being.

Are Science and Religion Compatible?

Up to the 1700s, the Catholic church had had a rocky relationship with the new field of scientific inquiry. That history, which involved the condemnation of Galileo, made it hard for the church to ward off the skepticism about religion that was afoot in society.

Back in the seventeenth century, the Italian astronomer Galileo Galilei, like the Polish astronomer Copernicus before him, had held that the earth travels around the sun, rather than the sun around the earth. In Galileo's time, however, people thought just the opposite: it was "common sense" that the earth was the center of the universe and that heavenly bodies such as the sun traveled around the earth. The ancient Greek philosophers had assumed this, and the notion seemed to be confirmed by the Creation account in the Bible. Unfortunately, the church condemned Galileo's findings as heretical. But Galileo's dedication to scientific truth never shook his faith in God, in the truths of the Bible, or even in the church that condemned him. He, like Isaac Newton, saw the discoveries of science as compatible with religion, not as contradicted by religious truth.

In 1992, on the 350th anniversary of Galileo's death, Pope John Paul II expressed regret for the church's error in condemning Galileo centuries before. The pope said the "sad misunderstanding" that there is a "fundamental opposition between science and faith" is a thing of the past.

Yet in the seventeenth and eighteenth centuries, science did seem incompatible with religion to those who had a limited understanding of both. Rather than contributing to a sense of wonder at God's creation, as science and scientific inquiry did for Galileo and Newton, the scientific attitude seemed to erode many people's belief in God. In an enthusiasm for science and rationalism, most philosophers of the Enlightenment tried to ease God out of the picture.

One offshoot of rationalism and empiricism was the movement called Freemasonry. The Freemasons, who were secretive bands of deists, believed in doing good works out of purely human motives. They opposed monarchies as well as the Catholic church. As time went on, this movement became a powerful force in reshaping Europe and the Americas.

Individualism, Secularism, and Nationalism: Revolution in the Making

Toward Shaking Off the Monarchies Naturally an emphasis on reason, and on arriving at truth through the senses rather than through religious revelation, affected the way people thought about government as well as religion and science. If all persons could reason to the truth, it followed that individuals were capable of directing their own destiny. Also, if God were nonexistent or at least uninvolved in the world, kings and queens could not claim that they held power through divine right, a right to rule given to them by God.

In another challenge to monarchical power, the French philosopher Jean-Jacques Rousseau held that society should be based on a genuine social contract, by which persons voluntarily surrender some of their individual freedoms in order to gain political liberty and the right to govern themselves as a society. Rousseau said that government, to be moral, must rest on the rational consent of the governed; it must uphold individual political rights. This notion of a republic ruled by the consent of its members was revolutionary, especially in countries headed by absolute monarchs. Such an idea threatened to turn traditional society upside down, as indeed it eventually did.

The Church Before the monarchies came tumbling down, the
Under Attack authority of the Catholic church came under attack.

In the 1600s, the French king urged religious nationalism—that is, that the French church rule itself through its own king-appointed bishops, instead of obeying the pope. The king even invaded the papal province of Avignon and threatened the Papal States in Italy. Although the papacy resisted the king's scheme, his moves signaled a more independent attitude on the part of nations with respect to the church in Rome.

The beginning of religious nationalism, along with the growth of rationalism and empiricism, illustrates the vulnerable position of the church in the 1600s and 1700s. Secularism, the exclusion of religious meaning or considerations from the affairs of life, was also beginning to take hold in people's mind and heart. This exclusion could be seen in the increasing trend to separate the church from the state and to make the church subservient to the state, even oppressed by it.

France Becomes The Age of Reason—an era that developed notions
a Secular Nation like the social contract and the rights of the individual—evolved into the Age of Revolution. The most drastic revolution occurred in France. For centuries the French peasants had teetered between poverty and outright destitution. Meanwhile, the small minority of nobles had lived in almost unimaginable wealth, with the clergy's approval and support. True, outstanding church figures like Vincent de Paul, Louise de Marillac, and John Baptist de La Salle dedicated their life to serving the poor. But the majority of the French clergy were loyal to and subservient to the monarchy. Those clergy depended on the nobles for positions and gifts. Furthermore, the monarchs' oppressive rule was still justified by "divine right," so religion seemed to have a hand in the oppression.

By the 1780s, discontent among the masses of French common people hit the boiling point. A national assembly passed reforms that radically curtailed the church's power and wealth as well as its authority over bishops and clergy. Yet even as the assembly argued over peaceful reforms, the storm of violent revolution was gathering.

From Revolution to Reign of Terror

In July 1789, a mob attacked the Bastille, which was a terrible prison in Paris that symbolized everything the people hated about the monarchy. This began the French Revolution, a movement whose program was "liberty, equality, fraternity." (Some of the same ideals and philosophies had inspired the American Revolution.)

The French national assembly continued to meet and became more radical. Along with all aristocrats, priests who refused to pledge their support to the Revolution were declared disloyal. Around forty thousand priests were hounded into exile. The death penalty was decreed for any exiled priest who returned to France. In 1792, French revolutionaries butchered over a thousand priests in the September Massacres. Finally, in January 1793, King Louis XVI was beheaded. The two-year Reign of Terror had begun.

Seeking to wipe out all opposition, the revolutionary "Committee for Public Safety" executed nearly thirty thousand people, among them many priests, sisters, and brothers. At one point, the leaders enthroned a woman, a stage dancer, as the "Goddess of Reason" in the Cathedral of Notre Dame in Paris. They implemented a new calendar that removed all Christian feast days. The revolutionaries declared a new religion, with belief in one Supreme Being; one dogma, or doctrine (the immortality of the soul); and one moral principle (to do one's duty).

The most bloodthirsty revolutionary leaders eventually killed one another off, and France fell into further chaos. Armies from neighboring countries, whose leaders were worried about the Revolution spreading, marched on France, at one point entering Paris itself.

Napoleon Versus the Church

Out of all the turmoil, one man, Napoleon Bonaparte, emerged to lead France. Napoleon restored order to France in 1795, at the price of a military rule that soon turned its gaze outward. In a few short years, Napoleon had conquered Western Europe and was threatening Russia. One of the prizes Napoleon had taken was Rome. Before long, he began acting as if he owned the church and the papacy.

In 1804, Napoleon ordered Pope Pius VII to come to Paris to crown him as emperor. At the ceremony, Napoleon instead crowned himself, thus publicly insulting the pope. In the next few years, Napoleon declared the Papal States to be the property of France, and he imprisoned the pope, mostly in solitary confinement, for six years. Pius's serene courage and his determination not to yield in matters of principle gained new respect for the church and the papacy.

By 1814, Napoleon was defeated by the combined forces of the other European nations. A limited form of the French monarchy was restored; the pope was given back rule over the Papal States; priests returned to their posts; and other Catholic institutions tried to begin anew. Having become a secular nation, France allowed freedom of religion. The church carried on its work in France, but its wealth and political power were gone. Nevertheless, the country's religious institutions multiplied, and thousands of French missionaries traveled to every part of the world.

Italy Unites The End of the Papal States

The Papal States, which had been placed back into the church's hands, did not stay with the church for long. Another revolution, this time in Italy, was in the making, and it would bring the church's territorial rule to an end.

For centuries Italy had been divided into small domains, called duchies, ruled by rival families. Finally a movement for a united Italy gained momentum. An army with Giuseppe Garibaldi at its head began uniting the peninsula. In 1848, Pope Pius IX had to escape from Rome, where a republic had been declared. The declaration of a republic, in effect, negated the Papal States as a sovereign state.

Pius IX saw the move toward reform and democracy as antichurch and antireligion, partly because many of the revolutionary leaders were Freemasons, who were opposed to the church. The pope refused to give up the Papal States. Popes had ruled those lands for eleven centuries, deriving from them income for church administration. Without the lands, the pope feared, he and future popes would be captive to a hostile Italian republic.

Despite the pope's opposition, a unified Italy was an ideal whose time had come. Nationalism triumphed. In 1861, with Italy newly united under a king, the pope's claim to the Papal States was no longer recognized. Pius IX called himself a "prisoner of the Vatican." In protest, no pope would set foot on Italian soil, staying within the Vatican from 1870 to 1929. The year 1870 signified the end of worldly power for the church of Rome.

More Nationalist Anticlerical Republics in Spain
Movements

Nationalism and secularism were gaining ground across the European continent in the nineteenth century. Off and on throughout the nineteenth century, republics that opposed the influence of the clergy replaced monarchies in Spain. Most of these republics were led by Freemasons. The church in Spain was suppressed, and some priests were executed. The republics closed seminaries and confiscated church property.

Why were the republics so antichurch? As in France and Italy, the church in Spain was often seen as rich and powerful, protected and courted by kings and queens. In addition, bitter memories remained of the Spanish Inquisition, when the nobility had used the church to crush political opposition. The pope was looked upon more as a foreign ruler than as a spiritual leader.

Anti-Catholic Pride in Germany

The church ran into difficulty in Germany as well. Otto von Bismarck, whose goal was to unite all the small German states into one Germany and make it a world power, created the German Empire in 1871, partly through war with France.

In order to unite Germany culturally as well as politically, Bismarck promoted the Kulturkampf ("culture struggle"), which was a campaign to take pride in all that was German. Bismarck saw the Catholic church as foreign. Laws restricting Catholic bishops, clergy, and schools controlled the church for fifteen years. One result was that many German priests, sisters, and brothers emigrated to the Americas to be missionaries.

Freedom for the Church in England and Ireland Ironically, while the church was suffering in countries that had remained Catholic after the Protestant Reformation, Catholicism was gaining some measure of respect in England. (Recall that Henry VIII had made the Church of England the state church in the 1500s.) Through the Emancipation Act of 1829, Catholics in England and Ireland, the latter of which was ruled by England, were finally free to practice their religion and were given complete civil rights. Rapidly the Catholic church re-emerged and became active.

One Englishman who took Catholicism seriously was John Henry Newman, an Anglican priest and leader of a renewal in the Anglican church. Newman was drawn to the Catholic church because it had historical roots leading back to the Apostles. In 1845, he converted to Catholicism and became a Catholic priest. His writings about his decision to convert and about the intellectual life made him a renowned figure worldwide, and he was honored by being made a cardinal.

Newman is well known for arguing that free intellectual inquiry and a liberal arts education are not only compatible with Catholic faith but are encouraged by it. For him, reason and faith were not at odds. In a church that was increasingly defensive and reactive against the world and modern culture, Newman's assertion was a breath of fresh air. It affirmed the deep respect for intellectual inquiry and for learning that had been so much a part of the church's heritage, going back to the ancient monastery schools and the great medieval universities. Many of today's Catholic liberal arts colleges and universities were founded with inspiration from Newman's collection of lectures, titled *The Idea of a University*.

The Pope's Spiritual and Moral Authority Pius IX was pope during the period when the church lost the Papal States. He led the church from 1846 to 1878—the longest papacy in history. During that period, he helped solidify the papacy's spiritual and moral authority. He proclaimed the dogma that Mary, Mother of Jesus, was free from original sin from the moment she was conceived; she is honored as such on the feast of the Immaculate Conception. Pius IX also encouraged the bishops of all countries to build seminaries in Rome. In this way, the Vatican could recruit the most capable young priests from other countries for its work, as well as influence and gain the loyalty of clergy throughout the world.

Concerned about the many philosophic and social movements that seemed to threaten the church, Pius published his *Syllabus of Errors,* which was a list of eighty errors that Catholics should reject. Among the errors were rationalism, freedom of religion, progress, and liberalism. Pius believed that the Catholic church should be protected and promoted by the state, that separation of church and state was a modern ill. He was clearly setting himself at odds with the movements of the times.

Finally, to further cement the spiritual authority of the papacy, Pius called all the bishops to Rome for Vatican Council I, held from 1869 to 1870. The main issue was the question of the pope's infallibility: Is the pope infallible—that is, incapable of error—when he officially (*ex cathedra,* meaning "from the chair of Peter") proclaims a doctrine of faith or morals? In 1870, the bishops answered with a firm yes, accepting and publishing the doctrine of papal infallibility.

It is important to recognize that only two doctrines have actually been defined *ex cathedra* by popes and thus are considered infallible. One is the Immaculate Conception of Mary, and the other is the Assumption of Mary. The doctrine of the Assumption says that Mary's body did not undergo bodily corruption after her death, but she was "assumed" into heaven.

The Spread of Capitalism, Marxism, and Darwinism

Other powerful forces and movements of the nineteenth century challenged the church. Increasingly the church was no longer in charge of world affairs, but instead it had to offer compassionate and wise help to a complex, hurting world.

The Ills of The nineteenth century saw the height of the Indus-
Industrial Society trial Revolution. Overseas trade flourished. Industrial
machines produced more goods, requiring more
markets. People flocked to the cities for industrial jobs. Such a dramatic change from the traditionally rural, farming way of life caused
problems: Cities developed crowded, filthy, and disease-ridden slums.
Factories exploited workers with terribly low wages and dangerous
working conditions.

Child Labor Abuses

Masses of children worked in mills and coal mines. Girls and
boys put in twelve- to sixteen-hour days, were beaten if they slowed
down, and earned only a pittance. Most never learned to read and
write. In fact, until well into the twentieth century, few laws protected children from abuse.

The story of Patience Kershaw, age seventeen, provides a
glimpse of the brutal life to which young people were subjected. She
told her story to a commission investigating the British coal mines:

My father has been dead about a year; my mother is living and has ten children. . . .

All my sisters have been hurriers [carrying baskets of coal from the
digging area of the mine to the main shaft], but three went to the mill.
. . . I never went to day-school; I go to Sunday-school, but I cannot read
or write; I go to pit at five o'clock in the morning and come out at five in
the evening; . . . I do not stop or rest any time [to eat]; . . . I hurry in
the clothes I have now got on, trousers and ragged jacket; the bald place
upon my head is made by thrusting the [coal baskets]; . . . I hurry the
[heavy baskets] a mile and more underground and back. . . . I hurry 11 a
day; . . . the getters [miners] that I work for are naked except their caps;
. . . sometimes they beat me, if I am not quick enough; . . . I am the
only girl in the pit; . . . I would rather work in the mill than in coal-pit.

The Marxist Answer: Class Struggle

Exploitation such as child labor abuses cried out for justice. One
response to the evils of industrial society came from Karl Marx, the
father of modern communism. In his books *Das Kapital* and *The
Communist Manifesto*, Marx blamed capitalism for the poor conditions of workers and advocated eliminating the private ownership of
the means of production.

Under capitalism, capital (the means of production and distribution—land, factories, railroads, mines) is privately owned and oper-
ated by a few for profit. Workers must sell their labor to owners for
whatever wage they can get. Marx was certain that in such an un-

equal system, where owners exploit the masses for their labor, class struggle was inevitable and would bring about a classless society. Marx dismissed religion as just a means of keeping people from rebelling against an unjust system. His theory of communism, later called Marxism, was part of the socialist thought that was gaining appeal among the common people in the industrial cities of Europe.

The Church Promotes Social Justice

Help for the Poor and the Workers

The Catholic church responded to the ills of industrialism in a number of ways. Welfare societies began in dioceses and parishes. Religious orders opened schools and hospitals specifically for the working class. Some church leaders supported strikes and the formation of unions. Among the advocates for workers, Henry Manning was notable; he, like John Henry Newman, had converted from Anglicanism to Catholicism and had become a priest and cardinal. In some countries, the church formed Christian democratic parties to represent the workers in parliaments. The church began to be identified with the cause of workers.

Beginnings of Modern Social-Justice Teaching

When Pope Leo XIII wrote his papal letter *On the Condition of Workers* (*Rerum Novarum*) in 1891, he did not realize that he was beginning a great modern legacy of Catholic social-justice teaching. In a way, his message told working and poor people that they did not have to turn to Marxism for justice, that the Catholic church was on their side. Leo's letter asserted that workers have rights to just wages and decent working conditions, to trade unions, and to collective bargaining with management. In the words of the papal letter:

The following duties . . . concern rich men and employers: Workers are not to be treated as slaves; justice demands that the dignity of the human personality be respected in them, ennobled as it has been through what we call the Christian character. . . . It is shameful and inhuman . . . to use men as things for gain and to put no more value on them than what they are worth in muscles and energy. (Number 31)

Leo criticized both extreme socialism and extreme capitalism. Although he upheld the right to own private property, he also emphasized the responsible sharing of private property. He insisted that Christianity had a different ideal to offer than either existing economic system did. Christianity emphasizes both the dignity of the human person and the common good of society. Leo's basic position still characterizes Catholic social-justice teaching in our own day.

Darwinism   A Challenge to the Biblical Creation Story

One other revolutionary development of the nineteenth century was the theory of evolution, formulated by the English scientist Charles Darwin. When his *On the Origin of Species* was published in 1859, it ushered in a period of doubt about God. Had God really created the world and human beings, just as the Bible recorded it? Or had the human species evolved from a lower life-form without direct creation by God? Those who believed that the Bible had to be understood as the *literal* truth could not accept the idea that Adam and Eve did not exist exactly as the Creation story describes. In short, Darwin's theory was scorned by many, but it eventually caused most people to re-evaluate their religious beliefs and helped bring about a distinction between scientific truth and religious meaning. Today Catholic scholars find no contradiction between a theory of evolution, which is about scientific fact, and the Creation story of the Bible, which is about religious meaning.

In response to questions about the Bible, Pope Leo XIII instituted a Vatican biblical commission, whose duty it was to apply new methods of archaeology and linguistics to biblical study. In addition, the Vatican archives were opened to scholars from all over the world. This encouragement of biblical scholarship would culminate in many of the decisions made by Vatican Council II, over seventy years later.

Conclusion

Stripped of its worldly power, the Catholic church once again became primarily a spiritual and moral force. Without the Papal States and without close relationships to corrupt monarchies and nobility, the church could be freer to go about the work that Jesus gave it to do—proclaiming the Gospel and carrying on Jesus' ministry in the world. Separated from the state and even at times oppressed by it, the church could criticize abuses in society rather than use its power to prop up the status quo. By the end of the 1800s, the church was identified more with the rights of workers and poor people than with the privileges of rich people and the ruling classes.

The revolutionary movements of the 1700s and 1800s posed enormous challenges to the church in Europe. On the other side of the Atlantic, in North America, the emerging church would find the ideals of democracy and separation of church and state more hospitable to the growth and flourishing of the church than those ideals were in Europe.

1. Are there any modern examples of "witch-hunts" in which an individual or group is persecuted? Who are some individuals or groups that serve as "scapegoats" in our society? What should Christians think about witch-hunts and scapegoating?
2. Can a person be a scientist and a person of faith? How can the two be reconciled and integrated?
3. Should the church affirm and embrace one form of government? What advantages accrue to the church when it stays free of politics?
4. Inventory all the ways in which the church fulfills its mission of social service and doing justice today. How are charity and doing justice part of your life?

13

The Church in North America

A Style of Its Own

WHILE THE CHURCH in Europe was racked by intellectual, religious, and political revolutions from the seventeenth through the nineteenth centuries, the church in the New World was growing. It was moving from the infancy of being colonial mission territory to the maturity of having its own particularly American identity.

As chapter 11 discussed, missionaries came along with the European colonizers to convert the native peoples in newly discovered lands. This was certainly the strategy of the church for evangelizing North America. In the countries now known as the United States and Canada, the church eventually did flourish, but not because huge numbers of the native peoples were converted. Instead, by 1900, Catholicism became the single largest denomination in both those countries because of the great flood of immigrants who came from Europe in the mid-1800s.

The story of the church in the United States and Canada begins with the missionaries.

Mission Territory

Chapter 11 covered the journeys of the Spanish explorers and missionaries to Latin America, including Mexico. The first Catholic missionaries to what is now the United States were Spanish Franciscan friars who accompanied explorers on their quests into the Southwest during the 1560s.

Seventy years later, French Jesuits sailed into the waters off of Canada's Nova Scotia (then called Acadia). Those French missionaries played a large role in opening up North America by helping chart the new territories' rivers, lakes, mountains, and valleys. Like the Spanish friars in the Southwest, the French priests worked among the native Americans—preaching to them, educating them in Western customs, and sometimes protecting them from exploitation.

Missionaries and Natives:
Viewing Each Other

Progress in converting native Americans was slow and generally discouraging. No doubt part of the problem was the way that the missionaries viewed the Indians. The Spanish friars tended to view native Americans as barbarians and sought to make them accept European ways. The French missionaries were considerably more respectful of the native American culture, but still they tended to misunderstand and demean it, referring to the native people as "savages" and "barbarians." French Jesuit Jean de Brébeuf was

Timeline . . .

1600
- Saint Augustine, FL, settled by Catholics.
- Spanish friars go with Southwest explorers.
- Santa Fe is founded.
- French Jesuits succeed among Hurons.
- Lord Baltimore granted land for Maryland settlement.
- Iroquois kill Jesuit missionaries.
- Maryland passes Act of Toleration.
- Pueblo Indians reject Christianity.

1700
- Colonial laws deprive American Catholics of churches, political office.

- Junipero Serra begins California missions.
- American Revolution begins.
- American priests elect John Carroll as first American bishop.

1800
- Sisters of Charity founded.
- Wave of Irish immigration begins.

- Wave of German immigration begins.
- Catechism commissioned by Council of Baltimore.
- Wave of Eastern European and Italian immigration begins.

1900
- Pope Pius X condemns Modernism.
- Alfred E. Smith loses presidential race by large margin.

- John F. Kennedy wins presidency.

known for his sensitivity to the natives. Father de Brébeuf gave an account of the missionaries' methods of teaching and relating to the friendly Hurons:

We call together the people. . . . I use the surplice [a loose white vestment] and the square cap, to give more majesty to my appearance. At the beginning we chant on our knees the Pater noster [Our Father], translated into Huron verse. . . . The Hurons, principally the little ones, who already know it, take pleasure in chanting it with us. . . . Then, having recapitulated what I said last time, I explain something new. After that we question the young children and the girls, giving a little bead of glass or porcelain to those who deserve it. The parents are very glad to see their children answer well and carry off some little prize. . . . Finally the whole is concluded by the talk of the Old Men, who propound their difficulties, and sometimes make me listen in my turn to the statement of their belief.

Brébeuf worked for many years among the Hurons, but in the end he was tortured and martyred by the Hurons' enemies, the Iroquois.

Native Americans had mixed reactions to the missionaries. Some tribes, like the Hurons, remained open to Christianity; other tribes showed unyielding hostility. Almost all Indian people recognized the foreign religion as a threat to their own religious traditions and way of life. They were quick to understand that the missionaries represented the front line of foreign domination. Native Americans also saw the Europeans as a threat to their physical well-being. As was the case in Latin America, thousands of Indians in North America died from diseases carried by Europeans. In the Spanish missions of the Southwest, Indians worked like slaves on mission farms under the watchful eyes of friars and soldiers. The beginnings of Catholicism in North America were tentative and sometimes scandalously brutal.

The Spanish Missions

In the Southeast. The Spanish explorers in the 1500s looked for gold in what is now Florida. They never found it, but accompanied by missionaries, they pressed on into the southeastern United States. Although a few Indians became Christian, others attacked the Spaniards, forcing them to retreat down the Mississippi River.

Despite those early failures, in 1565 the Spaniards built a settlement on the eastern coast of Florida and named it Saint Augustine. It was the first permanent Catholic settlement in what would later be the United States. By the mid-1600s, there were more than twenty-five thousand Christian Indians in Florida. The missionaries not only learned the native languages but also wrote books for the Indians. Shortly after 1700, however, most of the Spanish missionaries' work was destroyed when the English colonists from Carolina invaded Florida. The Indians were either killed or taken to Carolina as slaves.

In the Southwest. The first Europeans in the U.S. Southwest were Spanish explorers who came out of Mexico around 1540, looking for gold. They did not find gold, but they did find several nations of Indians living an advanced way of life in pueblos, or villages. Shortly before 1600, when a pueblo of Indians stood in the way of the colonists, the Spanish governor enslaved some of the Indians and mutilated others, cutting off a hand or a foot. This brutality made missionary work almost impossible, but the Franciscans stayed on even when the colony itself failed. In 1609, the town of Santa Fe was founded—the second permanent Catholic settlement within the area of what is now the United States. By 1630, there were roughly thirty-five thousand Christian Indians in the New Mexico region.

However, when Spanish traders raided Indian territory for slaves, the Pueblo Indians revolted, killing one-third of the Spaniards. Because Christianity and the Spaniards were connected, the Indians burned down churches and returned to their traditional religious practices. The Spaniards eventually reconquered the area, and missionary work began all over again. But by that time many Indians had left the territory in an attempt to escape the Spaniards.

In California. In 1769, Spanish friars, under the Franciscan Junípero Serra, began missionary activity in California. Because walking was less painful for Serra's half-crippled legs than riding a horse, he limped along the trails of California, teaching and baptizing thousands of native Americans. Serra established nine missions, among them San Diego, Santa Clara, and San Francisco. Eventually twenty-one missions were built by Spanish missionaries in California.

The Indians lived at the missions, and they soon began to learn not only the Catholic religion but European practices as well. Some friars led wisely, but others demeaned the Indians, treating them as slaves. The Indians' labor, a favorable climate, and the friars' agricultural know-how combined to make the California missions an agricultural and economic success. The mission residents cultivated vast orchards and vineyards and raised herds of cattle, supporting as many as two thousand persons on a single mission complex. Today, the vineyards and mission churches stand as reminders of the Spanish Catholic presence in the early history of North America.

The French Missions

Beginning in 1534, when French explorers landed on the shores of America just north of what is now the state of Maine, the French were attracted by the beautiful beaver furs that could be used to make hats in Europe. When France established a trading post and a small fort at Quebec in 1608, it was the beginning of New France, which the Indians called *Canada,* meaning "village" or "community."

To continue trade in beaver pelts, the French maintained good relations with the Indians and lived among them generally without disturbance. The French paid by barter for what they wanted, instead of taking it at gunpoint.. In return for beaver fur, they gave the Indians iron kettles, axes, knives, cloth, guns, and alcohol. The Indians helped the colonists learn how to survive and find their way through wilderness that had no roads and through hundreds of miles of rivers and lakes. The French were well received, particularly among the Hurons. But their friendship with the Hurons made the French into targets of the Iroquois tribes, who were the Hurons' enemies.

With the establishment of trading posts in what is now Canada and upstate New York, missionaries came to teach the Indians. The colony at Acadia had a school for both French and Indian children. Few Hurons were baptized in the next few years, though they were friendly to the missionaries. The French priests did not rush the native Americans into baptism before sufficiently instructing them in the Catholic faith. And such instruction was difficult, because the Indians kept on the move, living as nomads and rarely settling down for long in a village. The Jesuits had the most success with conversions.

Even when native Americans did become Christian, they remained subject to prejudice and fear. A story from the Fox Indians, of the Great Lakes region, describes the no-win situation often felt by Indian converts:

> Once there was an Indian who became a Christian. He became a very good Christian; he went to church, and he didn't smoke or drink, and he was good to everyone. He was a very good man. Then he died. First he went to the Indian hereafter, but they wouldn't take him because he was a Christian. Then he went to Heaven, but they wouldn't let him in—because he was an Indian. Then he went to Hell, but they wouldn't admit him there either, because he was so good. So he came alive again, and he went to the Buffalo Dance and the other dances and taught his children to do the same thing. ■

A Christian Indian's Dilemma

Courageous Christians. Among the missionaries to New France was the Jesuit Isaac Jogues, who in the mid-1600s lived for six years among the Hurons in the Albany area of New York. A war party of Mohawks, an Iroquois tribe, captured Jogues, tortured him, and used him as a slave during a yearlong captivity. Eventually he was rescued, and he went back to France to recuperate. But soon Jogues returned to the Hurons, and some months after his return, a band of Mohawks killed him. From 1646 to 1649 on the frontier, a total of eight French Jesuits were martyred in the New York region.

A few years after the death of Jogues, in the village where he was martyred, a girl was born to a Mohawk chief and a captive Christian Indian mother. The child, Kateri Tekakwitha, became an orphan when her parents died of smallpox, a disease brought in by the Europeans, but she was still raised as a Mohawk princess. At age twenty, she was baptized Catholic by a French Jesuit missionary. Kateri suffered greatly for her conversion; she was abused and ostracized by her relatives and tribe. Fearing for her life, she made a daring escape from the village, trekking two hundred miles through the wilderness, until she came to a village of Christian Indians near the place where Montreal stands today. She devoted the rest of her short life to helping people in need. She died at age twenty-four. Pope John Paul II beatified her, that is, declared her to be "blessed," which is one stage away from being declared a saint. Tekakwitha is the first native North American to be recognized this way.

In the mid-1600s in Quebec, two missionary developments were initiated by women. Marie Guyart, a French widow who joined the Ursuline order, journeyed to the New World as its first woman missionary. She was devoted to educating the Indian groups around Quebec and wrote grammar books, liturgies, and catechisms in Huron and Algonquin. By the time of her death, several more sisters had joined her from France to continue her work. Augustinian nursing sisters as well set up a clinic in Quebec to treat the sick French and native Americans. Both groups of women worked under harsh circumstances but ministered steadfastly.

A huge domain. By the end of the 1600s, French trappers, traders, and missionaries had extended the reach of France and Christianity to the south and west of New France. They had traveled the Great Lakes, and they had explored west to the Mississippi River and south on that river to the Gulf of Mexico, near the site of a later French colony that would be known as New Orleans. One explorer named the whole territory from north to south "Louisiana" after the French king Louis XIV.

French forts and villages sprouted up along the Ohio and Mississippi rivers and on the shores of the Great Lakes. By 1710, the land west of the English colonies was dotted with French trading posts. In these posts, the government of France took care of the religious needs of the colonists and traders.

In 1674, Francis Xavier de Montmorency Laval was made the first bishop of Quebec. He was a good organizer, and soon many villages in the diocese had parishes. Priests educated in the Quebec seminary took care of the French Catholics, while the missionaries—especially the Jesuits and Franciscans—taught the Indians. The number of Indian converts was never large. In his concern for the Indians, Bishop Laval let the traders know that it was wrong to use liquor as a way of doing business with, and basically manipulating, the natives.

France's defeat in the New World. New difficulties for the church in New France came from the European wars fought at various times during a seventy-five-year period, mostly during the 1700s. Part of the hostility was because France was Catholic while England was Anglican and Protestant. Eventually the French-English conflict crossed the ocean. Then the Indians came into the dispute—the Hurons on the side of the French and the Iroquois on the side of the English colonists, south of Canada.

Invaded by English settlers, French Catholics in the colony of Acadia refused to give allegiance to the king of England. As a result, many French Canadians were deported to various English colonies to the south, forced to leave behind their homes and farms. A large number who fled from English rule went all the way down to what is now the state of Louisiana, where many of their descendants, known as Cajuns, still live today.

By 1763, the war between the French and the English had ended with the Treaty of Paris, in which France gave Canada over to English rule. In 1774, the British Parliament passed the Quebec Act, giving French Canadians freedom to practice their religion and to hold elective offices. This somewhat pacified the French Catholics because they could then maintain their religious and ethnic identity. Some bitterness between French- and English-speaking Canadians persists to this day, however. The bitterness is most evident in a movement by French Canadians to separate the predominantly French province of Quebec from the rest of the nation of Canada.

The English Colonies

In search of religious freedom. Catholics in England in the 1600s were treated harshly, or at least were discriminated against; they were forbidden to own property or to vote. Consequently, many

English Catholics abandoned their church for the Anglican church. Most English settlers in America were Anglican, although some variation could be found: for instance, Puritans founded the Massachusetts Bay Colony, and Quakers founded Pennsylvania.

Catholics in England had an opportunity to escape discrimination when King James I gave Lord Baltimore, a Catholic, land for an American settlement that was named Maryland. Catholicism was still outlawed in England when the Maryland settlers arrived in 1634. The Maryland colony welcomed anyone who wanted to live there, and it passed an Act of Toleration, granting freedom of worship to all—an unusual move for that era. Although the leadership of the colony initially was Catholic, the majority of the settlers were Protestant.

Jesuits came to Maryland with the English Catholic colonizers. The Catholic governor granted land to the Jesuits so that they could support themselves. Thus, like the other pioneers, the Jesuits farmed, herded, milled grain, and oversaw all the other operations of their plantations. They hired some workers, and then they rode a circuit of plantations, covering three hundred to four hundred miles in a week, to administer the sacraments, celebrate Mass with Catholic families, and teach religion to the children.

Maryland Catholics still had to keep a low profile so that they would not stir up anti-Catholic sentiment. Even so, by 1704, when non-Catholic settlers far outnumbered Catholics in the colony, laws were passed against Catholics, depriving them of churches as well as the right to hold political office.

Fortunately, Catholics found religious freedom in the Pennsylvania colony, established by William Penn, a member of the tolerant Quakers, or the Society of Friends. In Philadelphia, Catholics were allowed to build a church, called Saint Joseph's. At the time, it was the only Catholic church allowed in the British Empire.

Independence: Good news for Catholics. As the British American colonists grew determined to break away from England, bigotry against Catholics decreased. The colonists knew that they would need all the unity they could muster for a fight with powerful Britain.

A Catholic statesman, Charles Carroll, was one of the signers of the Declaration of Independence. During the American Revolution, Catholic colonists wholeheartedly supported the war against England. Foreign Catholics as well came over from Europe to join in the struggle for independence; among these Catholics were the Polish soldier-heroes Tadeusz Kósciuszko and Kazimierz Pułaski, and the French general the Marquis de Lafayette. The help of France, a predominantly Catholic country, was vital to the American victory.

After the war, George Washington acknowledged the part Catholics had played in achieving the victory. With independence, the future looked promising for Catholics. The new Constitution's Bill of Rights gave to all U.S. citizens, among other rights, the freedom of worship. The Constitution provided for separation of church and state. As a new country, the United States offered relief from the religious bigotry and discrimination that were commonplace elsewhere. .

A Distinctly American Church

At the end of the American Revolution, only a handful of Catholic priests ministered in the colonies, mostly in Maryland and Pennsylvania. With such few numbers, it was difficult for priests to serve the thirty thousand or so Catholics who lived in the United States at the time. And for at least 150 years, the Catholic colonists had no bishop. In the larger towns, Catholic laypeople organized small parishes and tried to obtain the services of a priest whenever they could.

The church was poor, too. Finding the funds to support priests and build churches was extremely hard. The Maryland priest John Carroll (1735–1815), a cousin of Charles Carroll, was one of the first Catholics to help build a more robust U.S. Catholic church.

An American Bishop   Clearly, the young U.S. church needed a leader—a bishop—if it was to flourish. One problem was that the priests and most of the people they served did not want a foreign Catholic bishop in the United States. The U.S. Catholics were afraid that some would riot against a foreign Catholic bishop appointed by the pope. Because Catholics were finally being accepted in the new country, they were anxious not to revive the old bigotry against Catholicism. By special concession, the Vatican approved arrangements for a bishop to be elected by the U.S. priests rather than appointed by the pope. Father John Carroll was the overwhelming choice of the twenty-six U.S. priests at the election held in 1789, the same year that George Washington became the nation's first president.

Establishing Order

Bishop Carroll worked hard to establish order in U.S. Catholic parishes. Many priestless congregations had been running their own affairs and were not eager to have a bishop tell them what to do. Also, from 1790 to 1860, U.S. law required that every church congregation have a lay board of trustees that was responsible for church debt payments, pastors' salaries, and the hiring and firing of church personnel. This kind of democratic structure was not typical of the Catholic church.

Many U.S. Catholics, in the fervor of the new national democracy, wanted the church to be run democratically too, with the "voice of the people" being the "voice of God." Bishop Carroll's task was to maintain the support of dedicated Catholics while also taking firm control of church government.

The Need for Priests

With priests in short supply, Bishop Carroll established Saint Mary's, the first U.S. seminary, in Baltimore, Maryland, in 1791. He also directed the church west of the original thirteen states, which he organized into four huge dioceses. Seeing the pressing need for Catholic higher education, he helped start Georgetown College, which is now Georgetown University, in Washington, D.C.

Carroll also had to contend with the dilemma that non-British people were beginning to come to the United States, and priests who could speak the newcomers' languages were needed. In another communications problem, some of the French missionaries who still worked on the frontiers could not speak English.

Despite the difficulties, Carroll succeeded in planting a church that could grow in the United States. He was thoroughly American in style and spirit, committed to the principles of democracy and of separation of church and state, but he was also completely loyal to the Vatican. Under his leadership, the U.S. Catholic population grew from thirty thousand in 1790 to two hundred thousand in 1815.

American Sisters, American Saint For hundreds of years the Americas had been mission territory, served primarily by priests, brothers, and sisters of European origins. Then it came time for a particularly American form of the Catholic church to emerge. Bishop Carroll's leadership helped that Americanization come about. Another significant person in the process was New York-born Elizabeth Ann Seton (1774–1821), who was canonized in 1975 as the first saint born in the United States.

Elizabeth Ann Seton: Mother, Widow, Convert

The daughter of a well-educated Anglican father, Elizabeth mothered five children and was widowed before the age of thirty. Much against her family's and friends' wishes, she became a Catholic. The only parish in New York at the time served newly arrived, poor Irish immigrants. Elizabeth's peers were aghast that she was a member of that church, which they called "a horrid place of spits and pushing."

An Early Catholic School

After struggling to support her children in New York, Elizabeth moved to Baltimore at the encouragement of Bishop Carroll, to begin a small school. With further encouragement, she decided to start a religious community of women at Emmitsburg, Maryland, to run a school and orphanage there. This group, the Sisters of Charity, founded in 1809, was the first religious order to originate in the United States. The sisters wore the simple widow's garb of Mother Seton, as they called their leader, and led a rough, pioneer life that was characteristically American. Later the order joined the French Daughters of Charity, but several groups of sisters branched off as varieties of Mother Seton's Sisters of Charity. The schools these sisters started set the pattern for the Catholic parochial school system in the United States, a topic that will be discussed later in this chapter.

A Frontier Church　　With the expansion of U.S. territories west of the Appalachian Mountains in the early 1800s, thousands of settlers began moving westward on foot, on horseback, in wagons, and sometimes on flatboats. Many of those frontier people, especially the German and Irish people, were Catholic immigrants, so missionaries went with them. A number of the priests were French, and from among them came the pioneer bishops. Their dioceses spread over immense distances, so the bishops, as well as the few priests that there were, practically lived in the saddle, riding from one settlement to the next to give the sacraments and to instruct the people. The clergy lived a hard, impoverished life and often went hungry to serve the Catholics who were their responsibility.

The Crucial Role of Religious Communities

No matter how devoted and tough these early priests and bishops were, they had special help from the Catholic sisters who started schools, hospitals, and orphanages. Coming after Elizabeth Seton, leaders among the American sisters were Rose Philippine Duchesne, of the Sacred Heart order; Cornelia Connelly, founder of the Religious of the Holy Child; Katharine Drexel, who started the Sisters of the Blessed Sacrament and opened more than fifty houses of sisters to care for poor blacks and Indians in the South and Southwest; and Rose Hawthorne Lathrop (the daughter of Nathaniel Hawthorne), who started an order to care for people with incurable cancer.

Religious brothers and priests, such as Holy Cross Brothers, De La Salle Christian Brothers, and Franciscans, played significant roles in education on the frontier and "back East" as well. By the mid-1800s, Holy Cross Fathers had founded the University of Notre Dame in Indiana, Benedictine monks had founded Saint John's University in Minnesota, and the Society of Mary had begun Saint Mary's University in Texas.

Keep Going West

In the period just before the Civil War, the young United States continued to spread westward to what we now know as the Midwest. In addition, the areas that are now Texas, New Mexico, Arizona, and California were annexed to the United States after the Mexican-American War of 1846–1848. This new territory was inhabited by Catholic Mexican-Americans, but much of it was unsettled, and the land north of the newly acquired territories was inhabited only sparsely by tribes of native Americans. With new immigrants coming into the United States at the rate of two million every ten years, the land and work provided by the western areas were needed. Also, with the discovery of gold in California in 1849, poor immigrants had an extra incentive for "going west."

As the boundary of the United States gradually moved westward to the Rocky Mountains and down to Santa Fe from Oregon, Catholic missionaries went out to the new lands. Father Pierre Jean De Smet, a Belgian, was among the first to work with the Plains Indians, whose land was being invaded by U.S. settlers. On friendly terms with the Indians, he was free to come and go in safety. The U.S. government asked him three times to represent it at important Indian councils. Unfortunately, efforts at reaching fair and just settlements failed because of the continuing invasion by settlers.

An Immigrant Church

Poor and Uneducated   Subject to Discrimination

The majority of the immigrants who flooded into the United States after about 1830 were poor and uneducated, having suffered from bad times in their countries of origin. These immigrants hoped that they could build a new life.

Waves of Immigrants

From 1830 to 1860, the immigrants were mostly Irish. In fact, Irish immigration was the main cause for the jump in the Catholic population from about a half million in 1830 to over three million in 1860, making Catholicism the largest denomination in the country. Another wave of immigrants, from 1860 to 1890, brought German Catholics in numbers equal to that of the Irish immigrants. The third wave of immigrants, lasting from 1890 to the 1920s, came from Italy and Eastern Europe. (In the 1920s, immigration laws put the brakes on the influx of foreigners.) Because they did not know English, most of the immigrants lived with other people from their homeland, often crowded together in city slums.

Nativism: Anti-Catholic Bigotry

Anti-Catholic bigotry, although lessened by the bravery of Catholic patriots during the American Revolution, surfaced from about 1830 to the Civil War and periodically after that war. As the number of Catholics in the United States increased, the English-speaking Protestant majority became afraid of the Catholic immigrants coming into the country. Persons who called themselves nativists wanted the United States for "native-born Americans"—that is, for themselves (they forgot that the original native-born Americans were the Indians). The Irish immigrants who came to the Eastern cities took hard jobs, working on roads and on the Erie Canal, but they often earned enough to pay for their overseas relatives to join them. In time, many Irish Catholics moved into the American West. With their knowledge of English, they had an advantage over other newcomers when it came to finding employment and settling in, so they were considered an even greater cultural and economic threat to the "native-born."

Rumors and even publications by educated persons circulated claims that the Vatican and the Catholic immigrants were conspiring to take over the United States. Eventually, anti-Catholic sentiment developed into a political party, usually called the Know-Nothing Party because its members evaded questions by answering, "I don't know."

The Church Advocates for Workers and Poor People

Immigrant men found jobs as laborers, and they worked hard and long for little pay. Women found jobs that they could do at home, being paid a few cents for each piece of work they turned out. "Sweatshops," with horrible conditions, kept people working for long hours in unhealthy conditions. If workers tried to unite to bargain for better conditions, they were fired.

By 1886, a union known as the Knights of Labor had grown to seven hundred thousand members, many of whom were Catholic. When some bishops tried to get the Knights condemned by the Vatican, Cardinal James Gibbons, of Baltimore, wrote to Pope Leo XIII and went to Rome on the Knights' behalf. Not too long after, the pope wrote his encyclical *Rerum Novarum,* which strongly asserted workers' rights to just wages and decent working conditions.

The Catholic church responded in other ways to the needs of immigrant Catholics. Mother Frances Cabrini, herself an Italian immigrant, founded the Missionary Sisters of the Sacred Heart, to teach Italians in the parochial schools, to care for homeless children, and to nurse in hospitals. Such organizations as the Saint Vincent de Paul Society made it possible for Catholics to help one another with donations of clothes and furniture for the needy.

The Ethnic Churches During the late 1800s, the Know-Nothings ceased to be a powerful anti-Catholic force. The Catholic church had organized itself well with its own institutions, so it appeared that Catholics had smooth sailing ahead of them. But the emergence of ethnic churches caused new difficulties. Because the Irish comprised the first wave of Catholic immigrants

Péter Vay, a Hungarian bishop, came to the United States several times to look after the large population of Hungarian immigrants. When Our Lady of Hungary Church opened in Chicago in 1904, Bishop Vay was there. His account of the event expresses the then commonly held belief that the church and the Catholic school were absolutely necessary in helping the new immigrants adjust to the New World while keeping their Catholic and ethnic identity. Vay's account also provides a picture of parishioners' sacrifices to support their church.

At a little distance among the marshy pasture land I detected the small wooden structure. From its roof waved the American and Hungarian flags . . . harmoniously blending together. "That is the church, and the school is underneath," someone proudly volunteered.

. . . These simple folk have built it with their hard-earned savings, for the glory of God and the religious education of their children.

More than half the population of Chicago are foreigners. . . . [The Hungarians] are chiefly employed as butchers in the slaughter-houses, and as blacksmiths and carpenters in the Pullman establishment. . . .

The workmen and their families awaited me at the entrance of the building. For the greater part they were still dressed in their simple costume "from over the sea," and their whole demeanour showed that they had not long since arrived in these parts. Set adrift in that great city, without knowing the language, without friends or any one to advise them, these poor folks are at the mercy of chance.

. . . They have not only to be fed, they have also to be protected and educated. The church and the school are their only safeguards. As long as the people will go to church and are willing to have their children brought up on religious principles there is nothing to fear. ■

An Ethnic Church in Chicago, 1904

and there were so many of them—four and a half million from 1820 to 1920—most of the priests and bishops in the United States were Irish. Some ethnic groups, particularly the German Catholics, who came to the United States in huge numbers during the last half of the 1800s, wanted to practice their religion just as they had learned it and to preserve their native language. For many immigrant families, religious heritage was passed on through their native language and culture. Germans often resented the Irish priests and hierarchy, so they established German parishes with their own pastors.

Three booming cities of the time—Cincinnati, Saint Louis, and Milwaukee—became known as the German Triangle. German churches were the centers of their communities. The Mass was said in Latin, like it was in other parishes, and most of the devotional practices were similar to those of other Catholic ethnic groups. However, German Catholicism, like the Catholicism of other ethnic groups, had its own emphases. German parishes, for example, stressed excellence in church music. The parish choir was respected, and membership in it was an honor. In some cities, German inter-parish Catholic choirs put on magnificent concerts. Also, German parishes loved processions through their neighborhoods on saints' feast days. Often German Catholics published their own newspapers, and their parish schoolteachers taught in German. The parishes supplied a sense of continuity and tradition from the old country.

Eventually, German parishes asked Rome to form German dioceses in the United States. Pope Leo XIII turned down their requests—he stressed that nationality should not be the basis of decisions in the church, but that the church would take care of the needs of each ethnic church. Ethnic churches continued in the United States for many years, in some places continuing even into the present. Most major cities had German, Polish, Lithuanian, Italian, and Irish parishes. Within a block or two in a city, several different ethnic churches might be located, each drawing members of its own ethnic group.

Catholic
Parochial Schools

Catholic Problems with Public Schools

Until the mid-1800s, most Catholic children attended public school, if they went to school at all. School boards were almost entirely Protestant. Separation of church and state was the law of the land, but in practice the public schools were Protestant-oriented institutions. All students were required to read the King James version of the Bible (used by Protestants) and to recite Protestant prayers. In 1844, when a bishop of Philadelphia asked the school authorities if Catholic public school students could read the Catholic version of the Bible instead, the answer was a full-scale riot.

In the violence, three Catholic churches and a number of private homes were burned, and thirteen people were killed.

In New York in the 1840s and 1850s, about one-third of the Catholic children were in schools run by the Catholic church. Catholics there asked for a share of public school money, but the state legislature denied the request, saying that no financial help could be given to religious schools. Their request also brought heated reactions from many Protestants, causing the archbishop of New York to station armed guards around Catholic churches to discourage riots. Public schools were dominated by Protestant practices and points of view, and they stayed that way well into the twentieth century.

A School for Every Parish

Catholics became intensely committed to Catholic schools as a means of passing on the faith and supporting their children in a society that was often hostile toward them. Even if their children went to schools where a Protestant influence was not strong, Catholic parents still wanted their children to have good instruction in their faith. So as much as they were able, the mostly poor immigrants built their parish, or parochial, schools with hard-earned dollars. Many Catholic sisters and brothers dedicated their life to teaching the children, with only minimum necessities as their pay. Catholic families were proud of their schools, and the schools fulfilled a real need.

Catholicism was respected even by non-Catholics for its successful system of education. Catholic schools were so successful that in 1884 the Council of Baltimore (a U.S. bishops' council) ruled that within two years every parish *had to* have a Catholic school. The bishops also commissioned a catechism for all Catholics in the United States, a book that would guide Catholics in what they were to believe. The resulting Baltimore Catechism became the standard religion text for Catholic school children from then through the 1950s.

The decisions of the Council of Baltimore had an enormous impact on U.S. Catholicism and the development of Catholic identity over the next decades and even into our own time. For a variety of reasons, today not all parishes, or even most, have a parish school, but the Catholic school system is still recognized for its ability to educate with excellence and to pass on Catholic values.

Canadian Catholicism — Also a Church of Immigrants

Canada gained independent nation status by a union of British colonies that became the Dominion of Canada in 1867—unlike the United States, which became a nation through revolution. However, since 1774, when the British agreed to allow the people of Quebec the freedom to keep their French culture and religion, Canada had been divided into two parts along ethnic and religious lines: Quebec, which was mostly Catholic and French-speaking, and the remainder of the country, which was mostly Protestant and English-speaking.

In the nineteenth century, Catholic-Protestant tensions flared up in Canada as well as in the United States. But conflict over schools was not an issue in Canada. By the time of confederation in 1867, there was no legal wall between church and state as in the United States. Rather, the Canadian government helped each denomination run its own schools without interference in religious matters. This practice continues today, with Catholic schools funded by the state.

The Canadian Catholic church grew beyond French Canada through the large influx of immigrants, especially the Irish. By 1900, Catholics were the largest single denomination in Canada, numbering about 40 percent of the population. After the turn of the century, more and more Catholic immigrants settled in the Canadian West, most of them English-speaking. Bishops followed, and dioceses were organized to care for the Catholics.

Black Catholics   In America from the Beginning

One group usually not considered with Catholic immigrants is blacks. Evidence shows, however, that some black Catholics may have been in the New World from the time of the earliest colonies. The African Congo, where many slaves originated, became Catholic in the 1400s, when its king was converted by the Portuguese. Thus some of the slaves who arrived in Florida in the 1500s with the Spaniards may have been raised as Catholics in the Congo.

Many blacks converted to Catholicism in the United States through the Jesuits' evangelizing efforts in Maryland and Louisiana. In the nineteenth century, black religious orders were founded—the Oblate Sisters of Providence and the Holy Family Sisters—and black parishes were established. Unfortunately, opposition to slavery prior to the Civil War was not popular among U.S. Catholics, although a few priests and bishops spoke out against it. In 1839, the Vatican had condemned the slave trade, but some U.S. Catholics felt that this did not condemn the holding of slaves who were already in the United States. They argued that there are no condemnations of slavery in the Bible. In any case, at the time of the Civil War, there was no unified position on slavery in the U.S. Catholic church.

Thus, within the Catholic church, blacks faced discrimination. The first black priest ordained for the United States, Augustus Tolton, was refused admission to any American seminary, so he went to

Rome for his training and his ordination in 1886. Blacks also were not allowed to attend Catholic universities, and black parishes remained separated from predominantly white parishes until the 1960s.

Nevertheless, an active, committed, proud-to-be-Catholic black laity developed. Five Black Catholic Lay Congresses were held in the late 1800s. Participants were outspoken on the issue of racism, insisting that it was contrary to Catholic teaching. Their voices were some of the earliest to call for a social-justice consciousness in the church.

Democratic Ideals and the Church

The impulse of German Catholics and other ethnic churches to associate only with their own nationality and to preserve the religious ways of the old country was at odds with another tendency in U.S. Catholicism. That tendency was the movement to become more democratic and more integrated into American life. The latter position was promoted by Irish Catholics, who found it easier to adapt to U.S. culture, in part because they spoke English.

Tensions: To Americanize or Not The two tendencies—to be isolated versus to be assimilated—created great tensions in the Catholic church of the late nineteenth century. Some leaders felt that Catholics had to segregate themselves if they were to keep their faith within a society open to individual choices of all kinds. These leaders felt it was not possible to combine being an American with being a true Catholic, at least in matters concerning faith. On the other hand, the "Americanizers," represented by Irish members of the hierarchy, such as Cardinal James Gibbons and Archbishop John Ireland, argued that Catholics should participate fully as citizens of a democratic country in which church and state are separate. In 1894, Bishop Ireland declared the following: "There is no conflict between the Catholic Church and America. . . . The principles of the church are in thorough harmony with the interests of the Republic."

However, democracy and republicanism (representative government elected by the citizenry) were still new ideas, even in 1900. European church leaders knew what the republican revolutions had achieved in Europe: anticlericalism had swept through France and other countries, the Papal States had been stripped from the church, and the close ties of crown and cross had been destroyed. As a result, many officials in the Roman Curia mistrusted the American democratic style. They still saw the advantages of church and state working as one. Even the socially conscious Pope Leo XIII made a statement against the excesses of Americanism. His successor, Pius X, in 1907 made a sweeping condemnation of Modernism, a movement among European Catholic theologians that challenged traditional doctrines and advocated a more democratic structure for the church itself. Such Vatican pronouncements pulled in the reins on the Americanizers.

Marching into the Mainstream

Downplaying Catholic Divisions

Though the U.S. Catholic church in the early twentieth century was fairly isolated from the mainstream of American life, that was all beginning to change. Immigrants, mostly now from Italy and eastern Europe, poured into the United States up until World War I. The Catholic church was the largest denomination in the country. The war tended to unite Americans, and it united Catholics among themselves as well. German parishes, for instance, seeking not to be identified with the enemy, Germany, downplayed their German heritage and sought assimilation into the mainstream of U.S. life and the U.S. Catholic church.

After the war, however, America's door closed to great numbers of immigrants. Quota laws allowed only a certain number of immigrants to enter each year, with northern and western Europeans (who tended to be Protestant) allowed the greatest number. Growth of the Catholic population slowed considerably. But the children and grandchildren of earlier Catholic immigrants were becoming more established and began to enter the mainstream of American life.

Bigotry Again

Despite the gains of Catholics, the nativist prejudice that earlier Catholics had suffered reappeared with bitterness in the presidential election of 1928. New York governor Alfred E. Smith, a Catholic, was badly beaten on the presidential ballot amid attacks on the patriotism of Catholics. In spite of the sacrifices that Catholics had made in the war, many Americans were still afraid that a Catholic president would put his religion ahead of his patriotism—indeed that the pope would control the United States through a Catholic president.

From Poverty to Prosperity

In the 1930s, a worldwide depression left millions of people without work, homeless, and on the brink of starvation. Catholic social services increased their efforts to aid the needy, but some Catholic institutions had to close their doors when they ran out of funds. Nevertheless, the church continued to grow in numbers through the Great Depression and World War II.

After World War II, the U.S. Catholic church began an unprecedented building program. Many new Catholic colleges opened their doors in the 1950s. Most dioceses, whose only Catholic high schools had previously been owned and run by religious orders, funded the construction of their own schools. Catholics were totally committed to Catholic education. The once impoverished and illiterate Catholic population fast became the best-educated group in the country. New Catholic newspapers came off the presses at a remarkable rate.

Between 1945 and 1960, the Catholic population in the United States doubled and became more prosperous. Then the Irish Catholic John F. Kennedy was elected president in 1960, despite anti-Catholic rhetoric reminiscent of the Al Smith campaign. Kennedy's election and his term of office, though shortened by an assassination, dispelled people's fears surrounding a Catholic presidency. The Kennedy presidency clearly symbolized that the Catholic church had arrived as an accepted part of life in the United States.

Conclusion   In the colorful and varied history of the North American church, missionaries and teachers preached and taught in the wilderness, on the frontier, in sod huts, in city slums, and in stone cathedrals, to Dakota Indians, and to Italian immigrants. While growing into a distinctly American church, U.S. Catholics struggled against poverty and discrimination and questioned the structures and values of the wider society. In the process, they built a vital Catholicism in a democracy where church and state are separate. This had not been done before.

The dramatic, rapid growth of the North American church was due largely to the immigration of great numbers of European Catholics in the nineteenth and early twentieth centuries. With this growth, the church managed to develop its own institutions, such as schools and colleges, hospitals and social services, which enabled Catholics to become part of the mainstream and keep their Catholic identity.

Questions for Reflection and Discussion

1. Immigrants played an important role in American Catholicism. What new groups of immigrants have impacted the U.S. Catholic church?
2. U.S. Catholics have finally been included in the mainstream of American life. Does joining the mainstream make it harder to be critical of society's prejudices, assumptions, values, and structures? Is a more prosperous church any more faithful to the Gospels?
3. Do you agree with U.S. separation of church and state? Would society be better off if the state helped support churches?

14

World Church

Anguish in an Era of World Wars

THE CATHOLIC CHURCH, as it entered the twentieth century, had just seen a chaotic period of nationalist revolutions that stripped it of its worldly power. But, this loss of power enabled the church to gain moral and spiritual authority. Freed from secular concerns, the church rededicated itself to its mission of embodying Jesus in the world through teaching, preaching, and ministering.

Significantly, the moral stature of the papacy in the twentieth century would grow. By the time of the Vatican Council II, in the 1960s, the pope, as the leader of the largest religious body in the world, would be listened to not only as a spokesperson for Catholicism but as a moral advocate for the whole earth.

A Beloved Pope

Despite what was to come for the papacy, the twentieth century began with the pope still behind the walls of the Vatican. Holding to principle, popes were unwilling to set foot on Italian soil, which in 1870 had taken away the church's lands. The first pope to be elected in the new century was Pope Pius X (1903 to 1914). This warm, gentle man loved nothing more than being a pastor, and he carried that focus into his papacy. His concern was to make the sacraments more available to Catholics, reversing the popular tendency to regard the Mass and the Eucharist as remote and far above the faithful laypeople. By lowering the age for First Communion from adolescence to "the age of reason" (estimated at age seven) and encouraging all Catholics to receive Communion frequently, not just once a year, Pius X brought the Eucharist home to where it belonged—among the faithful.

This pope also encouraged a movement called Catholic Action, consisting of laypersons doing charitable work among poor people. Many of the Catholic social-service groups in dioceses and parishes today were rooted in the early Catholic Action groups.

Pius was a product of the nineteenth-century church in that he was wary of intellectual, cultural, and political movements in the wider world. In this respect, his papacy is symbolized well by the image of the pope as "prisoner of the Vatican." National moves toward democracy, the separation of church and state, and historical and scientific methods of studying the Scriptures were suspect to him. Pius looked unfavorably on efforts to adapt the church to modern times or to introduce democratic methods into the church. As seen in chapter 13, he condemned the theological movement known as Modernism. Nev-

Timeline . . .

- World War I begins.
- Pope Benedict XV calls for peace.
- Russian Revolution.
- Mussolini takes power in Italy. U.S. bishops advocate social-justice reforms.

1920
- Roaring Twenties usher in unbridled capitalism, social Darwinism.

- Lateran Treaty signed.
- Pope Pius XI condemns communism.
- Hitler made chancellor of Germany.
- Catholic Worker Movement founded.
- Pius XI denounces Nazism.
- World War II begins.
- Franco assumes power in Spain.

1940
- Religious in Far East perish as Japan enters World War II.
- Papal encyclicals encourage biblical scholarship, unity in church.
- Germany falls; atomic bombs force Japan's surrender.

- Pius XII excommunicates Catholics involved in communist activities.

- U.S. Catholic bishops decry racism.

1960
- Vatican Council II condemns use of weapons of mass destruction.

249

ertheless, Catholics all over the world loved him. It was not surprising when, forty years after his death, Pius X was declared a saint, the first pope to be canonized since the 1500s. He died on the eve of the First World War—a horrendous event that would change the face of Europe and even the nature of war itself.

A World Geared for War, a Church Geared for Peace

World War I, which began in 1914, was a new type of war. First, it was a total war—fought on land, sea, and *air*. Second, new technologies like the machine gun, poison gas, the submarine, and the airplane made the war far more deadly than past wars. (Besides, these technologies made war seem impersonal. Soldiers did not have to see the victims of their devastation and killing.) Third, this war entangled nations not only within Europe but outside it, including the United States and Canada. Countries struggled for global dominance.

A Pope as Advocate for Peace Millions of Catholics were caught up in the war, on both sides. Pope Benedict XV, who served from 1914 to 1922, used all his diplomatic skills to try to end the war. He condemned the war as unjustified, but his calls for peace were ignored amid the lust for power and the fervent nationalism. Benedict gave away vast sums of Vatican money for relief work among the thousands of people who were left homeless, sick, or wounded by the war. In fact, when Benedict died, the Vatican treasury was so depleted that it could not cover the expenses of the assembly of cardinals that was called to elect Benedict's successor.

The Aftermath of the War **A Time of Disillusionment**
By 1918 when Germany surrendered, millions of people had died in the war that was supposed to end all wars. The harsh conditions placed on Germany by the Allied victors (including Britain, France, the United States, and Canada) planted the seeds that would later grow into the Nazi Party and World War II. Although Pope Benedict warned the Allied powers not to totally humiliate Germany, his wisdom was ignored. After the war, Germany's economy broke down; many citizens starved; and humiliation, resentment, and anger boiled in its people. Besides the devastating loss of life and property on all sides, the war left a legacy of bitterness that split Catholics in Germany from those in France, Belgium, the Netherlands, and Italy. National pride and national humiliation overshadowed common religious heritage.

It was a time of enormous disillusionment with traditional and religious values. A mood of cynicism, exemplified by the morally loose Roaring Twenties, pervaded European countries, the United States, and Canada. People looked for nonreligious answers to their questions about life's meaning.

"Free Yourself from Religion"

The new science of psychology (literally, "the study of the mind") offered many people a perspective for looking at life and themselves. Enormously influential in this field was Sigmund Freud (1856–1939). Modern psychology has much to offer us in terms of understanding human behavior and treating mental illness, and Freud's contribution to the field was enormous. But his view of religion was heavily biased and even hostile.

According to Freud, the notion of God was simply a "projection of the unconscious." He saw religion and religious norms as merely society's means to control people, suppressing their natural desires and impulses until they became mature enough to direct themselves. In his view, religious faith was childish at best, harmful at worst, and definitely something to be "gotten over." Freud's view of faith, religion, and the role of religious values is generally not psychology's view today, but at the time when psychology was coming into vogue, his ideas dominated the field.

"Get All You Can"

Another perspective that people grabbed onto in the postwar time of disillusionment was a belief in unbridled capitalism. The meaning of life became "get all you can while the getting is good," regardless of the consequences for others. This approach left the social landscape strewn with the victims of cutthroat competition. Darwinism, the theory that biological species evolve over centuries through the "survival of the fittest," had become distorted into social Darwinism. This theory saw the process of survival operating in the social and economic realm, producing "superior" people, successful capitalists. In other words, if some of capitalism's victims—the poor, the unemployed, those who could not keep up with the competition—fell by the wayside, they were like the dinosaurs, who became extinct because they could not adapt to changes in the world's climate.

Social Darwinism provided a theoretical rationalization for the harm done by unchecked capitalism. Unjust conditions or low wages in the workplace were seen as necessary in order for owners of industry to triumph over their competitors. Compassion was out; winning was in.

An alternative to the social Darwinist approach in the United States

A Vision of Justice from the U.S. Bishops was proposed by the U.S. bishops in their *Program of Social Reconstruction*. When World War I ended, the bishops in 1919 issued a forward-thinking declaration—even radical for its time—setting forth the way that society should reform itself to be more just. The proposals in the declaration, as well as the bishops who made them, were harshly criticized by the business elite and politicians, but many of the ideas would later be reflected in new U.S. legislation. Indeed, the bishops' plan became a blueprint for change. The U.S. bishops advocated the following reforms, among others.

- Wage rates that would be at least sufficient for maintaining a family in decency—allowing employees to save and thus avoid poverty in times of sickness or accident and in old age (This was the intention behind later minimum wage laws.)
- Insurance for everyone, through a tax on employers, which would enable people's needs to be met throughout their entire life (This was the intention behind Social Security legislation.)
- The availability of medical care for wage earners and their families through group medicine (This is the intention of health insurance as a benefit for workers.)

Calling for a new viewpoint on the part of capitalists, the bishops reminded them, "The laborer is a human being, not merely an instrument of production; . . . the laborer's right to a decent livelihood is the first moral charge upon industry."

With Pope Leo XIII's encyclical on labor, *Rerum Novarum,* still fresh in mind, the U.S. bishops tried to apply the Gospel to economic and social life, presenting an alternative to the cynicism and disillusionment in the society at large. But around the globe, other, sinister forces were at work, steering the world toward another war.

The Rise of Totalitarianism

In times of social and economic chaos, when traditional values are being eroded, people sometimes turn to anything that will explain and regulate life for them, hoping that it will restore the order and good times for which they long. At such times, nations are quite vulnerable to totalitarianism, a total, all-encompassing system that orders national unity through a political ideology and upholds that unity with dictatorial means.

In a totalitarian country, all aspects of life are controlled by a single party, led by a dictator or a small group dedicated to the ideology. Opposition is usually eliminated by a politically controlled police force. The party also controls the media and education, which are used to manipulate the populace.

Two totalitarian systems came to power in the twentieth century: communism and fascism. Both systems tolerated religion only if it did not conflict at all with their ideology. Because the Gospel clearly conflicts with totalitarian thought, Christianity was typically suppressed under communist and fascist regimes.

Communism The Dream and the Reality

Karl Marx called for revolution by the oppressed working class, or proletariat, in capitalist societies. In the ideal Marxist vision, the workers would take control of the means of production and do away with private ownership of property. With the workers in charge, a classless society would emerge. Justice would finally come to the poor and oppressed workers.

Revolution in Russia

The first society in which people tried a Marxist revolution and succeeded was Russia, in 1917. But the workers did not actually take charge after the victory of the communists. Instead, the revolutionaries decided that the Communist Party would rule in the name of the workers. From 1918 to 1924, Vladimir Lenin led the party and the country of Russia, and before long he ruled the Union of Soviet Socialist Republics, or the Soviet Union—fifteen republics brought into a forced union. Central control of the economy was complete and rigid. Lenin ruled as a dictator, but his successor, Joseph Stalin, dictated the Soviet Union even more ruthlessly and violently.

Suppression of the Churches

The Soviet constitution theoretically allowed freedom of religion, but in practice the Christian churches, both Russian Orthodox and Roman Catholic, were suppressed. Supposedly in a classless workers' state, religion was "unnecessary"; people no longer needed the illusion of religion promising them happiness after death, because they had justice and happiness in *this* life. Thus, early on the Soviet Communist Party confiscated all church lands and dispersed priests, brothers, and sisters. In 1925, the party organized the League of the Godless to harass churchgoers. In 1929, the Law on Religious Associations decreed that citizens could not be instructed in the Christian faith, nor could they gather for prayer or discussion. All congregations had to register with the government. Those who chose to remain publicly Christian had limited opportunities for themselves and their families. Christians were forbidden by law to join the Communist Party, and party membership was essential to getting ahead.

The Church Reacts

In 1930, Pius XI, the pope from 1922 to 1939, called for a world-wide day of prayer for suffering Christians in Russia. In a papal encyclical, he condemned the errors of communism. Pius realized that communism as practiced in the Soviet Union stood in opposition to Christianity. Although the church shared the concern for workers that was implicit in Marxism, Soviet communism was unacceptable because it was totalitarian and atheistic. Only one ideology was permitted in the Soviet Union, and that one had no room for God or Christianity.

The Great Depression, which began in 1929, plunged the United States and much of the world into deep economic crisis. Millions of people were out of work, starving people stood in breadlines, and homeless people filled city streets. To those who were desperate for relief, the communist movement at least offered sympathy for their plight and a vision of a more just world.

In the midst of the depression, Dorothy Day, a young single mother, journalist, and recent convert to Catholicism, started a movement with Peter Maurin, a French peasant and wandering self-made philosopher. Day was longing to put her newly found faith into action. She had come from a radical socialist background and was passionately interested in justice for the poor, but she had parted ways with her old communist associates when she became Catholic. She and Maurin, who was steeped in the Catholic church's social teaching, were a good match to start the Catholic Worker Movement.

In 1933, in New York City, Day and Maurin published the first issue of *The Catholic Worker,* a newspaper addressing the plight of the poor and the workers. Soon afterward, they opened a house of hospitality, and then another one, to shelter and feed homeless and hungry people. The two founders relied on God's providence, shown in the generosity of people, to support the newspaper and their houses.

Day and Maurin intended that the Catholic Worker Movement, through its newspaper, would promote the social teachings of the Catholic church. Furthermore, Day and Maurin intended that the movement would not simply talk about social justice but live it out by doing works of mercy at a personal sacrifice—thus the houses of hospitality. As the need arose, they also joined picket lines to protest wars and injustices and even went to jail.

The first issue of *The Catholic Worker,* in May 1933, contained this message "To Our Readers":

Fascism An Ideology of Superiority

The other major totalitarian form of government that appeared on the global scene in the 1920s was fascism. Fascism stressed the dominance of one group, whether a social class or an ethnic group or a race, over another group. Fascist governments, which took total control of their countries' economies and promoted extreme nationalism, eventually dominated Germany, Italy, and Spain.

Italian, German, and Spanish Fascism

In Italy, the fascist leader Benito Mussolini proclaimed that Italy had to recover its proud Roman heritage and become an empire

For those who are sitting on park benches in the warm spring sunlight.

For those who are huddling in shelters trying to escape the rain.

For those who are walking the streets in the all but futile search for work.

For those who think that there is no hope for the future, no recognition of their plight—this little paper is addressed.

It is printed to call their attention to the fact that the Catholic Church has a social program—to let them know that there are men of God who are working not only for their spiritual but for their material welfare.

It's time there was a Catholic paper printed for the unemployed. The fundamental aim of most radical sheets is the conversion of its readers to Radicalism and Atheism.

Is it not possible to be radical and not atheist?

Is it not possible to protest, to expose, to complain, to point out abuses and demand reforms without desiring the overthrow of religion?

In an attempt to popularize and make known the encyclicals of the Popes in regard to social justice and the program put forth by the Church for the "reconstruction of the social order," this news sheet, *The Catholic Worker*, is started.

Today, more than sixty years after its founding, the Catholic Worker Movement lives on in more than one hundred Catholic Worker houses and in the Worker's newspapers. The movement continues to be a strong Catholic voice for social justice and peace. ■

The Catholic Worker Movement:
Catholic Social Teaching in Action

once again. Taking power in 1919, Mussolini promised to shape up the eroding national economy and to oppose communism. Civil ceremonies replaced religious ones—often in the form of mass rallies for the Fascist Party. Oppressive measures were used to discredit religious groups if they dared to oppose the party.

In Germany, fascism took the form of Nazism led by Adolf Hitler. The Nazis asserted that the German, or Aryan, people were superior to all other races and nationalities. Hitler claimed that national unity in Germany would be based on racial purity.

Spain, ruled by a communist-leaning government, persecuted the Catholic church in the 1920s. Church property was nationalized, education was completely secularized, and religious orders were suppressed and disbanded. In some places, extreme Spanish communists killed priests and religious brothers and sisters. A fascist rebel army led by General Francisco Franco ousted the communist government in 1939 after a bloody civil war, and Franco came to power. It was, on the surface, a victory for the church, because the Franco government gave official recognition and protection to the church. The church supported Franco as preferable to the communists. But Franco's rise to power was supported by Hitler and Mussolini; he ruled Spain as a repressive military dictator until 1975.

Church Reaction to Fascism in Italy

The church's reactions to the Italian and German forms of fascism were more complicated than its reaction to fascism in Spain. In Italy, the harsh measures that Mussolini used to control the country soon posed moral dilemmas for the church. (In the beginning of Mussolini's rule, the pope had not been compelled to condemn the dictator's actions, which were not yet as brutal as they would become.) Mussolini could not afford a condemnation by the church. In an effort to calm Catholic fears, the Italian Fascist Party opened talks with the church to reach an accord between Italy and the Vatican over the church's claims to Italian territory. These talks aimed to rectify the situation in which the pope remained a "prisoner of the Vatican" to protest Italy's taking the Papal States decades earlier.

After careful negotiations, the Lateran Treaty was signed in 1929. The papacy legally gave up any territorial claims in Italy and formally acknowledged the status of the ruling dynasty—the king, who was really just a puppet for Mussolini. The pope also agreed to stay out of Italian politics and to allow the government to approve the nominations of Italian bishops. In turn, the Italian government recognized the existence of the forty-acre Vatican City as an independent state and compensated the church for the previous loss of Rome and the

Papal States. Religious orders gained legal status, as did other church institutions. The Catholic religion could be taught in all secondary schools, and marriage throughout Italy would follow church law.

Mussolini viewed the state as superior to the church, but he could not push that notion into action without turning the Italian people, who were predominantly Catholic, against him. At one point, he tried to suppress the activities of Catholic Action groups. Pope Pius XI, no longer conciliatory toward Mussolini, publicly opposed the suppression. In 1931, the pope published the encyclical *Quadragesimo Anno* (*On Reconstructing the Social Order*), criticizing the absolutist state, which controlled all aspects of life. Mussolini backed away from his open crackdown on Catholic Action.

In the end, however, the pope could do little to stop Mussolini from swaying the masses of Italians toward backing the fascist dictatorship. The pope's criticisms of Italy's invasion of Ethiopia fell on deaf ears; most Italians thought that the invasion and victory were justified—indeed, even a source of national pride. Italy marched further along the road to fascism, soon joining into alliance with Hitler.

Pius XI and Church Reaction to Nazism

In 1937, Pope Pius XI needed all of his diplomatic skills and deep faith to deal with the Spanish civil war, Mussolini's strong-arm dictatorship, and the rising threat of Nazi aggression in Germany. Despite the danger of speaking out against Hitler and the Nazi government, Pius wrote a letter to Germany's Catholics, condemning Nazi brainwashing, and he had it smuggled into the country to be read from every pulpit one Sunday. Afterward, in a fit of rage, Hitler closed the presses that had printed the letter. Hitler then threw priests and laypeople into prison on trumped-up charges in an attempt to threaten the pope so that he would not criticize Nazism any further.

Pius continued to try to lead German Catholics away from Hitler. But when Pius died in 1939, Hitler and the Nazis controlled Germany absolutely. Their rise to power had fulfilled Pope Benedict XV's prediction at the end of World War I—that a Germany humiliated by the Allies' terms of peace eventually would seek power and revenge.

Cooperation of Christians

The Nazis chose the Jews, gypsies, and any other non-Aryans as scapegoats for their humiliation and defeat. In particular, they accused the Jews of conspiring to take over the German economy and industry—which the Nazis saw as part of an overall Jewish plot to subjugate the world. By being silent, most Germans, both Protestants and Catholics, cooperated in the suppression, if not the mass murders, of the Jews in Europe. Although some Christians and Catholics spoke out against the *Shoah,* the term Jews use for the Holocaust, and suffered grievously for it, most did not resist this great evil.

Many of the German Catholic bishops endorsed the Nazi regime, choosing not to follow the courageous example of Pius XI, who had dared to challenge Hitler. A Catholic political party in Germany voluntarily voted to allow Hitler to rule by decree. The Catholic trade unions were dissolved by their own choice. Catholic schools could operate, but they had to teach the Nazi party line. The Nazis methodically destroyed all church organizations and clamped down on the Catholic press. In effect, the German church let Hitler have his way. As the excesses of Nazi fascism became more flagrant, some church leaders did protest, but most were quickly silenced.

World War Again: Questions of Conscience for Catholics

As Hitler turned his ambitions beyond Germany, war swept through Europe, North Africa, the Middle East, and the Asian Pacific. The war lasted from 1939 to 1945. Japan joined forces with Germany and Italy in an effort to strengthen its own grip on much of Asia. The United States got into the war when Japan attacked Pearl Harbor in 1941.

The Role of Pius Pius XI's successor, Pope Pius XII (1939 to 1958), faced the terrible dilemma of how to resist Hitler while keeping Catholics safe. If he condemned the Nazis, he would alienate German Catholics, and the Nazis would step up persecution of the church in Germany and the occupied countries. But if the Vatican stayed neutral in the war, at least Catholics would not be killed and the Vatican itself would not be attacked by Hitler and Mussolini.

Pius decided to stay neutral. He realized that without the Vatican, the church would have no base from which to do any good. The pope had seen what happened when the Dutch bishops condemned the deportation of Jews: Nazi reprisals crippled the Dutch church. Finally, the pope realized that the church could not stop Hitler. Official neutrality, however, did not keep the pope from trying to ease the suffering of the war's victims. Four hundred thousand Jews were saved from death by seeking help from the Vatican. Also, the Vatican sent out an enormous amount of relief supplies to destroyed towns.

Pius XII's official stance of neutrality did not prevent him from being recognized as a hero after the war: the Israeli government awarded him a medal for saving Jews from death. However, some people have judged the pope and the church negatively because of the position of neutrality he took.

Catholic Resistance Within Hitler's Empire As discussed earlier, the vast majority of Catholics within Germany remained silent regarding the Holocaust. Nevertheless, some Catholics, both in Germany and in the German-occupied countries, did resist the Nazis. Their resistance took many forms, and their example still lives on, reminding us of what it means to be truly Christian, to be followers of Jesus. For instance:

- Franz Jaegerstaetter, a Catholic Austrian peasant farmer, was martyred in 1943 for refusing to serve in Hitler's army.
- Corrie ten Boom, in *The Hiding Place,* tells how her whole family risked their life to hide Jews from the Nazis in Holland.
- Edith Stein, born to a Jewish family but later a convert to Catholicism, was a German professor and writer of philosophy until the Nazis fired her because of her Jewish background. She became a Carmelite nun in Holland, but even in the convent the Nazis saw her as dangerous. She was taken from the convent by the S.S. police, sent to Auschwitz, tortured, and executed in the gas chamber.

Some Catholics resisting Hitler were driven to extreme, even violent, measures. Alfred Delp, a Jesuit priest, was a member of a group that tried to assassinate Hitler to stop the Nazi madness. Count Klaus von Stauffenberg, a Catholic, planted the bomb in the assassination attempt. The plot failed, and the whole group was executed.

Thousands of priests, religious, and laypeople were executed for other, less bold church activity. Cleverly, the Nazis persecuted only the lower ranks of the clergy and laypeople. The bishops who protested were left unharmed, but the bishops knew that the more they protested, the more often their priests and lay Catholics would "disappear" or be executed on phony charges.

Missionaries Suffer in Asia Japan had been taking land in Asian countries since early in the twentieth century. To gain power in Asia, it had to contend with the colonial powers of France, Britain, and the United States, which held territory in southern Asia. Sweeping south and west from its islands during World War II, Japan soon controlled most of the Far East. Europeans, Americans, and others resisting the Japanese were either killed or put into hellish prisoner-of-war camps. Those imprisoned included almost all the missionaries in the area. Many priests, religious, and laypeople died in the camps from a combination of disease, starvation, and overwork. Before the Allied victory of World War II, nearly an entire generation of missionaries perished in prisons in places like Singapore and the Philippines. After the war, missionary efforts were set back many years because of the losses.

The End **The Fall of Germany**
of the War   Germany's fall in May 1945 ended the war on the
European front and ended some of the greatest devastation in history. In the war, eighteen million Russians had been
killed by Hitler's forces; six million Jews had met death in concentration camps; millions of other people on both sides had lost their life.
Great cities of Europe and hundreds of towns and villages had been
flattened. Millions of people returned from prison camps or battle
lines to find their families dead and their homes destroyed.

The Atomic Bomb: A New Moment in History

On the Pacific front, the war between the Allies and Japan
dragged on into the summer following Hitler's defeat. In August 1945,
the United States brought the war to a sudden conclusion by its decision to drop a new, secret weapon, called the atomic bomb, on the
Japanese cities of Hiroshima and Nagasaki. The atomic bombs, also
called nuclear bombs, were small by comparison with the nuclear
weapons that have since been developed. Still, they were the most
destructive weapons the world had ever witnessed. Besides the enormous destruction and death they immediately caused, these bombs
released lethal radiation that killed victims more slowly and that had
long-term harmful effects. The Japanese knew that in the face of such
destructive capability, they had no choice but to surrender.

Most people in the United States at that time thought that drop-
ping the bombs on Japan was the right thing to do, because they believed that it hastened the war's end and thus spared U.S. soldiers'
lives. Most U.S. citizens did not realize just how destructive the
bombs were, nor did most people understand their long-term effects.
Catholics, with the exception of a few such as Dorothy Day, were
fairly unquestioning about the ethics of using nuclear weapons.

New Issues

As a result of World War II, a whole new array of problems confronted humankind. For perhaps the first time in history, huge civilian populations had been the direct targets of attacks. Weapons were
more deadly than ever before—the atomic bomb being the prime example. Germany's missiles had come into use late in the war, signal-
ing another advance in destructive capability.

Again, national boundaries were changing. The Soviet Union annexed parts of Eastern Europe as economically, politically, and militarily dependent client states. The cry for a Jewish homeland gave
impetus to the formation of the State of Israel. By the 1950s, France
and Britain were so weakened by the war that they lost most of their
colonies including almost all of Africa.

The Cold War and the Arms Race

A Race to Destruction   In global politics, the Soviet Union and the United States squared off as the world's two most powerful nations, with two very different forms of government and national ideologies. Allies during the war, they became hostile to each other once the war was over. The cold war commenced—enmity and conflict between the superpowers that was constantly threatening to break into a "hot," shooting war. Countries lined up on both sides of the conflict.

The nuclear arms race, a race to win weapons superiority, chewed up more of the superpowers' resources as they built tens of thousands of nuclear weapons. A new term illustrated the insanity of the nuclear arms race: MAD, or mutually assured destruction, was said to deter the superpowers from using the weapons.

Not until 1965, when the Second Vatican Council condemned the use of weapons of mass destruction, did U.S. Catholics begin to widely question their government's policy in having used atomic bombs in the past or in preparing to use them in the future.

Communist Persecution of the Church   **In the Soviet Union and Eastern Europe**
As the Soviets took over countries after World War II and installed communist governments, persecution of the church increased. Among the countries dominated by the Soviet Union were East Germany, Hungary, Czechoslovakia, Yugoslavia, Poland, Bulgaria, and Romania. Millions of Catholics lived in these countries, and more and more they were denied their right to worship. Priests and religious were exiled, jailed, or forced to leave their ministries for work in factories, farms, or forced labor camps. Catholic schools were confiscated by the government. Religious activity continued underground, but it did so at great risk. Some countries had national churches, but these churches were under the complete control of the communist government.

An example of the strategies used against the Catholic church in that era is found in the following instructions by the Czechoslovakian Communist Party:

The Vatican: You are to undermine the authority of the Vatican by all means, especially by attacks in the press, compromising articles and news items.

. . . To break down unity among the clergy, separate higher from the lower clergy, drive a wedge between bishops and clergy, also between the priests and their parishes. . . .

Attack the Catholic Church with all the usual weapons: unreasonableness of celibacy, economic power and wealth of the Church, the Church as a capitalist institution, moral delinquents. . . .

. . . Archbishops and bishops should be prevented from communicating with the Vatican otherwise than through the Government.

Pastoral letters must always have previous Government authorization.

Sermons of priests and all addresses to church associations should be censored and kept under rigid control. . . .

The Catholic clergy should be morally compromised, if necessary by means of woman agents.

In China

In 1949, Mao Tse-tung, after a long struggle for control of China, declared the creation of the People's Republic of China, a communist state. At the time, there were four million Chinese Catholics in China. Like the Soviets in their takeovers in Eastern Europe, the Chinese communists imprisoned or expelled all foreign missionaries. The Christian churches were dissolved. Mao stressed the need for Chinese nationalism and the destruction of all that was foreign and corrupt. Catholics lost their lives or had to go underground. Catholic worship eventually would be permitted, but only in a nationalized Chinese Catholic church, with its bishops approved by the government.

Resisting Communism

Pius XII used what influence he had to confront communism around the world. In 1949, he excommunicated Catholics involved in communist activities, denounced the communists' persecution of the church, and encouraged any efforts to resist communism.

Throughout Eastern Europe, people suffered during the cold war, which lasted from 1945 until 1989–1990. Then the Soviet bloc countries were liberated from domination by the Soviet Union, which also started to break up into independent, noncommunist republics. Catholics were free to practice their religion publicly. In China, however, the repression of the church continues, with underground Roman Catholics still subject to persecution if they are discovered.

Even as the church suffered the effects of the cold war in the 1940s and 1950s, the groundwork was being laid for the church to become an important reconciling force in the world. A Catholic renewal was beginning to grow that would reach its flowering in the Second Vatican Council, in the 1960s.

The seeds of renewal were planted in the 1940s and 1950s. First, in 1943, Pius XII issued two encyclicals that fostered a renewal of theology. In one encyclical, on the Scriptures, he approved modern scientific and historical methods of biblical scholarship, which encouraged Catholic theologians to get in touch with the roots of Christianity. In the second encyclical, on the Mystical Body of Christ, Pius highlighted the importance of all members of the church, laity included, and the need for unity in the church. In addition to these developments, an early, pre–Vatican II liturgical movement spurred a rediscovery of the early forms and spirit of Christian worship.

The renewal that was coming with the Vatican Council II would turn the church inward to find its own roots and outward to respond more compassionately to the whole human family. Major themes of Catholic social teaching—on justice, on peace and the arms race, on racial equality, on the distribution of the world's resources—were soon to be articulated. The church was to become a significant moral leader in efforts to reconcile the world's nations and peoples.

Conclusion A major theme for the Catholic church in the twentieth century has been how to respond to the struggle for dominance among the world's powers. During two world wars and the cold war, the church has had to constantly discern what the vision of Jesus would be on those conflicts. As an institution and as Catholic individuals, the church in the twentieth century has sometimes spoken out prophetically against oppression and war. But at times its voice has been raised only weakly.

Questions for Reflection and Discussion

1. What are today's Catholic Action groups?
2. As a result of World War I many people had become disillusioned with traditional religious values and practices. What contemporary experiences disillusion people about the effectiveness and value of organized religion or religious values?
3. How would you evaluate Freud's contention that religious faith is childish and that religion is simply society's way of controlling people?
4. Considering the just-war theory of Saint Thomas Aquinas summarized on pages 142–143, can the use of modern weapons of mass destruction ever be morally justified?
5. Do you think Catholics should have tried to more actively resist the spread of fascism? How would you respond if faced with such a decision today?

15

The Contemporary Church

On a Pilgrimage into the Future

THE SECOND HALF of the twentieth century has brought unprecedented growth in the Catholic church. The faith has spread throughout the globe. Gone are the days when the church was primarily European. Now more than 60 percent of all Catholics live in Asia, Africa, and Latin America, and that percentage is climbing rapidly. Besides the dynamic growth of the church, it has also been renewed in dramatic ways. The particular source of this renewal was the Second Vatican Council (1962–1965), called by Pope John XXIII.

The future of the Catholic church is bound to be full of surprises. The church is a community on a pilgrimage, making its way to God. Each step of the journey can bring joy and sorrow, revelations and confusion, love and hate. But even with great and unexpected changes, the church will continue its pilgrimage in the world, acting as Body of Christ and People of God, Institution, Sacrament, Herald, Servant, and Community of Disciples.

Reform and Renewal: Vatican Council II

By the middle of the twentieth century, the Catholic church had witnessed the devastation brought by two world wars; it had tried to prevent or eliminate the suffering of war; and the papacy was growing in its role as a moral force in the world.

As the church reached out to the world, theologians and biblical scholars focused on the church itself. Studies of the church's early worship and the Bible brought new insights into the church's identity and teachings. But the church's structures, liturgy, and expressions of its teachings had not significantly changed in hundreds of years, since the Council of Trent, in the 1500s. It became clear to some in the church that renewal was needed.

One monumental event—Vatican Council II—brought new light, hope, and direction to the church. One person—Pope John XXIII, inspired by the Holy Spirit—guided the church to that council.

Good Pope John

Pope John XXIII, elected in 1958, was not an aristocratic kind of leader. Instead he was approachable, warm, and humorous. He had started out in life as an Italian peasant named Angelo Roncalli, and he had served in the Italian medical corps during the First World War. But as a priest, Roncalli also was a

Timeline . . .

1950

- U.S. Catholic bishops decry racism.
- Pope John XXIII calls for ecumenical council.
- John XXIII opens Vatican Council II.
- Pope Paul VI meets with Patriarch Athenagoras to find common ground for dialog.
- Vatican Council II condemns use of weapons of mass destruction.
- Vatican Council II closes.
- Pope Paul VI delivers message of peace to United Nations.

1975

- John Paul II is elected pope.

- Catholic church publishes new *Catechism of the Catholic Church.*

2000

265

competent diplomat, with many years in the Near East and Paris as a member of the Vatican diplomatic corps.

At age seventy-six, Cardinal Roncalli was looking toward retirement from his position as archbishop of Venice. But when Pope Pius XII died, Roncalli, to his own amazement, was elected pope by his fellow cardinals. He was a compromise candidate, someone whom different factions in the College of Cardinals could agree on because he was not identified with any one strong view. Few observers expected much from him; most thought he would just be an interim pope, providing a short bridge to the next "significant" papacy.

But soon John XXIII's papacy took a different shape than that of his predecessors. He delighted the world by inviting all kinds of people to dine with him. Sometimes he wandered the streets of Rome, and he visited hospitals and prisons. He became known for telling warm, wonderful jokes.

But, John XXIII gave the church its greatest surprise when, in 1959, he called for an ecumenical council (worldwide council) of bishops. When asked where the idea had come from, John's answer expressed his sense that it had come directly from God: "My soul was illumined by a great idea . . . which I welcomed with ineffable confidence in the divine Teacher. And there sprang to my lips a word that was solemn and committing. My voice uttered it for the first time: a Council."

A Need to Renew

Ecumenical councils had been called before, but usually in times of great crisis for the church. The last one had been Vatican Council I, in 1869, when the church was under assault from many sides. But to the average Catholic in 1959, the church did not seem to be in crisis or facing great challenges. Most Catholics at the time could not perceive the problems that John clearly saw confronting the Catholic community. John understood all too well that the church was no longer a European institution but a worldwide community, made up of women and men with extremely diverse cultures, values, needs, and contributions to offer. The church also needed to respond to developments in technology, politics, economics, and science. So by calling a council, John XXIII hoped to open up the Catholic church to dialog with the whole world. Among other purposes, the council's aim was to promote the unity of all Christians and to study how the church could better understand and influence the rapidly changing world.

In spite of resistance from many sides in the church, the council opened in 1962. Although Pope John died in 1963, his spirit of openness would forever be associated with the council. In its three years of sessions, lasting until 1965, the world's bishops discussed with experts and debated among themselves many facets of church life and practice. They set new, fresh directions for the church's liturgy, its understanding of itself, its attitude toward other Christian denominations and non-Christian religions, and its relationship with the modern world. These directions have guided the church into the present.

The Liturgy: Finding Renewal by Going Back to the Sources

Since the Council of Trent, held in the 1500s, the form for all liturgical worship had been standardized and was followed throughout the entire church. For instance, the whole Mass, even the readings from the Scriptures, was said in Latin. Many elaborate prayers and rituals, added in the centuries before the Council of Trent, did not express the original intent of the Eucharist but were nonetheless included. The people's participation was limited: The priest faced the tabernacle (the box where the Eucharist was reserved), not the people. The people could try to follow the Latin Mass prayers using a missal (although these were not available for laypeople until the early twentieth century). Singing was minimal. Communion was received only in the form of the bread—and that was placed on the tongue by the priest. There were no lay readers or lay ministers of Communion. The focus of the Mass was on worshiping Jesus as God present in the Eucharist.

After looking at the ancient roots of Christian worship and at the ways the Mass had been altered through the centuries, the council bishops made significant recommendations. A more conscious community dimension was highlighted for the Eucharist, and eventually for all the sacraments. Clearly, the Mass today is different from the way it was in the 1950s: The prayers and rituals have been simplified to get back to their original intent. The local language is used. The priest communicates directly with the congregation. The scriptural readings are given great importance. The congregation participates through spoken responses and song. Communion is often received in the forms of both bread and wine. The liturgy today is designed to celebrate Jesus present among the community of believers, to support the faith and growth of the community, and to move the community to service and loving action in the world.

For some Catholics of the 1960s, the liturgical changes seemed to be drastic departures from tradition. But in reality, they were rooted in the earliest traditions of the church.

The Church's Understanding of Itself: Broadening Participation

Throughout this book, the words *Body of Christ* and *People of God* have been used to describe the church. These expressions point to the community dimension of the church, emphasizing that *all* members have important roles to play. This emphasis may seem ordinary to people now, but it was not common before Vatican Council II. Once again, by studying the roots of the church in the Scriptures and in other early church documents, the council bishops saw that they needed to shift the emphasis away from the church as a strictly hierarchical institution—one in which the pope rules, bishops and priests exercise authority under him, and everyone else follows along. They needed to stress the church as the entire community of the faithful who are the Body of Christ, or the People of God. The council bishops especially articulated this vision of the church in their document titled *Lumen Gentium* (*Dogmatic Constitution on the Church*).

This change in emphasis has brought much more lay participation and leadership into the church. Parish councils help direct the life of local churches. School boards, not just pastors or religious communities, manage most Catholic schools. Laypersons hold leadership positions from which they were excluded before Vatican Council II. (For instance, laymen, married or single, are now being ordained as permanent deacons. Laypeople are studying theology and the Bible, giving retreats, offering spiritual direction, and administering parishes.) In short, a broader spectrum of church members now takes responsibility for the life of the church.

Ecumenism: Reaching Out to Non-Catholics and Non-Christians

A most welcome direction encouraged by Vatican Council II was the ecumenical movement, the attempt to dialog and find common ground with other Christian denominations and other non-Christian religions. Pope John invited representatives from most non-Catholic Christian communities to attend the Second Vatican Council as observers. Since then, theological commissions from the Catholic church and other Christian denominations have studied points of similarity in their traditions and have sought to understand areas of difference. In local communities, prayer services involving different denominations have broken down some of the barriers separating Christians. Catholic and other Christian denominations now cooperate more fully in confronting social problems.

Three popes from recent decades—John XXIII, Paul VI (pope from 1963 until 1978), and John Paul II (pope since 1978)—have been personal examples of the attempt to heal divisions among Christians. Pope Paul VI surprised the world when, in 1964, he met with and embraced the Greek Orthodox Patriarch Athenagoras in Jerusalem. Neither the pope nor the leader of Orthodox Christians underestimated the existing differences between their communities, but the warmth of their meeting melted the ice that had formed through nine centuries of separation. The popes since Vatican Council II have encouraged many forms of cooperation and dialog with other Christians, such as shared ministerial training, common Bible translation projects, and further theological discussions.

The church's ecumenical outreach has extended beyond Christianity as well. In its *Declaration on Religious Freedom,* the Second Vatican Council affirmed the value of religious liberty and freedom of conscience for all people everywhere, not only Christians or Catholics. The bishops asserted that people must have the liberty to choose or to reject their own religion—that no religion, including Catholicism, should be the only one allowed by a given state.

Since the council, the Vatican has engaged in important dialog with Jewish leaders and scholars to heal the tragic wounds in Jewish-Christian relations, wounds perpetuated for centuries by misunderstanding and persecution of Jews. Great progress has been made. In another affirmation of traditions beyond Christianity, on two occasions Pope John Paul II has held gatherings of the leaders of the world's religions in Assisi, Italy, to pray for world peace.

Relationship with the Modern World: Openness and Loving Concern

At Pope John XXIII's urging, the Second Vatican Council opened avenues of discussion with all sectors of the modern world. The council reversed the suspicion and wariness that had previously characterized the church's attitude toward modern secular developments. One of the most famous quotes from the council, from its *Gaudium et Spes (Pastoral Constitution on the Church in the Modern World)*, states:

The joys and the hopes, the griefs and the anxieties of [people] of this age, especially those who are poor or in any way afflicted, these too are the joys and hopes, the griefs and anxieties of the followers of Christ. Indeed, nothing genuinely human fails to raise an echo in their hearts. (Number 1)

Thus the church declared its solidarity with the struggles and legitimate aspirations of people everywhere.

In the decades since Vatican Council II, the church has given flesh to those words. In countries where oppressive regimes have ruled, the church more and more has stood with the people and defended their cause. Church people have at times been killed because of their commitment to the oppressed. Popes since Vatican Council II have traveled worldwide to express the church's concern for the world's different cultures and peoples, especially for those who are poor and suffering. These popes have been eloquent defenders of human rights and promoters of justice and peace through their encyclicals. Likewise, national and regional conferences of bishops have issued major statements and pastoral letters that demonstrate the church's concern for the world.

The Second Vatican Council produced sixteen important documents setting the course of the church for decades and perhaps centuries to come. In recent years, the world's bishops became concerned that a unity of Catholic faith be guarded in the midst of the changes that resulted from the council. So in 1992, the church published *The Catechism of the Catholic Church,* a book that expresses Catholic teaching on the church's creed, the sacraments, the moral life, and prayer. This is the first such worldwide catechism since the *Roman Catechism* was developed in the 1500s, after the Council of Trent.

Glimpses of the Future: A Church Inspired by the Spirit

Looking back at the development of the church over almost two thousand years of history, we can surmise that the church's future will be filled with challenges and opportunities that will stretch the church in unexpected ways. The church of the year 2000 will have about 70 percent of its members in the developing world in Asia, Africa, and Latin America. This means that on the whole, Catholics will be poor and young, because these areas have significantly more poor and young people than the industrialized world. In all of these places, Jesus Christ is the source of faith and hope. In South and Central America, Jesus is often pictured as a liberator. In Africa, he is the source of life. And to many Asians, the image of Jesus as risen from the dead is most appealing. Indeed, Jesus is all of these and will always be the life-spring of the church.

As is undoubtedly apparent by now, Christians throughout the centuries, inspired by God's Spirit, have made the church what it is today. The church of the future, in turn, will be made by the people in it. The church changes, but it also retains its essential identity as

Christians and Catholics Throughout the World

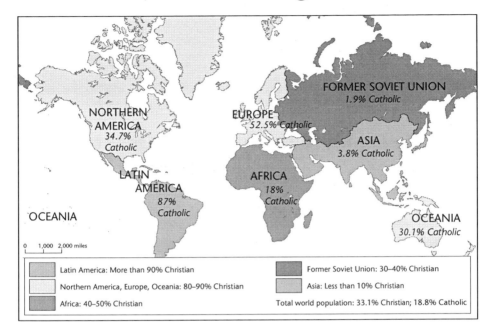

NORTHERN AMERICA
34.7% Catholic

FORMER SOVIET UNION
1.9% Catholic

EUROPE
52.5% Catholic

ASIA
3.8% Catholic

LATIN AMERICA
87% Catholic

AFRICA
18% Catholic

OCEANIA

OCEANIA
30.1% Catholic

0   1,000   2,000 miles

Latin America: More than 90% Christian

Northern America, Europe, Oceania: 80–90% Christian

Africa: 40–50% Christian

Former Soviet Union: 30–40% Christian

Asia: Less than 10% Christian

Total world population: 33.1% Christian; 18.8% Catholic

the community that embodies Christ in the world—at some times more obviously than at others. We can know with assurance that through trials and difficulties, and even sinful episodes, the church is inspired by the Holy Spirit to be Servant, Herald, People of God and Body of Christ, Institution, Sacrament, and Community of Disciples.

Some examples of how contemporary Catholics are living out these models of the church can give us glimpses of the church of the future.

Servant   Laypeople Offering Themselves for Service

In the future, we will see increasing involvement of laypeople in the servant role of Jesus. An article from the *National Catholic Reporter*, entitled "Minnesota Woman Washes Feet of Walking Wounded," gives an example of a laywoman living out the mission of Jesus to be a servant to the world:

Mary Jo Copeland has washed the feet of hundreds of society's "walking wounded."

That is an incidental service provided to some of the 400 to 500 poor and homeless who come daily to her Sharing and Caring Hands day shelter near the new Target Center [in Minneapolis], where the Minnesota Timberwolves play professional basketball.

Copeland soaks the blistered feet of children and adults with worn-out or ill-fitting shoes, rubs them and soothes them with an ointment. Many are given new shoes and socks from the center's ample supply.

"Our Lord taught us to serve," says the suburban Catholic woman, who sees the suffering Christ in the poor. Jesus, she explains, "gave us an example by washing the apostles' feet. I believe the poor are our way home to God." . . .

About a thousand volunteers—many from suburban churches—assist Copeland at the shelter. Like Copeland and associates, no one is paid. "I believe that volunteers are more caring and sensitive than those who receive paychecks for their services," she says.

The shelter attracts people who do not qualify for assistance from other agencies. They come for food (a church brings in each noon meal), clothing, a shower, dental care, counseling or other help, along with something Copeland described as even more important—"a sense of dignity as human beings, and a feeling of being loved." . . .

Copeland started the shelter, she said, because she remembers what it is like to be hungry, poor and unloved. She was born in Rochester, Minn., to alcoholic, abusive parents. She was not allowed to take a bath, and schoolmates would make fun of her body odor and ragged clothing.

Although lonely, she says she learned in parochial school that God's love is unconditional and to believe that God had some special task in mind for her. The prayer of St. Francis of Assisi became her prayer.

At one time, Copeland planned to become a nun, she said. But at age 18, she married Dick Copeland, and they have 12 children. As the youngest child neared school age, Mary Jo became a volunteer for Catholic Charities at a storefront location.

After three years, she decided to open her own shelter. . . .

Asked how long she plans to operate the shelter, the 49-year-old Copeland said: "Until I go to heaven. I have promised God that for the rest of my life I will be his hands, his heart, his feet and his mouth." (15 November 1991)

Herald Solidarity with the People

We have seen that in its role as Herald of the Good News, the church historically has not always been sensitive to the cultures it has evangelized. Sometimes church missionaries imposed European culture, rather than appreciating the special gifts and strengths of the people to whom they were preaching the Good News.

Missionaries today think of their work as not only bringing the Good News to foreign lands but also discovering God in the people they are sent to serve. Rather than trying to impose their own culture on people, missionaries attempt to live in solidarity with them, learning to appreciate how God is working through the people. A poem by a lay missionary volunteer to Chile, in South America, illustrates this sense of solidarity:

My life is becoming more and more
    intimately intertwined
with those of my Chilean friends
    and North American housemates:

Sharing the birth and baptism
    of Vicente and Raquel's son,
Sharing Teresa's pain over the unjust detention
    of her son,
Dancing at our costume party with friends here
    in the *población* [village].

Spending the day with Lily:
singing, hiking in the foothills,
    washing clothes and sewing,
Praying for a friend who has been forced into hiding,
Helping Humberto with his exercises
to regain muscle strength and coordination.

Accompanying those who are ill,
and gratefully receiving visitors when I was ill.
Sharing, crying, and laughing
with Chilean peers during our recent retreat.

People like Angelica and Sara
are touching me profoundly with their lives—
their simplicity, questioning, and service to others
amid the illness, poverty, and at times
desperate situations of their own lives.

I am learning a deeper sense of humility.
Be assured, however, that I am happy here—
thankful for the gift of life and the opportunity
    to be living the struggles and challenges
with the people in La Faena.

(Anne Attea)

People of God and Body of Christ **Finding Christ in the Eucharistic Community**

The liturgical renewal prompted by Vatican Council II gave fresh meaning to the Eucharist. Changes in the Mass enabled Catholics to see more clearly their relationship to one another through the Body of Christ; that is, the Body of Christ is shared as Jesus' body and blood in the Eucharist, but it is also lived out as a community. Daniel Ponsetto, a youth minister and author, offers a reflection on an experience of Sunday Mass at his parish when the reality of the Body of Christ was revealed to him:

Sunday, on the feast of Corpus Christi [the Body of Christ], which also happens to be the name of our parish, I had one of those revelatory experiences. Excitement filled the air that day, because the parish community was going to have a picnic on the church lawn after Mass. During the liturgy, as I made my way forward to the altar to receive the Eucharist, I suddenly became aware of all those around me who were also coming forward for communion. Unexpectedly, I found myself wanting to look deeply into their faces: the middle-aged woman with a tired-looking face, the old man across from me, slightly hunched over and moving with difficulty. I was struck by the immensity of life embodied in the people who surrounded me and processed with me: some young, some old; some rich, some poor; some whole, some broken; some beautiful, some unseemly. All with a history. All on a journey. I couldn't take my eyes off of them.

I suddenly found myself overwhelmed by the sense that I was connected to these people, to these lives. More than as a mere participant in the eucharistic liturgy, I saw my life—in all of its complexity—as a part of something much larger. I was seized by a deepened understanding that I was, with these others, the body and blood of Christ, living, breathing, hoping, joyful, and sorrowful. (*Praying Our Stories*, page 85)

Institution **Working with Other Christian Churches**

The church as an institutional structure is facing many challenges, not the least of which is the declining number of priests. The shortage of priests is a serious dilemma for the church, but it is also an opportunity to broaden the ministries performed by lay Catholics. The Catholic church of the future will increasingly involve the laity in leadership positions.

With the strides made in the ecumenical movement, the church as institution is also cooperating with other Christian denominations on action for social justice. We are seeing this in many projects, such as in the following one, happening in Brooklyn, New York:

The Catholic Diocese of Brooklyn, the Episcopal Diocese of Long Island and the area's Lutheran Church, Missouri Synod, reached agreement with

New York City's government and home owners' associations to build as many as 1,300 single-family dwellings for lower-middle-class families, to enable them to become first-time home owners. The church group calls itself East Brooklyn Congregations and leads the Nehemiah housing movement, named for the prophet who reconstructed Jerusalem.

The group hopes to build 700–800 row houses in an area of East New York known for drugs and violence. . . .

. . . The group has already constructed about 2,300 two- and three-bedroom homes in the past eight years. (Quoted in *National Catholic Reporter*, 30 October 1992)

Sacrament, Community of Disciples

God Revealed in a Small Christian Community

In recent decades, many Catholics have discovered their Catholicism anew in small Christian communities that gather to pray, reflect on the Scriptures, celebrate, share in work projects, and simply live their lives together in faith. Some of these—like communities of the Catholic Worker Movement started by Dorothy Day and Peter Maurin (see pages 254–255)—are focused on doing the works of mercy. Many communities, such as those in the RENEW movement in the United States, are inspired by basic Christian communities, the small groups of Catholics that emerged in Latin America as a means of relating the Gospel to everyday life and offering support in living out the faith.

Small groups such as these express the church as a Community of Disciples. They are the wave of the future for the church. The following account by Hilary Gutman, from a Catholic Worker house in Rochester, New York, illustrates that such communities, too, are often where the church's role as Sacrament, as revelation of God, can be seen:

It was a crisp autumn day. Women had been straggling across the field to the big, century-old, yellow house all afternoon. The community of Bethany House, a Catholic Worker emergency shelter for women and children, was slowly gathering for its weekly celebration of the Eucharist. This loosely knit group was made up of women who were all former guests of the shelter. They came now for support; they came to relieve their loneliness. They came with children tucked two to a stroller built for one; they came limping; they came babbling, carrying on conversations only they understood. They came as God's special gift to us, and tonight would be no exception.

Because most of these women came from backgrounds where celebrating birthdays was not economically possible, an important part of the women's weekly gatherings had been the celebration of birthdays, both their own and their children's. Balloons, streamers, presents, cake, and ice cream were all part of the evening. This Wednesday we were celebrating four-year-old Biesha's birthday. Several years ago, Biesha, her mother, and her two brothers were guests of the house when their father was first incarcerated. Now, settled in their own apartment, the family continued to rely on the shelter for emotional and physical support.

Short and slight for her age, Biesha danced around the house, eyes shining, as we prepared to celebrate the liturgy. This, she knew, was to be a special evening for her. Her brown skin gleamed with a soft aura against her crisp new turquoise dress. Secretly, she whispered in my ear that she hoped she would get a Barbie doll for her birthday.

As the drama of the liturgy unfolded, so did the poignancy of the people's prayers. Some prayed to find a job. Others prayed that they could make it again—but this time without drugs. There were prayers, too, for friends still in prison. And there was a special prayer for Biesha, that she might grow gracefully in age and wisdom. As we joyfully shared robust hugs with each other during the exchange of peace just before Communion, I found Biesha had attached herself to my leg like a little vine.

I held this beautiful child in my lap while the eucharistic bread was passed from person to person, while each of us held the host until all could receive together. As I sat on the floor with the Eucharist in my right hand and my left arm wrapped around Biesha, I wondered about the Divine Presence in my midst. I thought of Jesus and his birth into poverty; I thought of his short, abruptly ended life. I thought about Biesha and all that her few years had held already, and I wondered, What will she be like at thirty-three? Was I holding the Divine in my right hand or in my left? And what about the Presence I felt and knew at the core of my very being? There was no answer. God was so real. We were three, but we were One; the Trinity in profound Reality.

Conclusion If any lesson or hope for the future can be gained from studying the church's history, it is certainly that the church has always been gifted with the abiding presence of the Holy Spirit. Through times of persecution, internal strife and divisions, and even sinful, misguided mistakes, the church has never been abandoned by God. After all its trials, the church has endured in truth and love. Even when corruption seemed to tear the church apart, the Spirit of God through people in the church called the church to renewal.

Individual Christians have listened to the Spirit over the centuries: Paul listened to Christ on the road to Damascus, Augustine felt the move to conversion in his garden while reading the Scriptures, Teresa of Ávila listened to the call to reform her order, Francis of Assisi heard the invitation to the simple life, Louise de Marillac listened to God through the cries of the poor in France, lay volunteers have discovered God in the people they serve, and contemporary urban Catholics recognize Christ in the people they encounter at Mass. Perhaps today the presence of God's Spirit with the church is more apparent than ever, as we witness the lives of Catholics whose faith and commitment to the Gospel seems as fresh and lively as that of the early Christians.

What the church will be in the future depends on how well the people who make up the church can listen for the Spirit of God in their own lives and circumstances. Below, a Maryknoll Lay Missioner working in Hong Kong expresses the source of hope for the future of the church:

> God, my life, my way, my hope, my *future*,
> I never thought of you as my future.
> I always worried about my future—
> what was I going to do?
> It is so nice to think of you as my future,
> like I can relax
> instead of trying to figure everything out.
> We will move on, but remember: you are our hope.
> Amen.
>
> (Mary Kondrat)

Questions for Reflection and Discussion

1. What kind of role do you think a pope can and should play in the modern world? Should popes try to exert influence only among Catholics?
2. Reflect on the activities that used to be done only by priests but are now often done by laypeople. How do you feel about this change?
3. Complete this sentence: One thing I would like to see that would promote unity among the world's people is . . .
4. What are two ways that you might be able to serve other people?
5. Reflect on the church's history as presented in this book. Recall five images, events, or people that you found inspiring. Why these five? In what ways do they call you to action?

Index

A

abbots, 121–122, 128–129, 135
Acadia, 229, 232, 234
Act of Supremacy (England), 182
Act of Toleration (Maryland), 235
Acts of the Apostles, 27, 29–30, 43, 45, 51
adult baptism, 116, plate 8
Africa, 157, 170, 205–207, 244, 260
African Americans, 244–245
Age of Reason, 216–218
Age of Revolution, 218–221
Albigensians, 147, 149, 151–152
Alexander VI, Pope, 165, 169, 191
Ambrose, Saint, 77–79, 80, 90, 106, 142
American Indians, 192–193, 194, 196, 229–234, 239
Americanism, 245–246
American Revolution, 219, 235–236
Anglican church, 181–183, 211, 222, 235
Anglo-Saxons, 107–108, 118–119
Antioch, 32–33, 34–35, 44, 89
anti-Semitism, 12, 99, 134
Antony of Egypt, 74–75, 100, 103, 205
apostates, 64
Apostles, 24–27; eucharistic language of, 14; fourth-century church and, 67; institutional church and, 17; Jewish opposition to, 28–29; legacy of, 54; papal authority and, 176; servant church model and, 19. See also Acts of the Apostles
Aquinas, Saint Thomas, 110, 142–143, 153–154
Arabs, 128, 145, 154, 206
Arianism, 68–70, 73; barbarians and, 88, 96; Goths and, 96–97; in Milan, 78, 79
Aristotle (philosopher), 110, 140, 154
Asia, 197–205, 259
Asia Minor, 33, 43
Athanasius, Saint, 69–70
atomic bomb, 200, 260
Augsburg Confession, 178

Augustine of Canterbury, Saint, 107–108
Augustine of Hippo, Saint, 79–86, 90, 142, 205, 276
Augustinians, 193, 205, 233
Australia, 207–208
Avignon papacy, 159–161
Aztecs, 192–193

B

Baltimore Catechism, 243
baptism, sacrament of, 116
barbarians: Arianism and, 88, 96; conversion of, 112, 118–119, 193; Gregory the Great and, 107; invasions of, 58, 85. See also Franks; Goths; Vikings
Barnabas (companion of Saint Paul), 32–34, 35, 41
Basil, Saint, 76, 105
Bede, Saint, 113, 115
Benedict XV, Pope, 250, 257
Benedictine monasticism, 103–105, 112, 119, 129, 133
Bible: Darwinism and, 226; Galileo and, 217; King James version of, 242; Latin Vulgate version of, 77; Luther and, 176–177; modern scholarship on, 226, 262–263; printed, 164; terms for, 13; Wycliffe on, 168. See also Christian Testament; Hebrew Scriptures
bishop of Constantinople, 89, 127–128, 144
bishop of Rome, 60, 64, 89. See also papacy
bishops: early church, 60, 64, 67, 69, 70, 84; Dark Ages, 93, 95, 99, 121–122, 124, 126, 128–129; High Middle Ages, 135, 136, 150; Late Middle Ages, 168; sixteenth century, 182, 184, 191; nineteenth century, 196–197, 223, 238; twentieth century, 204, 252, 258, 259, 270
Black Death, 157–158, 161, 164, 165, 211, plate 11

German bishops, 124, 126
German emperors, 128, 135, 136, 146
German immigrants, 238, 239, 242, 246
Germany: Christianity in, 113–114;
Frankish empire and, 120; in Late
Middle Ages, 161; Nazism in, 257–258;
in nineteenth century, 222; Peasants'
Revolt in, 178–179, plate 12; Protestant
Reformation in, 175, 177, 178–179; Third
Crusade and, 146; witch burning in,
212; in World War I, 250, 257; in World
War II, 259, 260
Gibbons, Cardinal James, 240, 245
Gnosticism, 68
Gospels, 50–52
Gothic cathedrals, 137–138, plate 9
Goths, 79, 85, 86, 88, 96, 105
Great Papal Schism, 161–163, 168
Gregory I (the Great), Pope, 95,
105–108, 113, plate 7
Guadalupe, Virgin of, 193–194
guilds, 134, 139, 165
Gunpowder Plot, 211

H

Hebrew Scriptures, 13, 47, 52, 54
Henry VIII, King (of England), 181–183,
222
Herald church model, 18–19, 272–273
heresies, 67–71, 147, 149, 175–176,
177–178, 181, 217
hermits, 74, 75–76, 100
High Middle Ages, 132–155
Hildegard of Bingen, Saint, 148–149
Hitler, Adolf, 12, 256, 257, 258–260
Holocaust, Jewish, 11–12, 257–258, 259
Holy Land, 144–145, 146, 185–186
Holy Roman emperors, 128, 135, 146,
150
Holy Roman Empire, 128, 135, 171, 179
Holy Spirit, 27, 31, 36, 271, 276–277
humanism, 164
Hundred Years' War, 158, 159–160
Huns, 88

I

Ignatius of Loyola, Saint, 185–186, 189
indulgences, 145, 167–168, 173–176
Industrial Revolution, 224
infallibility, 223

infant baptism, 116
Innocent III, Pope, 136, 146, 147, 149,
158–159
Inquisitions, 149–151, 163, 183, 185,
221–222
Institution church model, 16–17, 268,
274–275
Ireland, 123, 222
Irish convicts, 207–208
Irish immigrants, 238, 239, 240, 245
Irish monasticism, 100–103, 113, 116
Islam, 108–110, 113, 126, 169; Crusades
against, 144–147; in North Africa, 205;
in Philippines, 201; scholarship and,
115, 140–141, 147; Spanish Inquisition
and, 163, 183
Israel, 258, 260
Italy: Roman era, 88, 96–97; Middle Ages,
119, 139, 157, 159, 161, 169; nineteenth
century, 221, 239; twentieth century,
256–257, 258

J

Japan, 198–200, 258, 260
Jerome, Saint, 76–77, 105
Jerusalem: bishop of, 60; Council of,
35–36, 44; early Christian delegation
from, 34–35; famines in, 33, 44; Muslim
recapture of, 145, 146; Paul the Apostle
in, 35–36, 45; pilgrimages to, 145;
Roman destruction of, 52, 54; Temple
in, 28; women in, 62
Jesuits, 185–186; in China, 202–204; in
Japan, 198–199; in New World, 193, 196;
in North America, 229–230, 232–234; in
Nova Scotia, 229; in Philippines, 200; in
Southeast Asia, 204; in United States, 244
Jesus Christ: Apostles and, 24–27; in
church history, 12; Greco-Roman deities
and, 39; institutional church and, 17; as
Jew, 12, 52; as Messiah, 25, 28, 30; as
Mother, 162; Mystical Body of, 16, 263,
268, 274; natures of, 68–70, 71, 73,
88–89, 90; papal authority and, 176; real
presence of, 166, 177; Resurrection of,
26, 42; as Sacrament of God, 18; Saul of
Tarsus and, 29–30; Servant church
model and, 19; universal appeal of, 270;
wilderness experience of, 74
John Paul II, Pope, 217–218, 233, 269
John XXIII, Pope, 265–267, 269

Judaism: Apostles and, 24–25; Christian awareness of, 11; early church and, 22–23, 27–37, 52, 54, 57; ecumenical movement and, 269; First Crusade and, 145; Greco-Roman Gentiles and, 39, 44; Islam and, 109; in Late Middle Ages, 163, 183; Nazism and, 257–258; Paul the Apostle and, 45; in Philippi, 41; in Thessalonica, 42. *See also* anti-Semitism

Julian of Norwich, Saint, 162

Justinian I, Emperor (Eastern Roman), 98–100, 110, 134

just-war theory, 142–143

K

Kildare (Irish monastery), 103

Know-Nothing Party, 240, 241

Koran, 109, 140

L

Lady of Guadalupe, 193–194

Las Casas, Bartolomé de, 196

Last Supper, 19, 25. *See also* Eucharist, sacrament of

Late Middle Ages, 156–171

Lateran Treaty (1929), 256–257

Latin America, 192–197, 275, plate 16

Latin kingdoms (Middle East), 145

Latin language, 14, 108, 141, 204

Latin Mass, 94, 120, 127, 166, 242

lay participation, 16, 263, 268, 274

lay volunteer groups, 271–272

Leo I (the Great), Pope, 87–89, 90, 107

Leo XIII, Pope: on Americanism, 245–246; biblical scholarship and, 226; German-American parishes and, 242; *Rerum Novarum,* 225, 240, 252

liturgy, 52, 120, 127; languages of, 127, 204; music of, 107, 242; pre–Vatican Council II movement for, 263; Vatican Council II and, 13–14, 267. *See also* Eucharist, sacrament of; Mass

Louisiana, 233, 234, 244

Lumen Gentium, 18, 268

Luther, Martin, 174–180

Lutheran church, 178–180, 183

M

Manichaeism, 80

Marillac, Louise de, 214, 219, 277

marriage, sacrament of, 14, 144

Martel, Charles, 110, 113, 114

Marxism, 211, 224–225, 253–254

Mary, Virgin: Assumption of, 223; devotion to, 166, 194; Guadalupe appearance of, 193–194; Immaculate Conception of, 223; Pentecost and, 26

Maryknoll Missioners, 206, 277

Maryland, 235, 237, 244

Mass: Chinese, 204; in German Triangle, 242; Luther on, 177; medieval, 94–95, 127, 166; Vatican Council II and, 13–14. *See also* Eucharist, sacrament of; liturgy

Medici family, 169

mendicant orders, 149, 151–154, 155, 193, 201, 203. *See also* Dominicans; Franciscans

Merton, Thomas, 75, 82–83

Mexico, 192–194, 231

Milan, Edict of, 65–66, 70

missions, 130, 190–209, 221, 272–273; to Africa, 170, 205–207; to Asia, 197–205, 259; to Britain, 107–108; to China, 202–204, 262; to Netherlands, 113, 115; to North America, 229–234, 237, 238; to Russia, 127; to Scandinavia, 124; to Slavs, 124, 126–127

Modernism, 246, 249

monasticism:

—**early,** 73–77, 90, plates 4 and 6

—**Dark Ages,** 100, 103–105, 110, 113; feudalism and, 121–123; private confession and, 116; scholarship and, 115; urban growth and, 133–134; wealth and, 93

—**sixteenth century,** 182

—**eighteenth century,** 196–197

—*See also* Benedictine monasticism; mendicant orders

More, Saint Thomas, 176, 182–183

Muhammad (prophet), 108–109

music, church, 107, 242

Mystical Body of Christ, 16, 263, 268, 274

N

Nagasaki (Japan), 198, 200, 260
nationalism: High Middle Ages, 134–135;
Late Middle Ages, 159, 163, 168;
sixteenth century, 173; seventeenth
century, 219; nineteenth century, 207,
221–222, 245; twentieth century, 250, 262
Native Americans, 192–193, 194, 196,
229–234, 239
nativism, 240, 246
Nazism, 12, 250, 257–260
Nero, Emperor (of Rome), 46, 52, 53
Netherlands, 113, 115, 259
New Testament, 13, 46–47, 49, 52, 73
Nicaea, Council of, 69, 78
Nicene Creed, 69, 71, 73
Ninety-five Theses, 174–175
Norsemen, 120, 123–124, 125, 126
North America, 170, 190–191, 206,
228–247
Nova Scotia, 229, 234
nuclear weapons, 200, 260

O

Old Testament, 13, 47, 52, 54
On Reconstructing the Social Order
(Pius XI), 257
On the Condition of Workers (Leo XIII),
225, 240, 252
Order of Friars Minor. *See* Franciscans
Order of Preachers. *See* Dominicans
Orthodox Eastern church: Council of
Chalcedon and, 89; early medieval
worship in, 93, 96; ecumenical
movement and, 269; Fourth Crusade
and, 146; Lutheranism and, 180; Slavs
and, 127; Western split from, 141, 144,
154, 169–170. *See also* Russian Orthodox church

P

paganism: Celtic, 100; Frankish, 97;
Germanic, 114; Greco-Roman, 39;
Roman, 46, 59, 61, 67, 70
Palestine, 144–145, 146, 185–186
papacy: early, 86–88, 90; Dark Ages, 110,
112–113, 117–118, 119, 127–128, 130;
High Middle Ages, 135, 136, 140, 144;
Late Middle Ages, 156, 159–161,

167–168, 169; Renaissance, 164–165;
sixteenth century, 176, 183, 186;
seventeenth century, 219; eighteenth
century, 204; nineteenth century, 223;
twentieth century, 249, 256–257, 269,
310. *See also* bishop of Rome
Papal Schism, 161–163, 168
Papal States: Middle Ages, 117–118, 119,
160; seventeenth century, 219; nineteenth century, 221, 223; twentieth
century, 256–257
parochial schools, 238, 242–243
*Pastoral Constitution on the Church in
the Modern World,* 269
patriarch of Constantinople, 89,
127–128, 144
Patrick, Saint, 100–102, 114
Paul VI, Pope, 269
Paul, Saint: Augustine and, 81; Barnabas
and, 33–34; on Body of Christ, 16;
conversion of, 29–30, 276, plate 2;
epistles of, 46–47, 49; Gentile converts
and, 37; Greek language and, 14; in
Jerusalem, 35–36, 45; legacy of, 54;
missionary journeys of, 32, 33–34,
39–40, 41–46; in Rome, 45–46;
Stephen's martyrdom and, 24; tomb of,
128
Peasants' Revolt, 178–179, plate 12
Pelagianism, 84–85
Pennsylvania, 235
Pentecost, 26–27, plate 1
People of God church model, 16, 263,
268, 274
Pepin the Short, King (of the Franks),
114, 115, 117–119
persecution: in England, 211; in
Germany, 212, 257–258; in Japan,
198–200; in Lyons, 57–58; in Roman
Empire, 46, 53, 59, 61, 64, 84, plate 3; in
Uganda, 207. *See also* nativism
Peter, Saint, 25, 46, 128; Avignon papacy
and, 159; bishop of Rome and, 60;
Gentile converts and, 34–35, 37; papal
authority and, 176; Paul the Apostle
and, 32; Pentecost sermon of, 27;
Samaritan converts and, 31
Philippines, 200–202, 259, 270
Pius X, Pope, 246, 249–250
Pius XI, Pope, 257
Pius XII, Pope, 258, 262–263, 266

Second World War, 200, 202, 246, 250, 258–260
seminaries, 223, 237
serfs, 120, 121, 123. *See also* feudalism
Serra, Junípero, 231
Servant church model, 19, 271–272
Seton, Saint Elizabeth Ann, 237–238
simony, 129
slavery: in Africa, 206; Children's Crusade and, 146; Daughters of Charity and, 214; Justinian Code on, 99; in New World, 195, 196, 244; in Philippines, 200. *See also* serfs
Slavs, 124, 126–127
small Christian communities, 44, 275–276
social justice: nineteenth century, 225, 245; twentieth century, 252, 254, 270, 271–272, 274–275
Soviet Union, 253–254, 260, 261–262. *See also* Russia
Spain: Middle Ages, 109, 161, 170, 183; sixteenth century, 186–187, 191, 192–197, 200, 244; eighteenth century, 201; nineteenth century, 201–202, 221–222; twentieth century, 256
Spanish Inquisition, 163, 183, 185, 221–222
Spanish missionaries: in China, 203; in Japan, 199; in New World, 193–196, 229, 230–231; in Philippines, 200–201

T

Tekakwitha, Kateri, 233–234, plate 15
Temple of Jerusalem, 28
Teresa of Ávila, Saint, 186–188, 189, 276–277, plate 13
Tertullian (church father), 62–63
Tetzel, John, 173–174
Theodoric, King (Arian), 96–97, 103
Theodosius, Emperor (of Rome), 67, 70, 79
Thomas Aquinas, Saint, 110, 142–143, 153–154
totalitarianism, 252–253
Tradition (church), 168, 177
transubstantiation, 166, 168, 177
Trent, Council of, 154, 176, 183–185, 189, 267, 270
Turks, 144–145, 169–170, 185–186

U

United States, 236–247; bishops of, 252; church-state relations in, 236, 242, 245, 246, 247; in cold war, 261; Japan and, 260; Philippines and, 202. *See also* American Revolution
universities, 139–141, 175, 186, 222, 238
urban life, 133–134, 137, 165, 224
usury, 99, 134

V

vassals, 120–121, 123
Vatican, 163, 168, 226
Vatican Council I, 223, 266
Vatican Council II, 249, 261, 262, 263, 265–270; biblical scholarship and, 226; Council of Trent and, 184–185; *Declaration on Religious Freedom,* 269; denominational reconciliation and, 189, 268–269; *Dogmatic Constitution on the Church,* 18, 268; liturgical reforms of, 13–14, 267, 274; *Pastoral Constitution on the Church in the Modern World,* 269
Vikings, 120, 123–124, 125, 126
Vincent de Paul, Saint, 213–214, 219
Virgin of Guadalupe, 193–194

W

witch-hunts, 212, 213
women, 62–63, 99, 275–276
women religious: American, 238, 240; Chinese, 204; European, 153; French, 214; Irish, 103; Italian, 105
working class, 225, 240, 252
World War I, 246, 250, 252, 257
World War II, 200, 202, 246, 250, 258–260
Wycliffe, John, 168

X

Xavier, Francis, 197, 198, 199

Z

Zwingli, Ulrich, 180

Acknowledgments *(continued)*

The scriptural quotations contained herein are from the New Revised Standard Version of the Bible. Copyright © 1989 by the Division of Christian Education of the National Council of the Churches of Christ in the United States of America. Used by permission. All rights reserved.

The excerpt accompanying plate 10 is from *Clare of Assisi: Early Documents,* edited and translated by Regis Armstong (Mahwah, NJ: Paulist Press, 1988), pages 35–36.

The words quoted on page 18 from *Dogmatic Constitution on the Church,* number 1, and the words quoted on page 269 from *Pastoral Constitution on the Church in the Modern World,* number 1, are found in *The Documents of Vatican II,* Walter M. Abbott, general editor (New York: America Press, 1966), pages 15 and 199–200. Copyright © 1966 by the America Press.

The words of Justin on page 48, and the words of Tacitus and an anonymous source on page 53, are from *Eerdmans' Handbook to the History of Christianity* (Grand Rapids, MI: Wm. B. Eerdmans Publishing Company, 1977), pages 127, 71, and 69, respectively. Copyright © 1977 by Lion Publishing, Berkhamsted, Herts, England.

The account of Blandina's martyrdom on pages 57–58 is excerpted from *Early Christian Spirituality,* translated by Pamela Bright and edited by Charles Kannengiesser (Philadelphia: Fortress Press, 1986), pages 39–49. Copyright © 1986 by Fortress Press. Used by permission of Augsburg Fortress.

The statement by Ignatius of Antioch, quoted on page 59, is from volume 2 of *The Lives of the Saints,* originally compiled by the Reverend Alban Butler, later edited, revised, and supplemented by Herbert Thurston (London: Burns, Oates, and Washbourne, 1930), page 4.

The Nicene Creed, as quoted in part on page 69, is the English translation of the Nicene Creed by the International Consultation on English Texts.

The words quoted on page 69, reflecting the position of Athanasius at the Council of Nicaea, were originally written by Clement of Alexandria in his "Exhortation to the Greeks," 1.8.4. The words used here are quoted from *The People of the Creed: The Story Behind the Early Church,* by Anthony E. Gilles (Cincinnati: Saint Anthony Messenger Press, 1985), page 72. Copyright © 1985 by Anthony E. Gilles.

The extract on page 75 is from *The Wisdom of the Desert: Sayings from the Desert Fathers of the Fourth Century,* translated and written by Thomas Merton (Norfolk, CT: New Directions, 1960), pages 3–8. Copyright © 1960 by the Abbey of Gethsemani. Reprinted by permission of New Directions Press.

The words of Ambrose on page 79 are from his "Sermon Against Auxentius," as quoted in volume 2 of *The Faith of the Early Fathers,* selected and translated by W. A. Jurgens (Collegeville, MN: Liturgical Press, 1979), page 165. Copyright © 1979 by the Order of Saint Benedict, Collegeville, Minnesota.

The excerpt from Augustine of Hippo's *Confessions* on page 81 is from *Augustine of Hippo: Selected Writings,* translated by Mary T. Clark (New York: Paulist Press, 1984), pages 125–126. Copyright © 1984 by Mary T. Clark. Used with permission of Paulist Press.

Augustine's sayings on page 81 is from *The People of the Creed,* by Anthony E. Gilles, page 72.

The excerpts on pages 82–83 are from *The Seven Storey Mountain,* by Thomas Merton. Copyright © 1948 by Harcourt Brace Jovanovich; renewed 1976 by the Trustees of the Merton Legacy Trust. Reprinted by permission of Curtis Brown and Harcourt Brace and Company.

The quotation of Augustine on page 85 is from *The Essential Augustine,* selected and with commentary by Vernon J. Bourke (Indianapolis: Hackett Publishing Company, 1974), page 176. Copyright © 1974 by Vernon J. Bourke.

The quotation of Bede on page 108 is from his *History of the English Church and People,* translated by Leo Sherley-Price, revised by R. E. Latham (Harmondsworth, Middlesex, England: Penguin Books, 1968), page 71. Copyright © 1968 by Leo Sherley-Price.

The quotation on page 114 is from *The English Correspondence of Saint Boniface,* translated and edited by Edward Kylie (New York: Cooper Square Publishers, 1966), pages 53–54.

The rules set forth by Charlemagne and quoted on page 118 are from *A History of Christian Missions,* by Stephen Neill (Harmondsworth, Middlesex, England: Penguin Books, 1964), page 80. Copyright © 1964 by Stephen Neill.

The quotation on page 125 is from *Lion of Ireland,* by Morgan Llywelyn (New York: Playboy Paperbacks, 1981), pages 38 and 45–47. Copyright © 1979 by Morgan Llywelyn. Reprinted by permission of Houghton Mifflin Company. All rights reserved.

The lyrics on page 142 by Bertrand de Born are quoted from *A Distant Mirror: The Calamitous Fourteenth Century,* by Barbara W. Tuchman (New York: Alfred A. Knopf, 1978), page 16. Copyright © 1978 by Barbara W. Tuchman.

The words of Hildegard of Bingen on pages 148–149 are reprinted from *Hildegard of Bingen's Book of Divine Works with Letters and Songs,* edited by Matthew Fox (Santa Fe, NM: Bear and Company, 1987), pages 273–275 and 361. Copyright © 1987 by Bear and Company, P.O. Box 2860, Santa Fe, NM 87504. Used with permission.

The extract on pages 151–152 is from *Massacre at Montségur: A History of the Albigensian Crusade,* by Zoé Oldenbourg, translated by Peter Green (New York: Pantheon Books, 1962), page 93. Copyright © 1961 by George Weidenfeld and Nicolson and Pantheon Books, a division of Random House. Used by permission.

The extract on page 153 is from *The Wisdom of St. Francis and His Companions,* by Stephen Clissold (New York: New Directions Publishing Corporation, 1979), page 32. Copyright © 1978 by Stephen Clissold.

The extract on pages 157–158 is from *Narcissus and Goldmund,* by Hermann Hesse, translated by Ursule Molinaro (New York: Farrar, Straus and Giroux, 1968), pages 218–220. Translation copyright © 1968 by Farrar, Straus and Giroux. Reprinted by permission of Farrar, Straus and Giroux.

The extract on page 160 is from *Saint Catherine of Siena as Seen in Her Letters,* translated and edited by Vida D. Scudder (London: J. M. Dent and Sons, 1911), pages 131–132.

The excerpt by Julian of Norwich on page 162 is from *Julian of Norwich: Showings,* translated by Edmund Colledge and James Walsh (New York: Paulist Press, 1978). From the Classics of Western Spirituality series. Copyright © 1978 by the Missionary Society of Saint Paul the Apostle in the State of New York. Used with permission.

Savonarola's words on page 169 are from *The Unarmed Prophet: Savonarola in Florence,* by Rachel Erlanger (New York: McGraw-Hill Book Company, 1988), pages 238–239. Copyright © 1988 by Rachel Erlanger.

The quotation on pages 173–174 and the second quotation on page 178 are from *The Western Tradition,* volume 1, *From the Ancient World to Louis XIV,* by Eugen Weber (Lexington, MA: D. C. Heath and Company, 1972), pages 332 and 341. Copyright © 1990 by D. C. Heath and Company.

The words of Martin Luther quoted on page 176 are from volume 2 of *Readings in Church History,* edited by Colman J. Barry (Westminster, MD: Newman Press, 1967), page 21. Copyright © 1965 by the Missionary Society of Saint Paul the Apostle in the State of New York.

The words of Melanchthon quoted on page 178 are from *The Reformation,* by Owen Chadwick (Harmondsworth, Middlesex, England: Penguin Books, 1972), pages 65–66. Copyright © 1972 by Owen Chadwick.

The quotation of Dorothy Day on page 187 is from *The Long Loneliness: The Autobiography of Dorothy Day* (New York: Harper and Row, Publishers, 1952), page 140. Copyright © 1952 by Harper and Row, Publishers.

The first quotation of Teresa of Ávila on page 187 is from *Saint-Watching,* by Phyllis McGinley (New York: Viking Press, 1969), page 93. Copyright © 1969 by Phyllis McGinley.

The excerpt on page 187 from Teresa of Ávila's *Interior Castle* is from volume 2 of *The Collected Works of St. Teresa of Ávila,* translated by Kieran Kavanaugh and Otilio Rodriguez (Washington, DC: ICS Publications, 1980), page 284. Copyright © 1980 by the Washington Province of Discalced Carmelites, ICS Publications, 2131 Lincoln Road NE, Washington, DC 20002.

Teresa of Ávila's poem on page 188 is from volume 3 of *The Collected Works of St. Teresa of Ávila,* translated by Kieran Kavanaugh and Otilio Rodriguez (Washington, DC: ICS Publications, 1985), page 386. Copyright © 1985 by the Washington Province of Discalced Carmelites, ICS Publications, 2131 Lincoln Road NE, Washington, DC 20002. Used with permission.

On page 195, Bartolomé de Las Casas's description of Latin American native peoples is from "Las Casas: Defender of the Indians," an interview with Helen Rand Parish by James S. Torrens, in *America,* volume 167, 25 July 1992, page 31.

The extract on page 198 is from *Saint Francis Xavier (1506–1552),* by James Brodrick (Garden City, NY: Image Books, 1957), page 252. Copyright © 1957 by Doubleday and Company.

The quotations on pages 212 and 224 are from *The Western Tradition,* volume 2, *The Renaissance to the Present,* by Eugen Weber (Lexington, MA: D. C. Heath and Company, 1972), pages 432–434 and 615. Copyright © 1990 by D. C. Heath and Company. Used with permission.

Vincent de Paul's words on page 214 are from *Monsieur Vincent: The Story of St. Vincent de Paul,* by Henri Daniel-Rops, translated by Julie Kernan (New York: Hawthorn Books, 1961), page 75. Copyright © 1961 by Hawthorn Books.

The extracts on pages 5 and 215–216 are from *Meditations for the Time of Retreat,* by John Baptist de La Salle, translated by Br. Augustine Loes (Winona, MN: Saint Mary's College Press, 1975), pages 47, and 50 and 80. Copyright © 1975 by the Christian Brothers Conference. All rights reserved.

The second extract on page 216 is from *De La Salle: Meditations,* edited by W. J. Battersby (London: Waldegrave, 1964), page 400. Copyright © 1964 by Waldegrave Publishers.

John Paul II's words quoted on page 218 are from *Catholic Trends,* 7 November 1992, page 3.

The excerpt on page 225 from *On the Condition of Workers*, number 31, is from *Justice in the Marketplace: Collected Statements of the Vatican and the United States Catholic Bishops on Economic Policy, 1891–1984*, edited by David M. Byers (Washington, DC: United States Catholic Conference [USCC], 1985), page 21. Copyright © 1985 by the USCC.

The words of Jean de Brébeuf on page 230 are from *The Jesuit Relations and Allied Documents: Travels and Explorations of the Jesuit Missionaries in North America (1610–1791)*, edited by Edna Kenton (New York: Albert and Charles Boni, 1925), pages 115–116. Copyright © 1925 by Albert and Charles Boni.

The Fox Indian story on page 232 is quoted from *Native American Testimony: An Anthology of Indian and White Relations*, edited by Peter Nabokov (New York: Harper Colophon Books, 1979), page 68. Copyright © 1978 by Peter Nabokov.

The words of Elizabeth Ann Seton quoted on page 237 are from *Mrs. Seton: Foundress of the American Sisters of Charity*, by Joseph I. Dirvin (New York: Farrar, Straus and Giroux, 1962), page 171. Copyright © 1962 by Farrar, Straus and Giroux.

The extract on page 241 and the quotation of the U.S. Catholic bishops on page 252 are taken from volume 2 of *Documents of American Catholic History*, edited by John Tracy Ellis (Wilmington, DE: Michael Glazier, 1987), pages 557 and 607. Copyright © 1987 by John Tracy Ellis. Used by permission of Liturgical Press.

The words of John Ireland on page 245 are quoted from *Christianity: A Social and Cultural History*, by Howard Clark Kee and others (New York: Macmillan Publishing Company, 1991), page 720. Copyright © 1991 by Macmillan Publishing Company.

The extract on page 255 is from *Dorothy Day: Selected Writings*, edited by Robert Ellsberg (Maryknoll, NY: Orbis Books, 1992), page 51. Copyright © 1983, 1992 by Robert Ellsberg and Tamar Hennessey. Used by permission of Orbis Books.

The extract on pages 261–262 is from volume 3 of *Readings in Church History*, edited by Colman J. Barry (Paramus, NJ: Newman Press, 1965), pages 498–499. Copyright © 1965 by the Missionary Society of Saint Paul the Apostle in the State of New York.

The words of Pope John XXIII on page 266 are quoted from *Pope John XXIII: Shepherd of the Modern World*, by Peter Hebblethwaite (Garden City, NY: Doubleday and Company, 1985), pages 316–317. Copyright © 1984 by Peter Hebblethwaite.

The *National Catholic Reporter* news article quoted on pages 271–272, "Minnesota Woman Washes Feet of Walking Wounded," by Willmar Thorkelson, 15 November 1991, is used by permission.

The poem on page 273 by Anne Attea, and the prayer on page 277 by Mary Kondrat, are from *Open Hearts, Helping Hands: Prayers by Lay Volunteers in Mission*, compiled by Carl Koch and Michael Culligan (Winona, MN: Saint Mary's Press, 1993), pages 36 and 75. Copyright © 1993 by Saint Mary's Press. All rights reserved. Used by permission.

The first extract on page 274 is from *Praying Our Stories: Reflections for Youth Ministers*, by Daniel Ponsetto (Winona, MN: Saint Mary's Press, 1992), page 85. Copyright © 1992 by Saint Mary's Press. All rights reserved.

The *National Catholic Reporter* news article quoted on pages 274–275, 30 October 1992, is used by permission of Catholic News Service.

The quotation by Hilary Gutman on pages 275–276 is from "A Trinitarian Presence," in *Womenpsalms*, compiled by Julia Ahlers, Rosemary Broughton, and Carl Koch (Winona, MN: Saint Mary's Press, 1992), pages 18–19. Copyright © 1992 by Saint Mary's Press. All rights reserved. Used by permission.

The words of Oliver Wendell Holmes on the back cover are from *Time Capsules of the Church*, by Mitch Finley (Huntington, IN: Our Sunday Visitor Publishing Division, 1990), page 6. Copyright © 1990 by Our Sunday Visitor Division, Our Sunday Visitor.

Photo Credits

Alinari, Art Resource, NY: plate 5
The Bettmann Archive: plate 12
Bridge Building Images: plate 15; P.O. Box 1048, Burlington, VT 05402. Copyright © 1986. All rights reserved.
Bridgelan, Giraudon, Paris: plate 13
C. M. Dixon, Photo Resources: plate 8
Giraudon, Art Resource, NY: plate 7
Giraudon, Paris: plate 14
Sonia Halliday Photographs: plate 9
Erich Lessing, Art Resource, NY: plates 3 and 6
Nicaraguan Cultural Alliance: plate 16
Richard Nowitz: plate 4
Scala, Art Resource, NY: plates 1, 2, 10, and 11